Pacific Crest Trail Project:

Calypso

Pacific Crest Trail Project:

Calypso

by Nikki "Calypso" Oniu

ISBN: 979-8-218-78670-0

Artwork and text: Nicole Oniu

Book design and editing: Tim Royce

Foreword: Mark Taylor

Photographs: Nicole Oniu, Bogdan Oniu, Mark Taylor, Zac Walker, Nathan Grathwhol, Sam Heilbroner, Sophie Bearman, Trevor Valencia, Bill Cole, and Vicente Pomparo

For Bogdan, whose question provoked a journey within a journey.
Born from the trail and water of the Pacific Crest Trail,
this book is a testament to your unwavering love and encouragement.
Thank you for being my greatest adventure.

Table of Contents

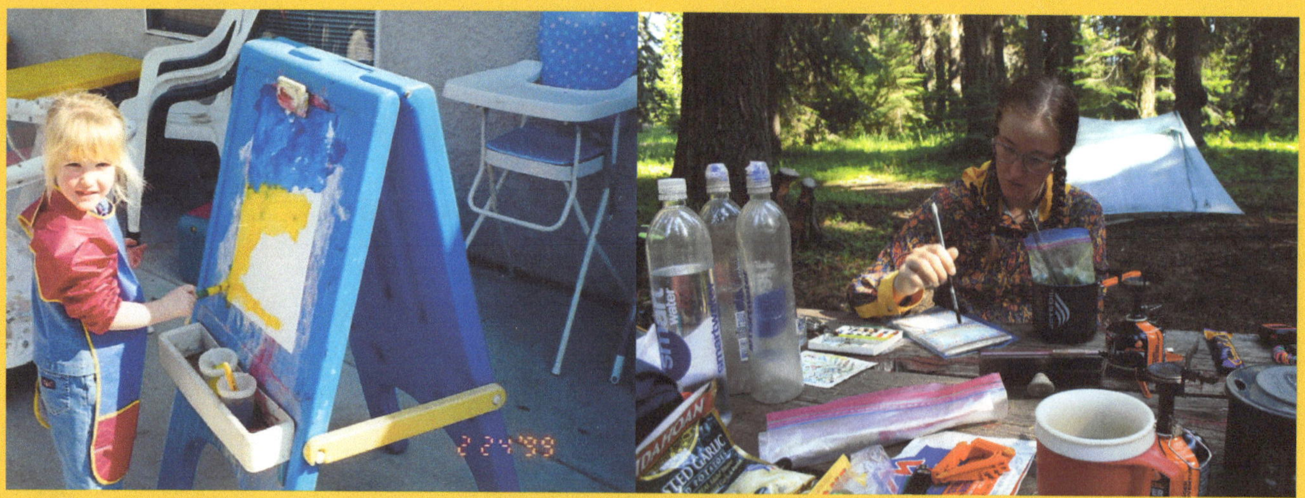

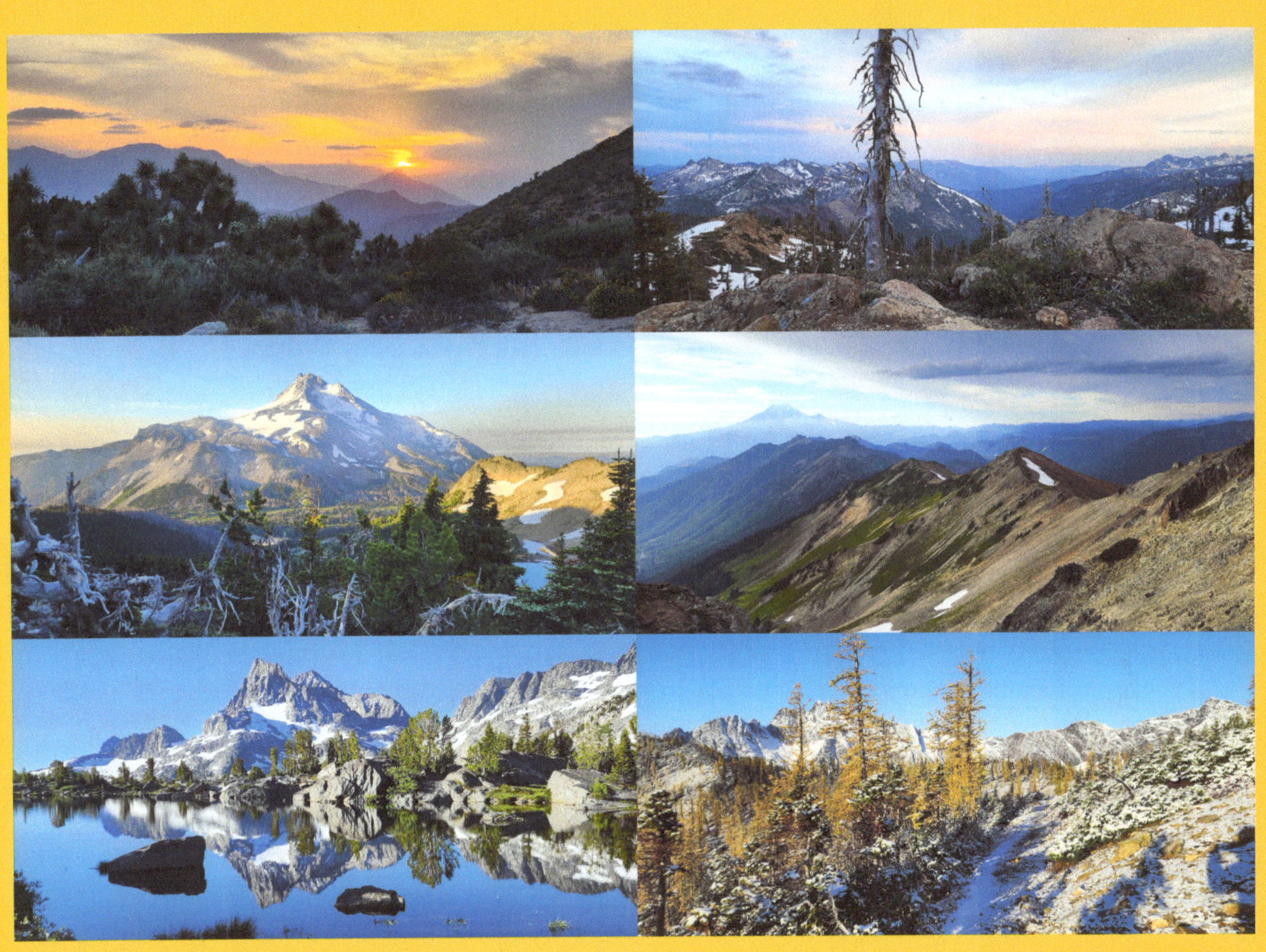

With views like these, finding inspiration
to paint came effortlessly.

Foreword

Something had changed when I joined my daughter Nikki to hike all of Oregon during her 2023 Pacific Crest Trail thru-hike. Although I taught her how to backpack when she was a child, hiking with her this time was different. Nikki, known on the trail as Calypso, has always pursued life with determination and purpose. Since childhood and throughout her military career, her mom and I watched as she faced challenges, sought new adventures, and found success that went beyond personal achievement in academics or career.

That success has always been about more than her own goals. Nikki invests deeply in the people around her, forming lasting friendships and creating connections that endure long after the trail ends. Her leadership skills extended naturally to the PCT, where her fellow hikers recognized and respected her quiet strength. By the time I joined her, she was a well-oiled machine, steady and efficient. I quickly realized there was an obvious role reversal—I was now the one learning from her, learning from her grit, her discipline, and the experiences that shaped her journey.

As a section hiker, I had always enjoyed what I called "prime time" hiking: choosing stretches of the PCT in ideal seasons and avoiding the thru-hiker bubble. Because of this, it took me 15 years to earn a trail name. When I joined Nikki on trail, I was given instant credibility from the hikers we hopscotched with for over 421 miles from Callahan's to Cascade Locks. That credibility came from the admiration Nikki had already earned. Whenever decisions needed to be made about schedules, routes, or plans, the question inevitably arose: "What's Calypso doing?" People trusted her judgment, not only because of her steady presence, but because she had a way of seeing situations from different angles. At the end of our shared Oregon journey, I was finally given a trail name, one I carry with immense pride: CD, Calypso's Dad.

Nikki's gift for perspective, which guided her on the trail, is also what allows her to capture the world so vividly in her paintings. She has always been an artist at heart, drawing inspiration from the wilderness and carrying her creative drive into every stage of life. On the trail, at the end of long days when I could do little more than recover, Nikki still had the energy and discipline to paint. Each night she captured in watercolor a moment from her hike, an impression of trail life that most of us could only attempt to put into words. Through her art, she allows us to see the PCT as only a thru-hiker can.

Each painting became more than just a landscape. It is a reflection of life unfolding on the trail: the people, the places, and the shared experiences that shaped her journey. This book is more than just a record of miles hiked or days endured. It is a collection of moments: experiences, impressions, and insights seen through the eyes of a daughter who hiked with conviction, with creativity, and with heart. It is my honor to introduce you to her story, as Calypso's Dad.

-CD

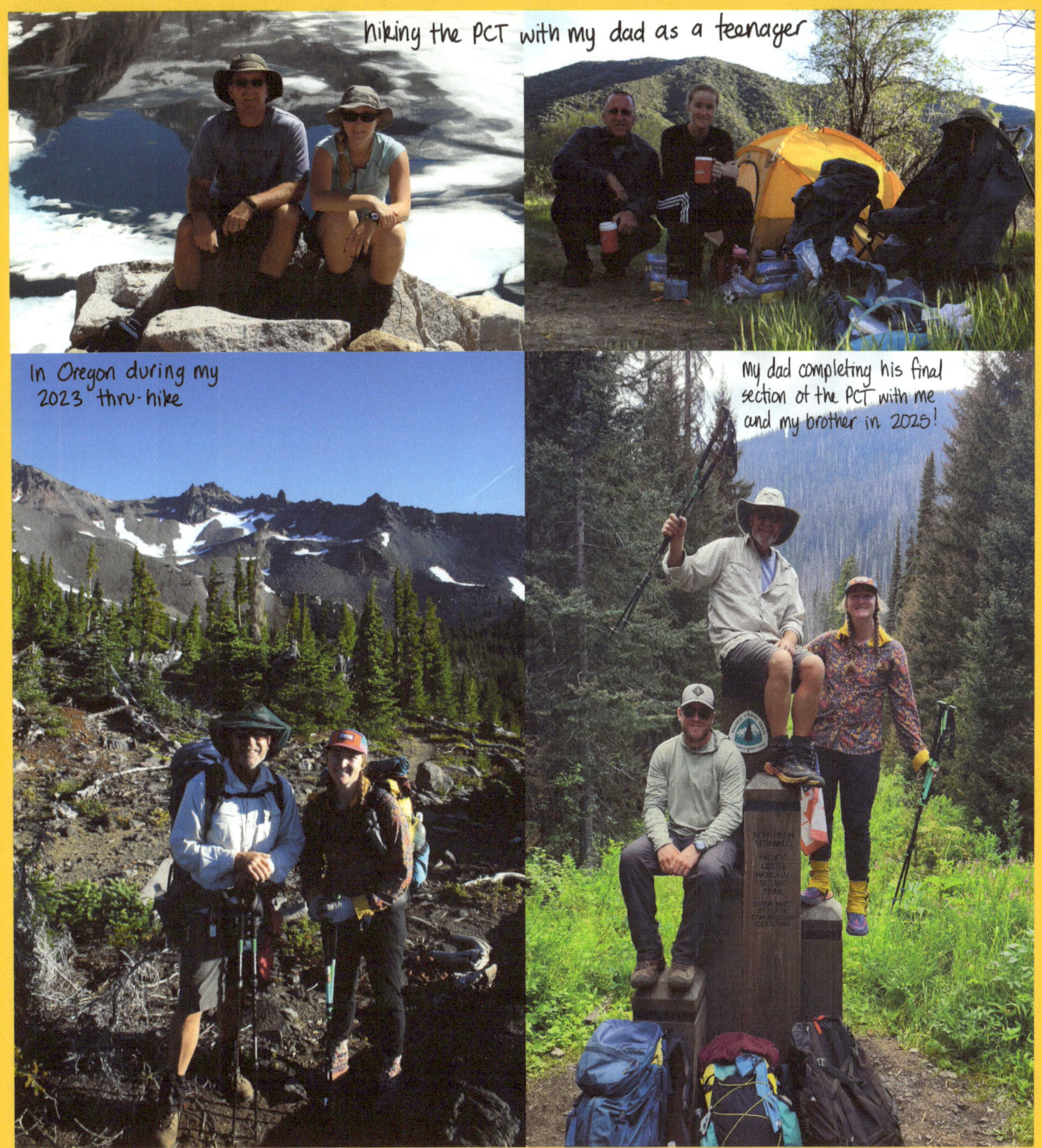
hiking the PCT with my dad as a teenager
In Oregon during my 2023 thru-hike
My dad completing his final section of the PCT with me and my brother in 2025!

Introduction

The Pacific Crest Trail is so much more than just a 2,655-mile footpath through the mountains of the West Coast stretching from Mexico to Canada. For me, it has been a touchstone to ground my soul in the wilderness throughout my life. It is a testament to the simplicity of life's core components within a singular purpose: to walk. It became my masterclass in self-discovery with constant lessons of self-directed resilience and decision making. It is where I learned that my body is strong and will adapt to the demands I place upon it. It brutally forced me to learn how to care for myself mentally and physically so I could perform with mindfulness and without injury. The trail is where I forged new connections with strangers who became friends and strengthened the existing bonds of my closest friends and family. Although the trail was often a profoundly solitary experience for me, it paradoxically fostered an exceptional sense of community. Finally, the wilderness is where I tempered myself as an artist, finding inspiration in the rugged landscapes and resources.

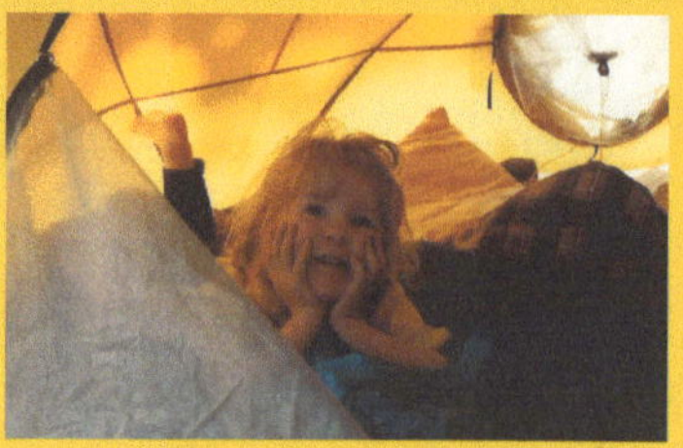

My connection to the PCT began long before I ever dreamed of thru-hiking. My first recollection of trail is from when I was an elementary school kid in Porterville, California hearing stories from my dad and brother hiking a trail together among towering granite peaks and cold alpine lakes in the Sierra Nevada. Around that time, my dad set an ambitious goal to section hike the entire PCT. As my brother got older and opted to adventure with friends, my dad needed a new hiking partner. Who better than his 12-year-old daughter?

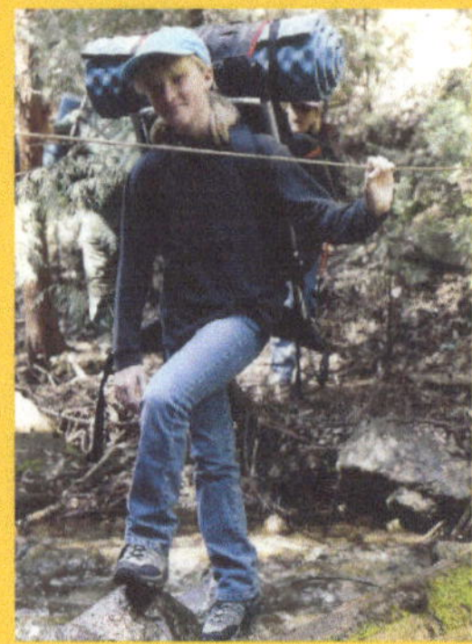

During each spring and summer break from school, my mom would drop my dad and me off at remote trailheads where we would embark on 80- to 120-mile section hikes of the PCT. These weren't just hikes; my dad is known for planning backpacking treks that are lessons in persistence, resilience, and self-reliance. My introduction to backpacking was wearing heavy leather hiking boots and carrying all my own gear in an adult male 80L backpack while climbing through the deserts of Southern California and mountains of the Sierra Nevada. We would average 17 miles and end every day with tired legs, sore feet, and very hungry bellies. These hikes were formative experiences where I saw what it takes to be a PCT hiker, where I began to appreciate the sublime beauty of the wilderness, and where I learned that all it takes is all you have.

Hiking on the PCT with my dad in my early years culminated in a post-high school graduation trek from Kennedy Meadows South to the summit of Mount Whitney. Shortly after that hike, I embarked on another significant chapter of my life: joining the military. I graduated from the Air Force Academy where I earned a Bachelor of Science and learned lessons in leadership for my career as an officer. Most importantly, it is where I formed lasting friendships, spent every summer hiking to the summits of 14ers, snowboarded and skied millions of vertical feet in the Rocky Mountains, and fell in love with Bogdan. I was commissioned and served for seven years on active duty as an intelligence officer at three duty stations with several deployments around the world. Amidst my military career, the PCT remained a persistent dream, and when the time came for me to separate from active duty, I knew it was my opportunity to attempt a thru-hike.

There is no way for me to share every meaningful experience I had on trail. In fact, I don't think I could put it in writing if I tried; instead, my experiences are documented in my paintings and snippets from my journal. If you haven't read the description on the back of the book yet, now is a good time to pause and read about how these paintings came about. If you look closely at the dates and locations on the paintings, you'll notice they are out of geographical order which deserves some explanation because this book follows my personal journey along the Pacific Crest Trail in 2023.

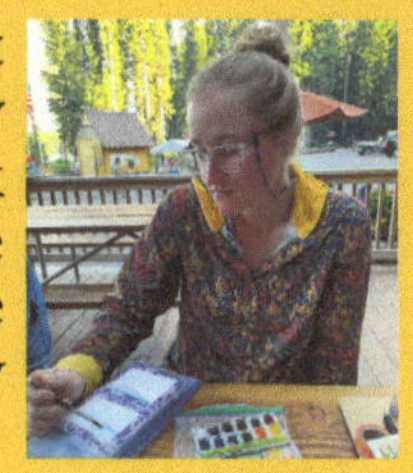

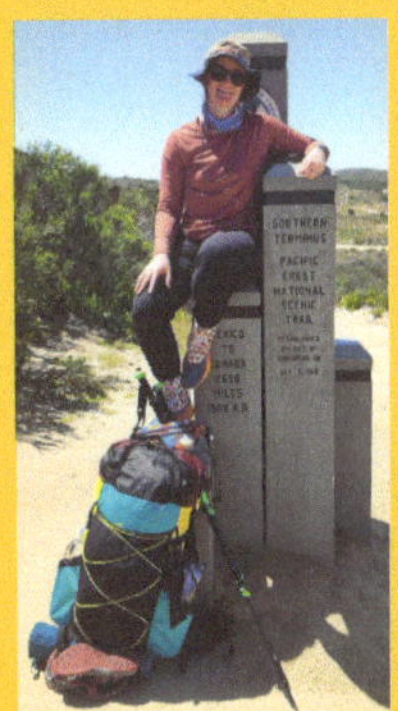

The first steps I took heading north from the Southern Terminus felt like a monumental undertaking. I had a plan to walk a continuous footpath from Mexico to Canada, but I would quickly embrace the need to re-evaluate due to weather and fire. As I earned my trail legs in the desert, the reality of approaching the unforgiving landscape of the Sierra Nevada set in. The winter leading up to the 2023 thru-hiking season brought the mountains of Central California record breaking snowpack followed by a springtime cycle of melting and late-season snow storms. The conditions were destroying bridges over backcountry river crossings and testing the limits of search and rescue teams who were pleading for hikers to reconsider their plans. Having grown up with these mountains as my backyard, I assessed the risk of entering the conditions as a solo hiker and reflected about the experience I wanted to have during this thru-hike attempt.

I decided on a flip-flop thru-hike that would allow me to avoid the snow conditions in higher risk terrain and would also optimize hiking earlier through areas that are commonly closed during fire season. I planned to finish hiking NOBO (northbound) from the Southern Terminus to Kennedy Meadows South. I would then flip up to Northern California to hike NOBO from Chester to the Northern Terminus. Finally, I would return to Chester and hike SOBO (southbound) through the Sierra Nevada to complete my hike at Kennedy Meadows South.

Leaving behind the blooming cacti and sun-scorched expanses of the desert, I stepped into Northern California where the landscape was a canvas of contrasts. The volcanic terrain and scorched forests from fires of years past eventually gave way to lush green forests and snow-capped peaks looming on the horizon. My days became moving meditations as my footsteps crunched on ice-crusted snow and softened on carpets of fallen needles. Northern California, Oregon, and Washington imbued my flip-flop thru-hike with a dynamic chapter to explore with both my feet and my brushes. As I was nearing Stevens Pass, three sections of the trail going north caught fire and closed. This prompted my second flip-flop decision to leave the 180 miles from Stevens Pass to the Northern Terminus undone while I went back to Chester to hike SOBO through the Sierra Nevada.

Although a double flip-flop hike was not my original intention, nor my second intention, hiking SOBO through the Sierra Nevada in mid-August and early September was a dream because the season provided a sense of solitude with a quieter connection to the trail. The days were filled with warm, golden sunshine and temperatures that were perfect for hiking. Afternoon thunderstorms were humbling, while the nights were crisp, cool, and clear. This was the exact experience that I imagined while making my first flip decision.

After connecting my footpath at Kennedy Meadows South, returning to Northern Washington in the autumn to tackle the final stretch of the PCT was an intense test of resolve. The fire closures were no longer enforced, but the trail had traded one challenge for another. The familiar green landscape of summer had given way to a symphony of fall colors, with deep oranges and reds on the low-lying foliage and a stunning, vibrant yellow illuminating the tamarack trees. This beauty was accompanied by a relentless and chilling rain, which eventually gave way to the first persistent layers of snow. Each step through the cold, wet conditions was a battle of mental fortitude, demanding every last ounce of resilience I had to give. When I finally arrived at the end of my journey with Bogdan there to surprise me at the Northern Terminus, the moment was surprisingly anticlimactic. It felt like a silent punctuation mark. In the end, it was less about the destination and more about the incredible effort and community it took to get there. The paintings in this book represent the periods, commas, ellipses, question marks, and exclamation points that all together formed the incredible story of my thru-hike of the PCT.

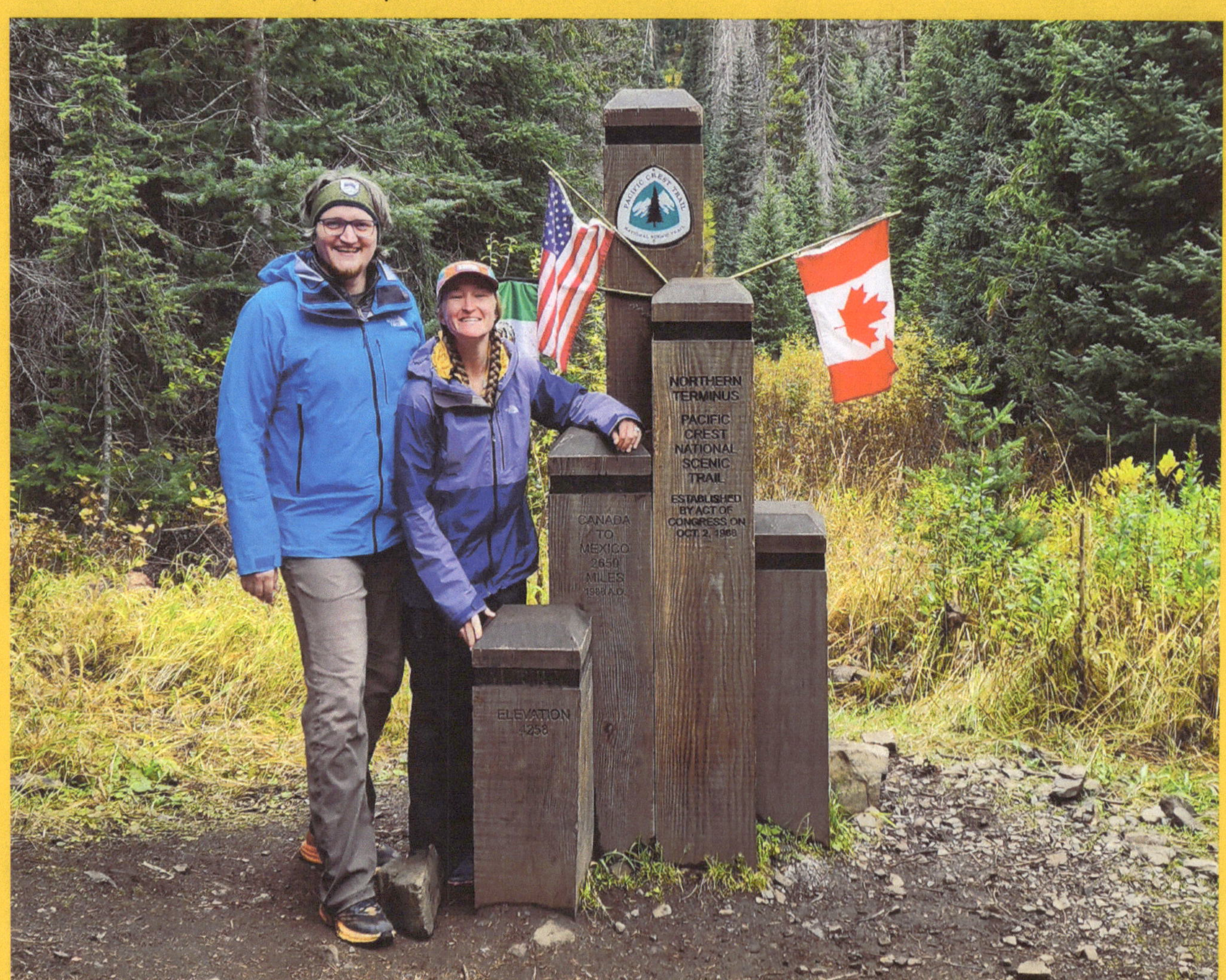

How to read my trail project:

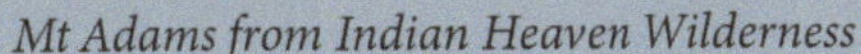
Mt Adams from Indian Heaven Wilderness

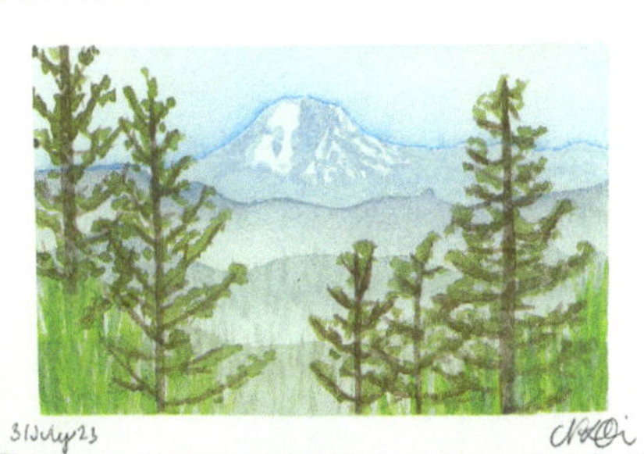

Big Huckleberry Trailhead to Blue Lake	
Trail day:	106
Hiking day:	89
Trail miles:	2189.2 - 2208.0
Hiking miles:	18.34
Ascent:	+3852'
Descent:	-1959'
Minimum elevation:	2799'
Maximum elevation:	4984'

slug the same color as pickled jalapeno.

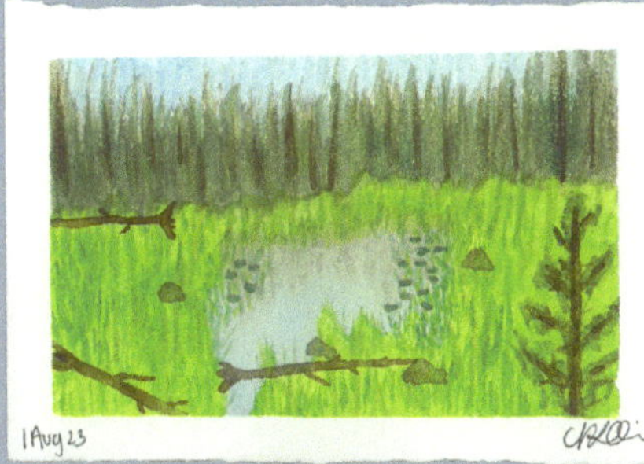

Blue Lake to Indian Heaven Wilderness	
Trail day:	107
Hiking day:	90
Trail miles:	2208.0 - 2229.7
Hiking miles:	22.19
Ascent:	+2979'
Descent:	-3196'
Minimum elevation:	3367'
Maximum elevation:	5197'

A Marshy Meadow with Lily Pads in Indian Heaven Wilderness

86

description of the painting

where I started the day

where I ended the day

days since I started

days spent hiking

trail miles according to Far Out

hiking stats according to my Garmin watch

random thoughts from my journal or mantras that kept me going

same same... next day

Southern California

The Desert

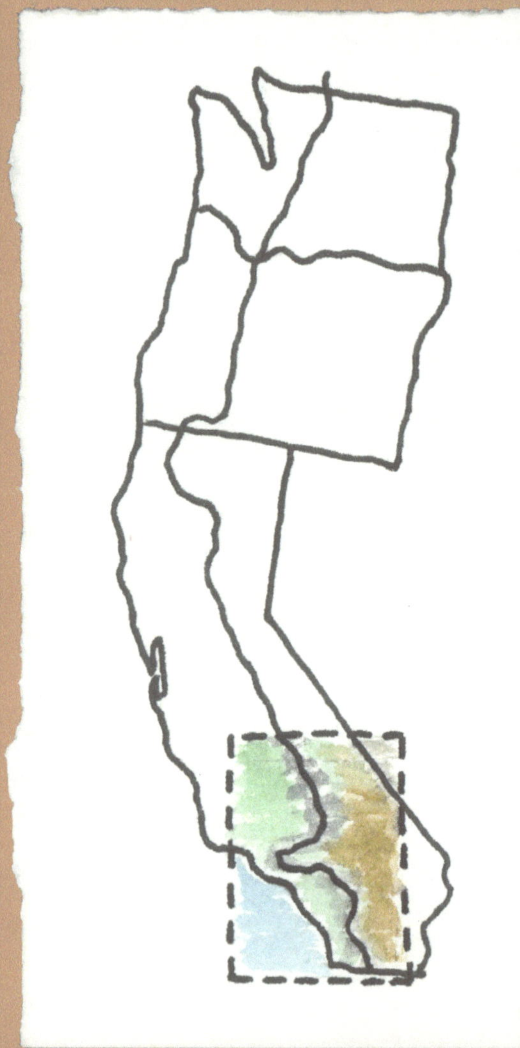

Northbound: Southern Terminus at Campo, CA to
Kennedy Meadows South, CA

April 17 to June 2, 2023

Trail days:	47
Hiking days:	41
Trail miles:	0.0 - 703.4
Average miles per hiking day:	17.16
Fewest miles per hiking day:	5.23
Most miles per hiking day:	31.84

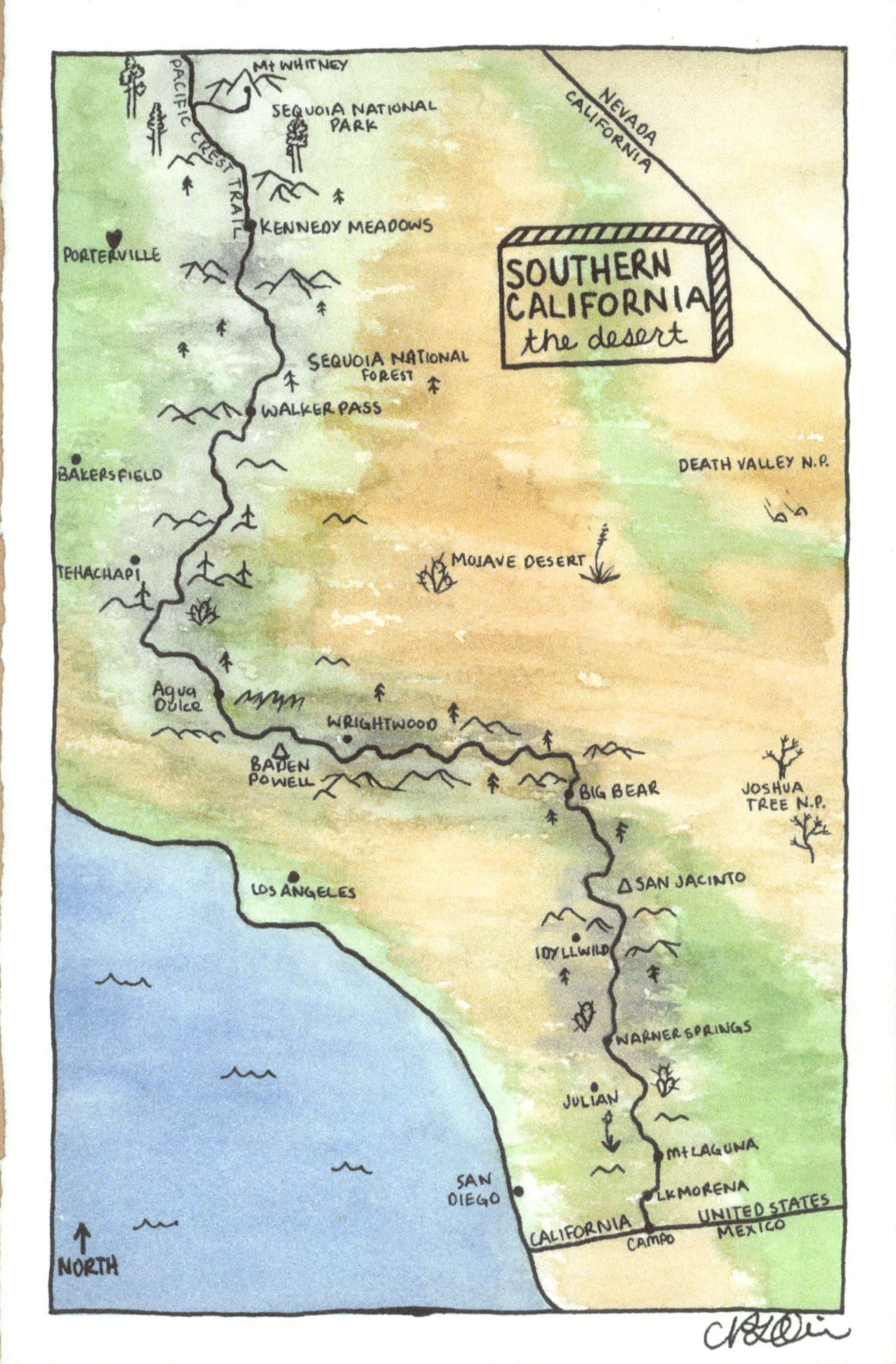
SOUTHERN CALIFORNIA
the desert
Mt WHITNEY
SEQUOIA NATIONAL PARK
PACIFIC CREST TRAIL
NEVADA
CALIFORNIA
KENNEDY MEADOWS
PORTERVILLE
SEQUOIA NATIONAL FOREST
WALKER PASS
BAKERSFIELD
DEATH VALLEY N.P.
TEHACHAPI
MOJAVE DESERT
Agua Dulce
WRIGHTWOOD
BADEN POWELL
BIG BEAR
JOSHUA TREE N.P.
LOS ANGELES
SAN JACINTO
IDYLLWILD
WARNER SPRINGS
JULIAN
Mt LAGUNA
SAN DIEGO
LK MORENA
UNITED STATES
MEXICO
CALIFORNIA
CAMPO
NORTH

The Border Wall between Mexico and California

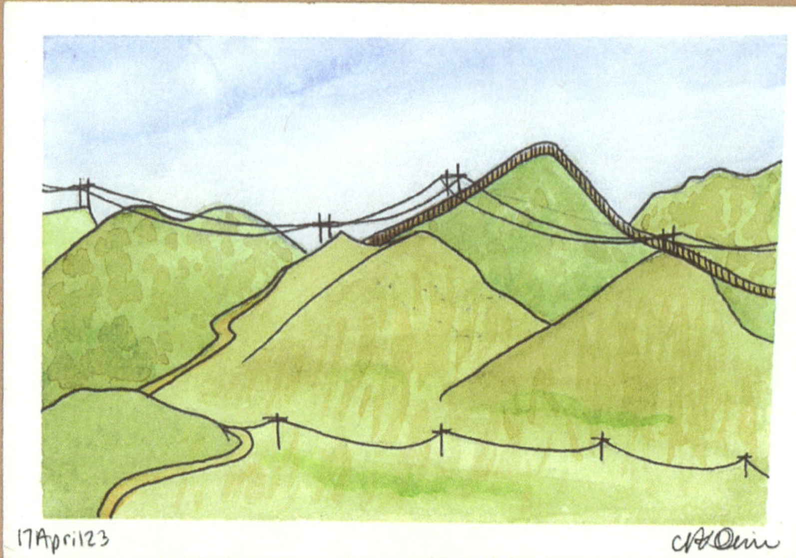

U.S.-Mexico Border to Campo

Trail day:	1
Hiking day:	1
Trail miles:	0 - 5.1
Hiking miles:	5.23
Ascent:	+495’
Descent:	-889’
Minimum elevation:	2373’
Maximum elevation:	2906’

Then it was just me and the trail.

I've adapted my eating schedule to snacking all day long.

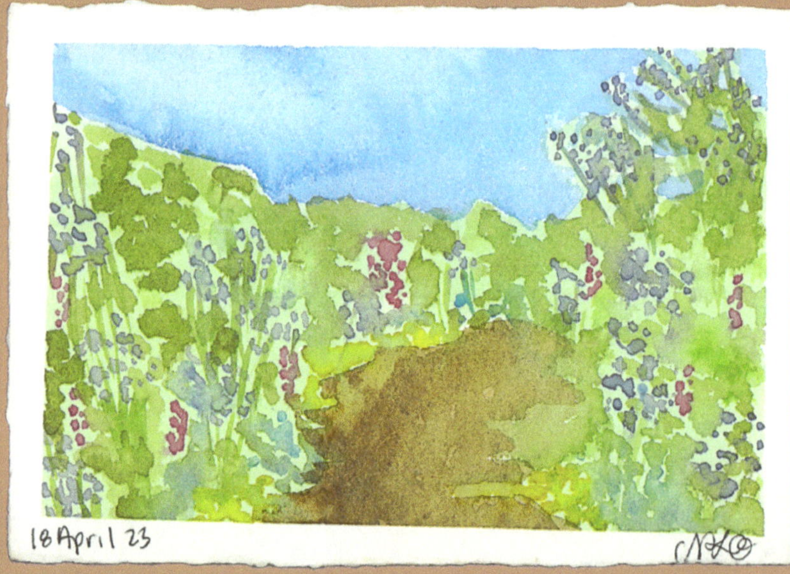

Campo to Lake Morena

Trail day:	2
Hiking day:	2
Trail miles:	5.1 - 20.0
Hiking miles:	15.60
Ascent:	+2700’
Descent:	-2188’
Minimum elevation:	2329’
Maximum elevation:	3524’

Wildflowers during a Super Bloom

Rocks above Kitchen Creek Falls

Lake Morena to South of Mt Laguna

Trail day:	3
Hiking day:	3
Trail miles:	20.0 - 36.1
Hiking miles:	16.45
Ascent:	+3349’
Descent:	-1129’
Minimum elevation:	3051’
Maximum elevation:	5299’

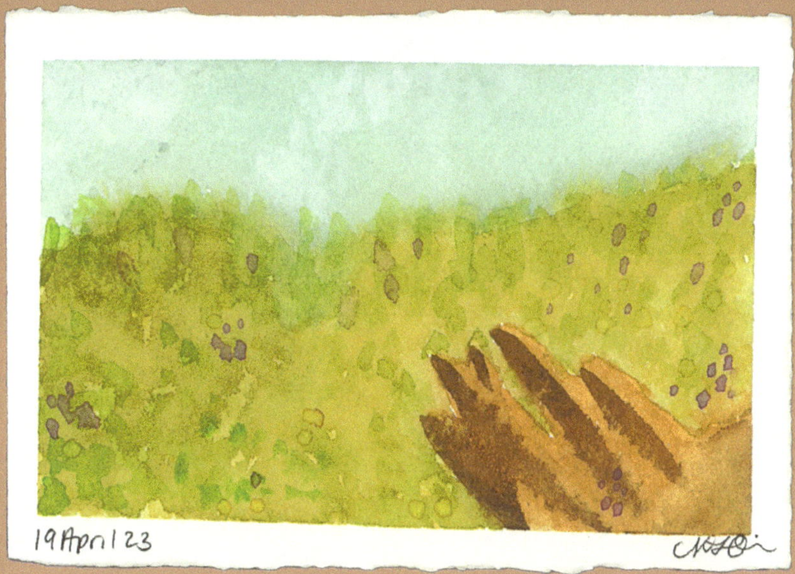

...the name Calypso. It feels right.

South of Mt Laguna to Mt Laguna Campground

Trail day:	4
Hiking day:	4
Trail miles:	36.1 - 47.2
Hiking miles:	13.63
Ascent:	+1903’
Descent:	-1663’
Minimum elevation:	5205’
Maximum elevation:	6016’

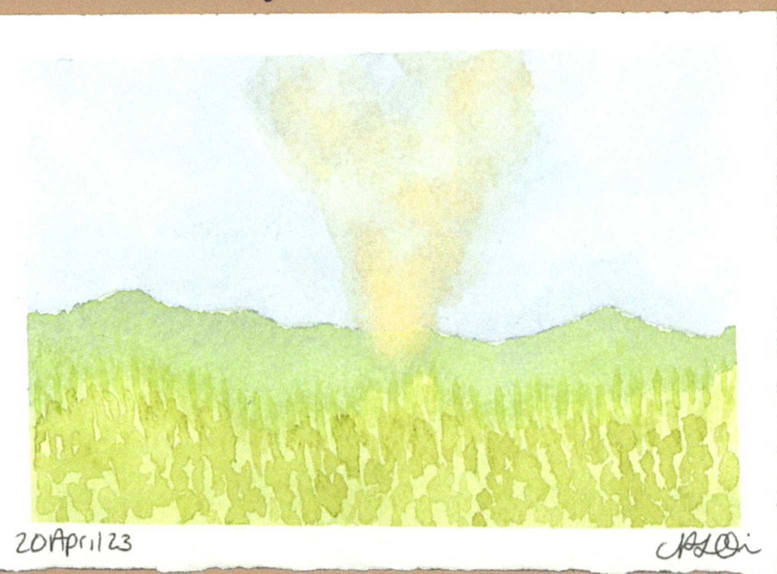

Smoke from a Control Burn near Mt Laguna Campground

Ascent from Pioneer Mail Picnic Site to Kwaaymii Point

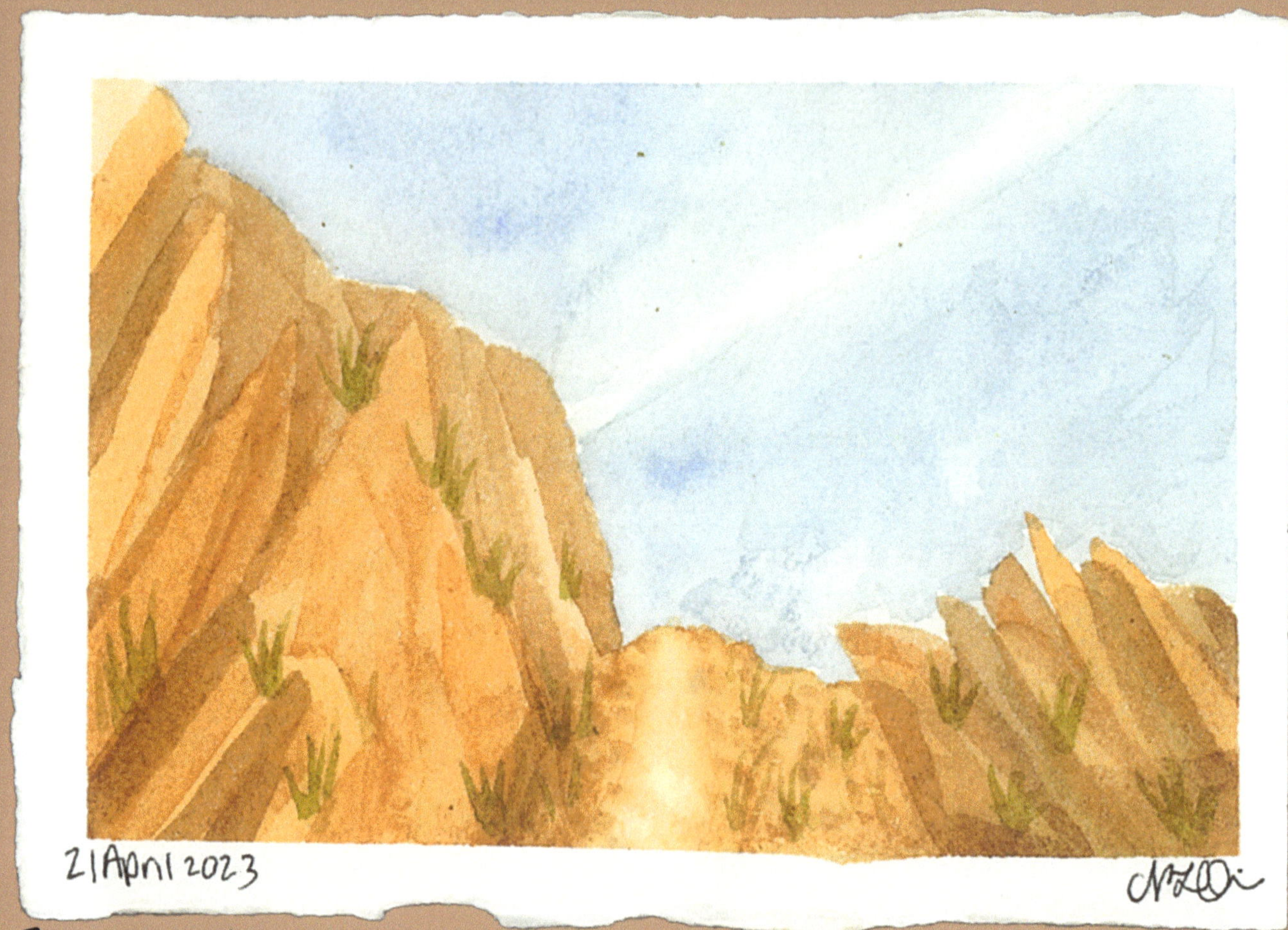

Today I reminded myself that I can do hard things.

Mt Laguna to Rodriguez Water Tank

Trail day:	5	Ascent:	+2230’
Hiking day:	5	Descent:	-4121’
Trail miles:	47.2 - 68.4	Minimum elevation:	3669’
Hiking miles:	21.80	Maximum elevation:	5581’

Descending into Shelter Valley

Rodriguez Water Tank to Scissors Crossing

Trail day:	6
Hiking day:	6
Trail miles:	68.4 - 76.3
Hiking miles:	7.96
Ascent:	+669’
Descent:	-2047’
Minimum elevation:	2260’
Maximum elevation:	3657’

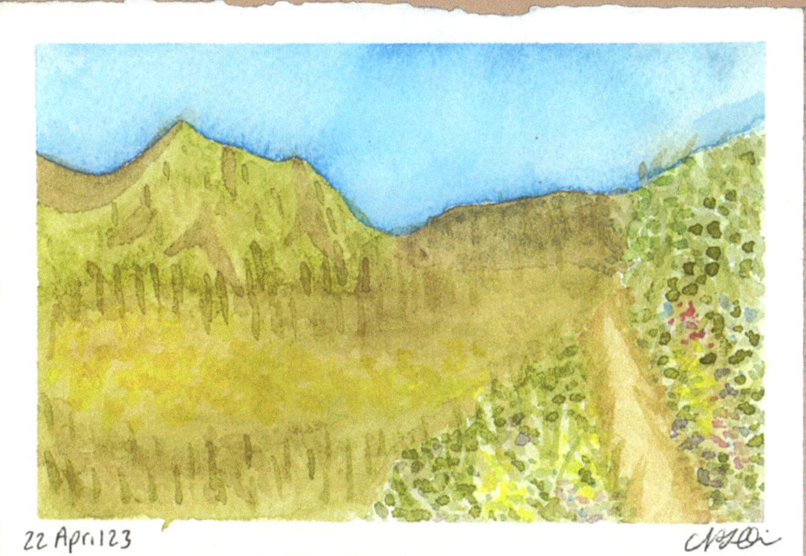

I tended to my feet, painted, and drank a lot of water.

Scissors Crossing to Windy Ridge

Trail day:	7
Hiking day:	7
Trail miles:	76.3 - 94.4
Hiking miles:	18.27
Ascent:	+3062’
Descent:	-1027’
Minimum elevation:	2257’
Maximum elevation:	4312’

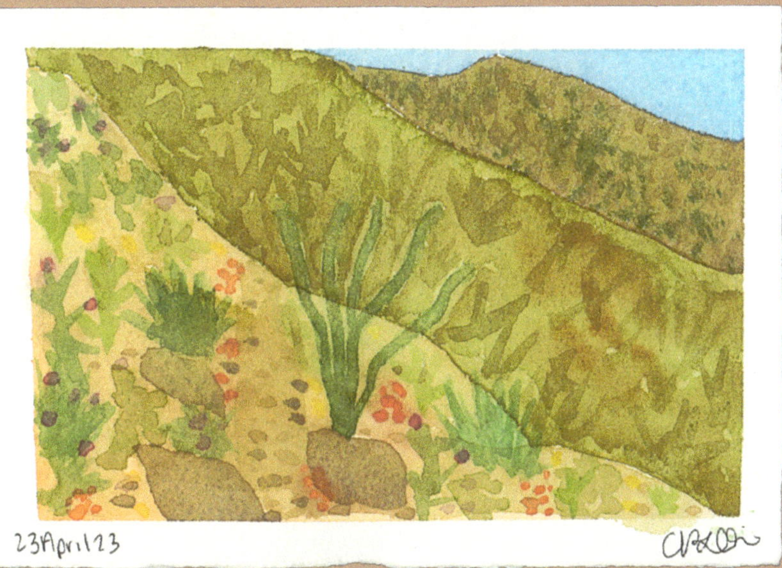

Ascent from Scissors Crossing

Crossing Agua Caliente Creek near Warner Springs

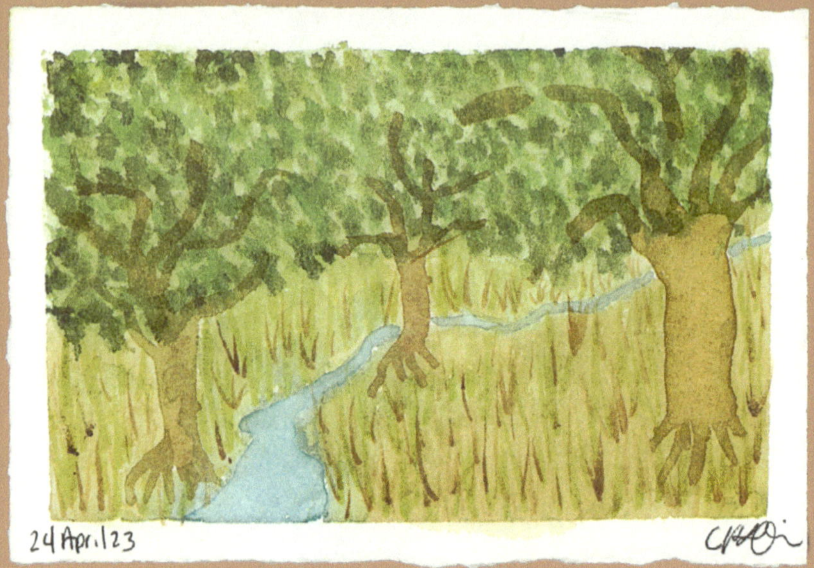

Windy Ridge to Warner Springs

Trail day:	8
Hiking day:	8
Trail miles:	94.4 - 109.5
Hiking miles:	18.58
Ascent:	+1426'
Descent:	-2691'
Minimum elevation:	3051'
Maximum elevation:	4385'

We had a shoes-off feet-soaking break before the climb.

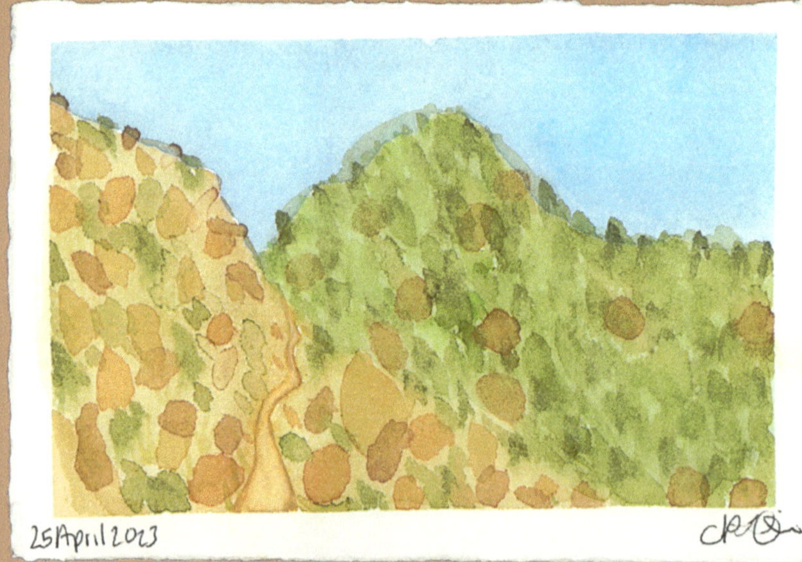

Warner Springs to Mike's Place

Trail day:	9
Hiking day:	9
Trail miles:	109.5 - 126.9
Hiking miles:	18.05
Ascent:	+3330'
Descent:	-1407'
Minimum elevation:	2910'
Maximum elevation:	5231'

Fields of Big Red Boulders Leading to Mike's Place

Looking North toward Apache Peak from Comb's Peak Ridge

Mike's Place to Coyote Road

Trail day:	10
Hiking day:	10
Trail miles:	126.9 - 142.9
Hiking miles:	16.74
Ascent:	+2142'
Descent:	-3133'
Minimum elevation:	3376'
Maximum elevation:	5606'

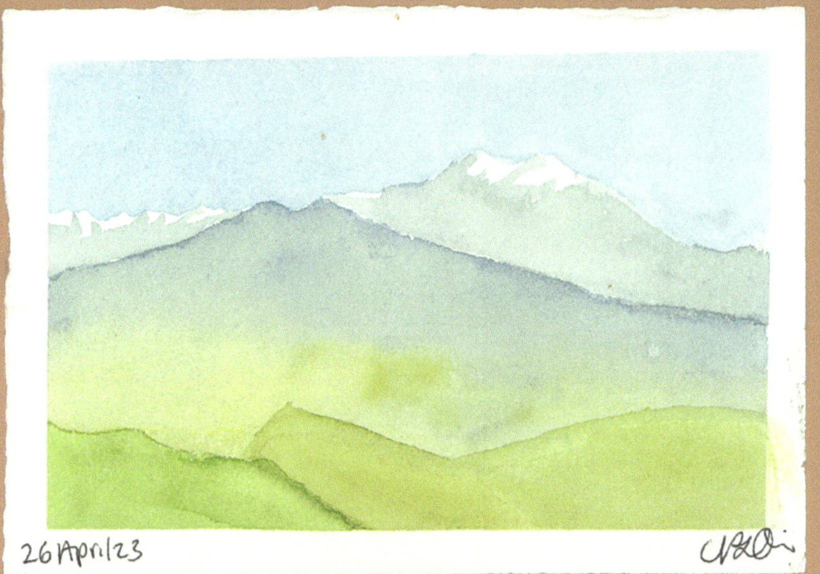

Coyote Road to Highway 74

Trail day:	11
Hiking day:	11
Trail miles:	142.9 - 151.8
Hiking miles:	8.99
Ascent:	+1670'
Descent:	-829'
Minimum elevation:	4099'
Maximum elevation:	5067'

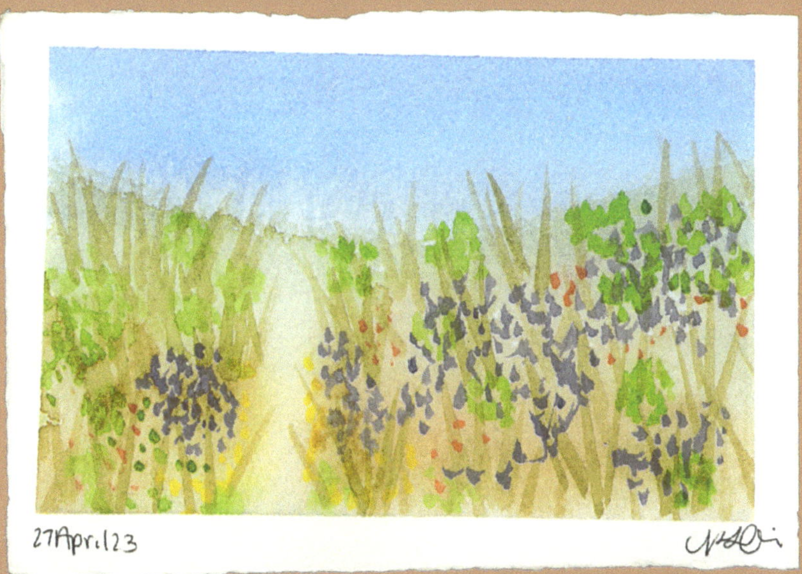

Wildflowers on the Way to Paradise Valley Cafe

Looking North at Mt San Jacinto

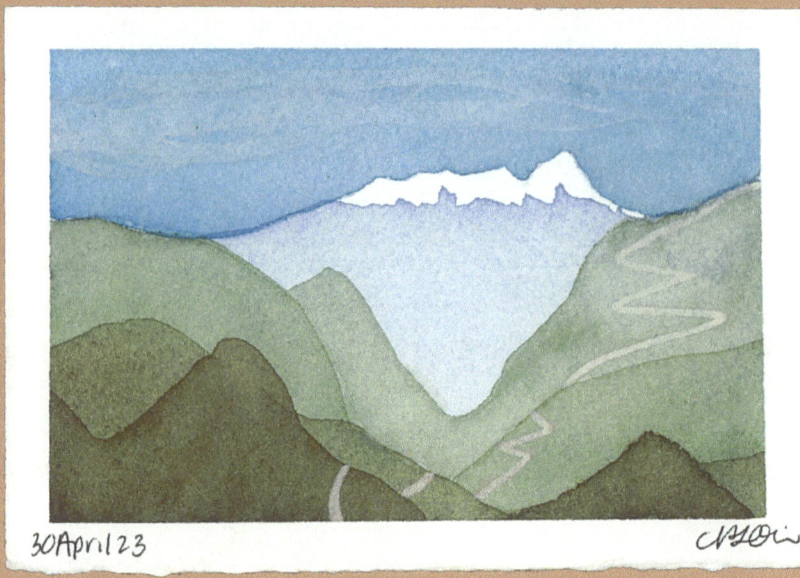

Highway 74 to the San Jacinto Range

Trail day:	14
Hiking day:	12
Trail miles:	151.8 - 157.4
Hiking miles:	5.66
Ascent:	+1274’
Descent:	-495’
Minimum elevation:	4896’
Maximum elevation:	5732’

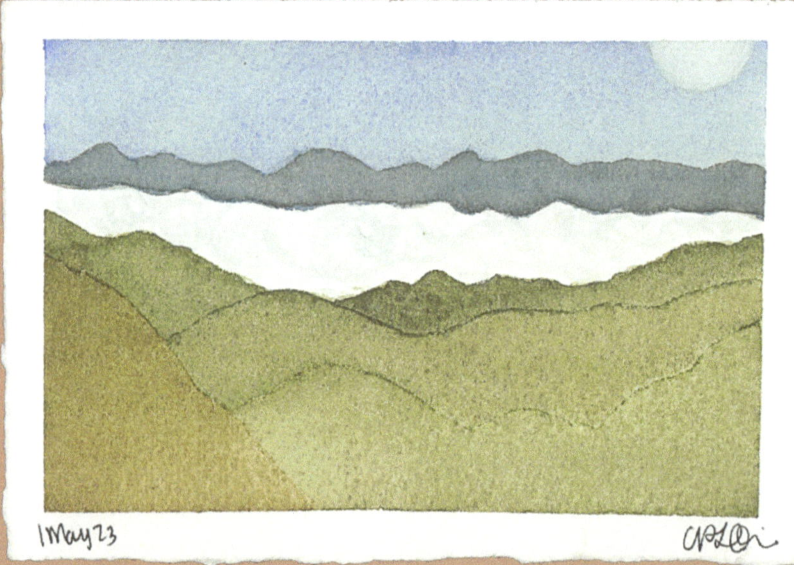

San Jacinto Range to Spitler Cutoff

Trail day:	15
Hiking day:	13
Trail miles:	157.4 - 168.5
Hiking miles:	14.60
Ascent:	+4140’
Descent:	-2784’
Minimum elevation:	5432’
Maximum elevation:	7224’

Sea of Clouds Looking West toward Idyllwild

A Frosty Sunrise from Spitler Cutoff Overlooking Palm Springs

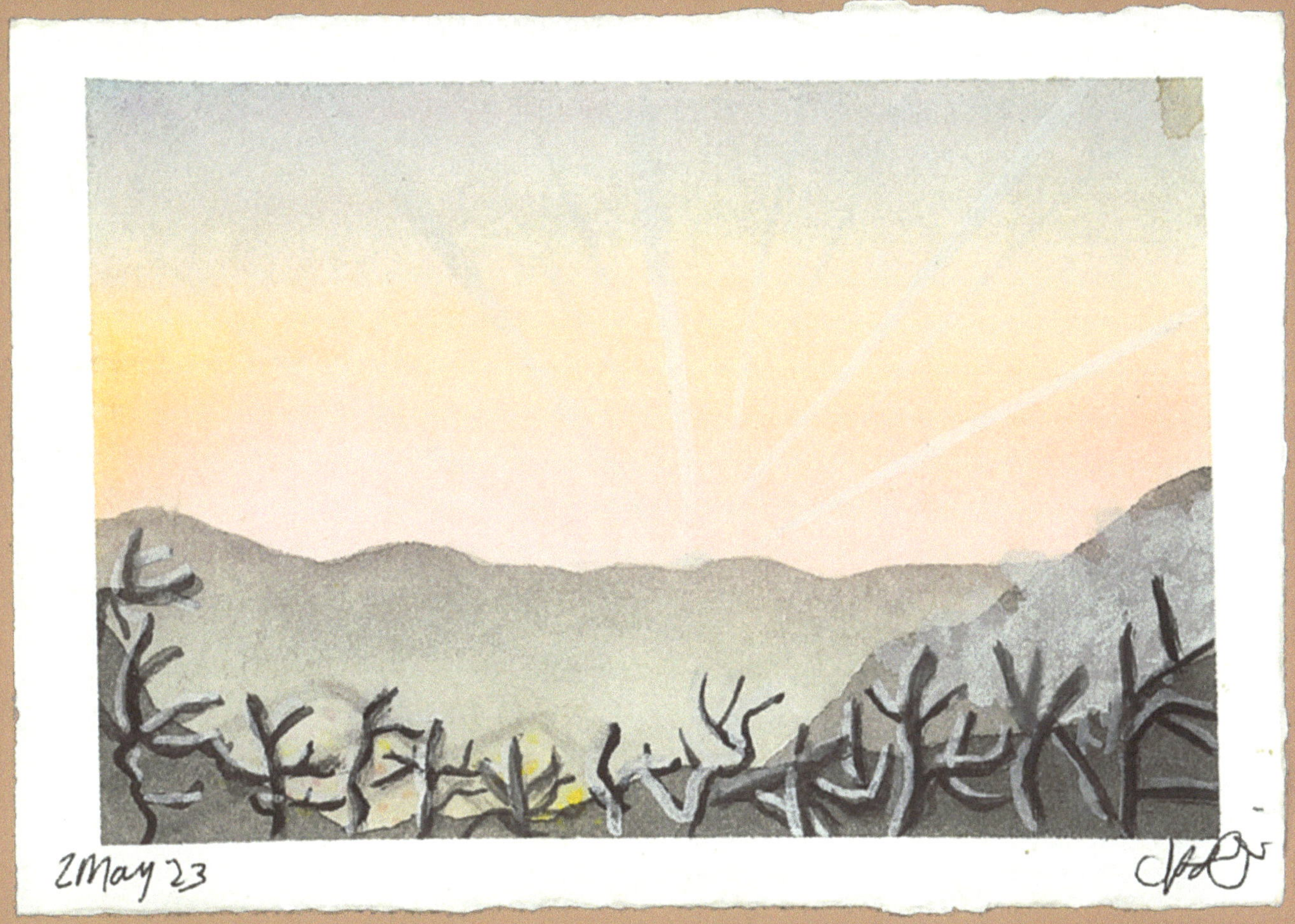

Spitler Cutoff to Strawberry Junction

Trail day:	16	Ascent:	+4186’
Hiking day:	14	Descent:	-3051’
Trail miles:	168.5 - 183.4	Minimum elevation:	6865’
Hiking miles:	15.59	Maximum elevation:	9085’

Crossing Snowfields in the San Jacinto Range

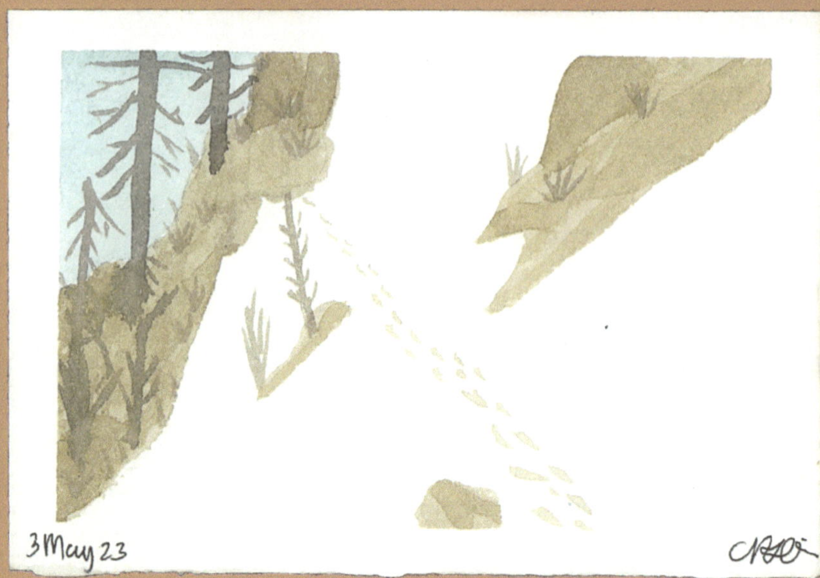

Strawberry Junction to I-10

Trail day:	17
Hiking day:	15
Trail miles:	183.4 - 207.0
Hiking miles:	25.70
Ascent:	+2887'
Descent:	-9806'
Minimum elevation:	1207'
Maximum elevation:	9005'

Wow today was a slog.

The miles went quick today.

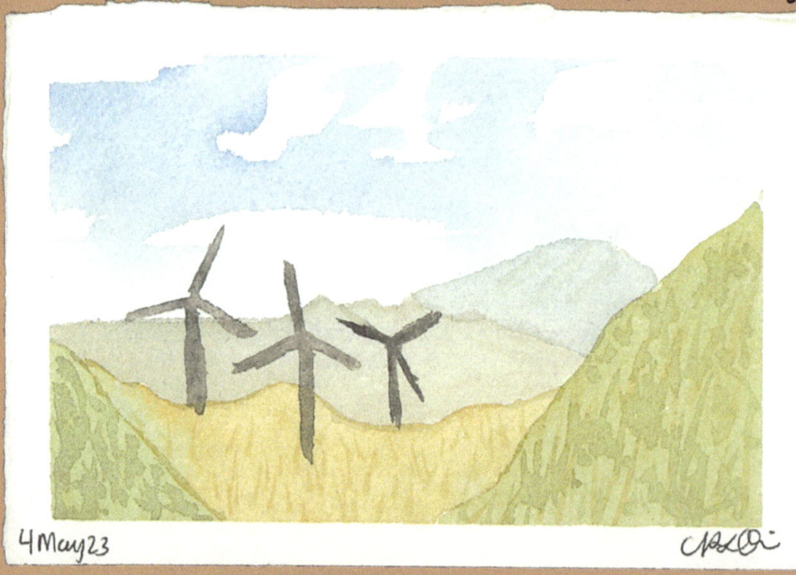

I-10 to Whitewater Preserve

Trail day:	18
Hiking day:	16
Trail miles:	207.0 - 218.5
Hiking miles:	12.77
Ascent:	+2818'
Descent:	-1886'
Minimum elevation:	1187'
Maximum elevation:	3266'

Climbing to Whitewater Preserve Looking South toward Mt Torro

Crossing Whitewater River

Whitewater Preserve to Mission Creek

Trail day:	19
Hiking day:	17
Trail miles:	218.5 - 236.9
Hiking miles:	20.16
Ascent:	+5890'
Descent:	-1458'
Minimum elevation:	2096'
Maximum elevation:	6673'

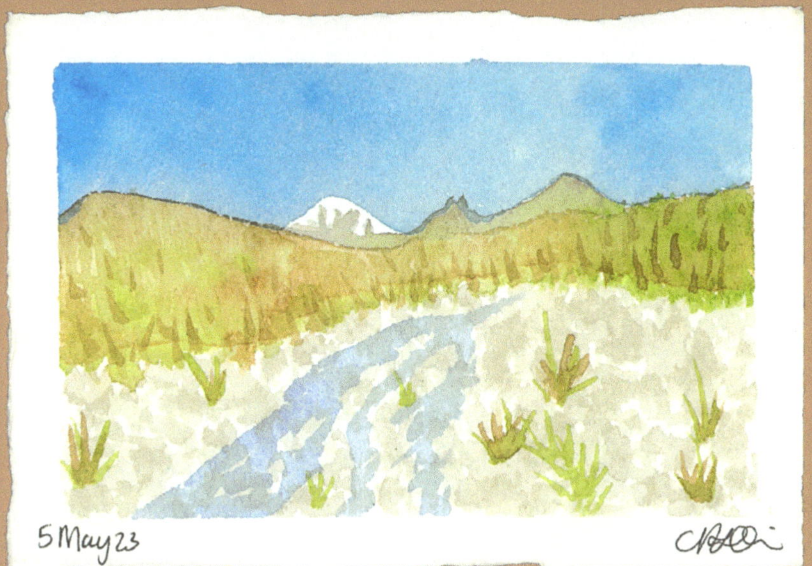

Mission Creek to Arrastre Trail Camp

Trail day:	20
Hiking day:	18
Trail miles:	236.9 - 256.2
Hiking miles:	19.76
Ascent:	+3844'
Descent:	-2869'
Minimum elevation:	6680'
Maximum elevation:	8740'

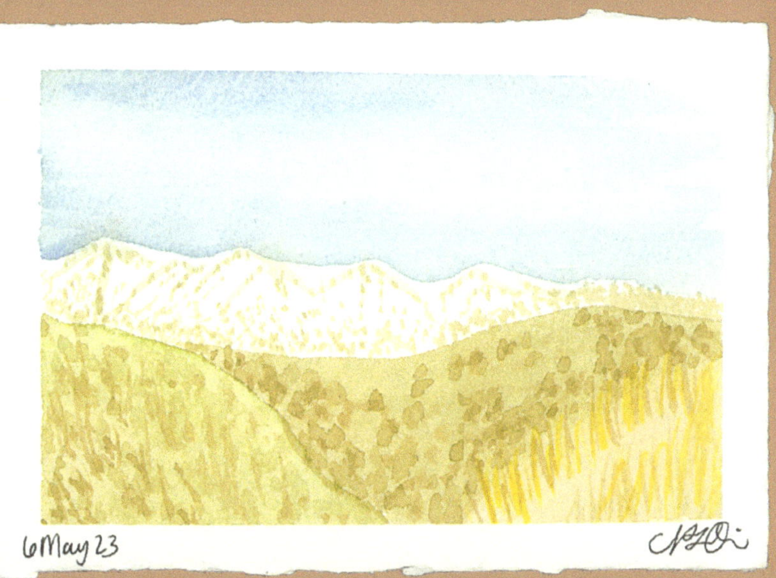

Climbing into Big Bear Looking at Sugarloaf Mountain

Looking East toward Johnson Valley and the Mojave Desert

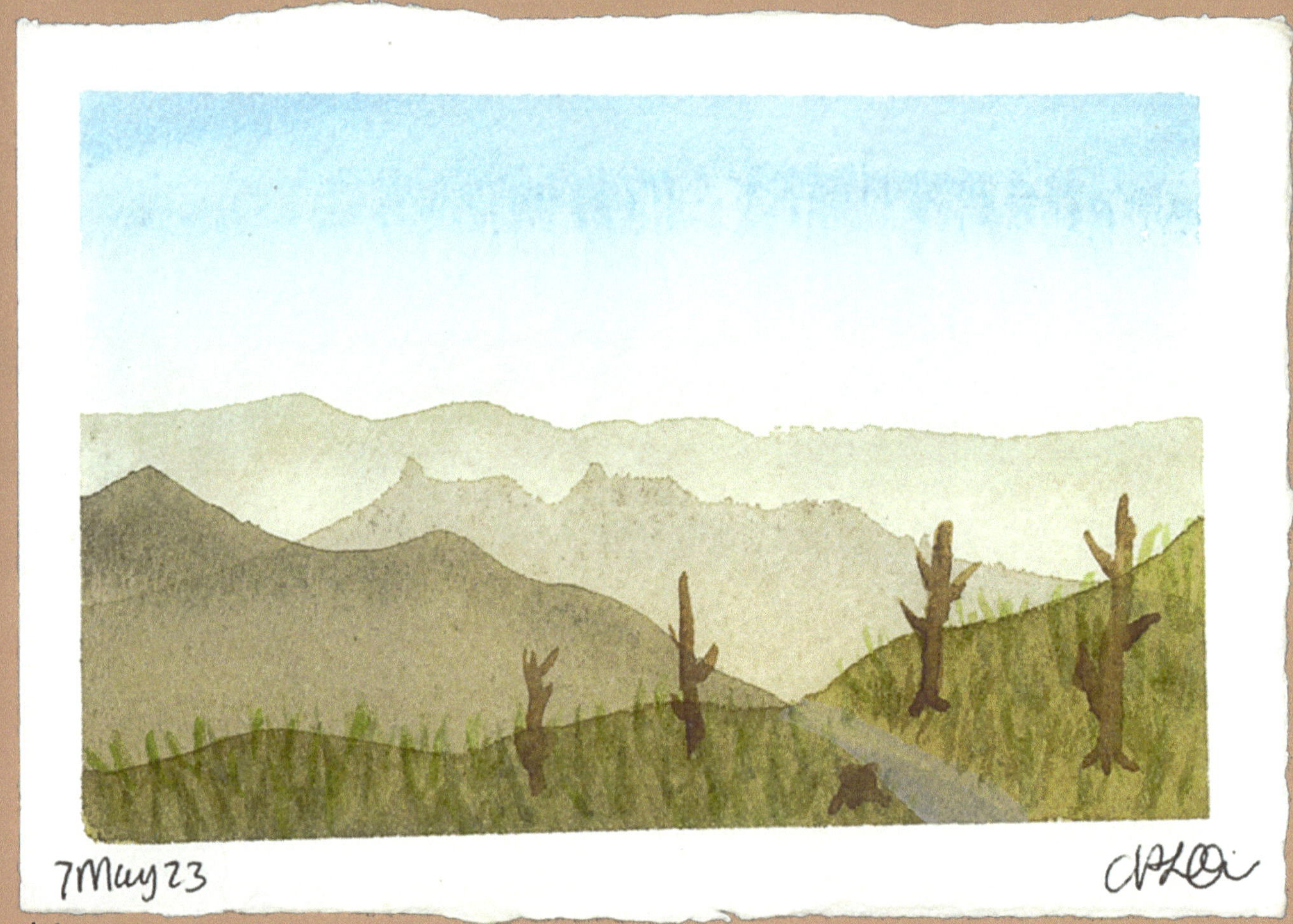

After the enlightenment, the laundry.

Arrastre Trail Camp to Highway 18

Trail day:	21	Ascent:	+1006’
Hiking day:	19	Descent:	-1846’
Trail miles:	256.2 - 266.1	Minimum elevation:	6765’
Hiking miles:	10.46	Maximum elevation:	7688’

Looking across Big Bear Lake at the Ski Runs

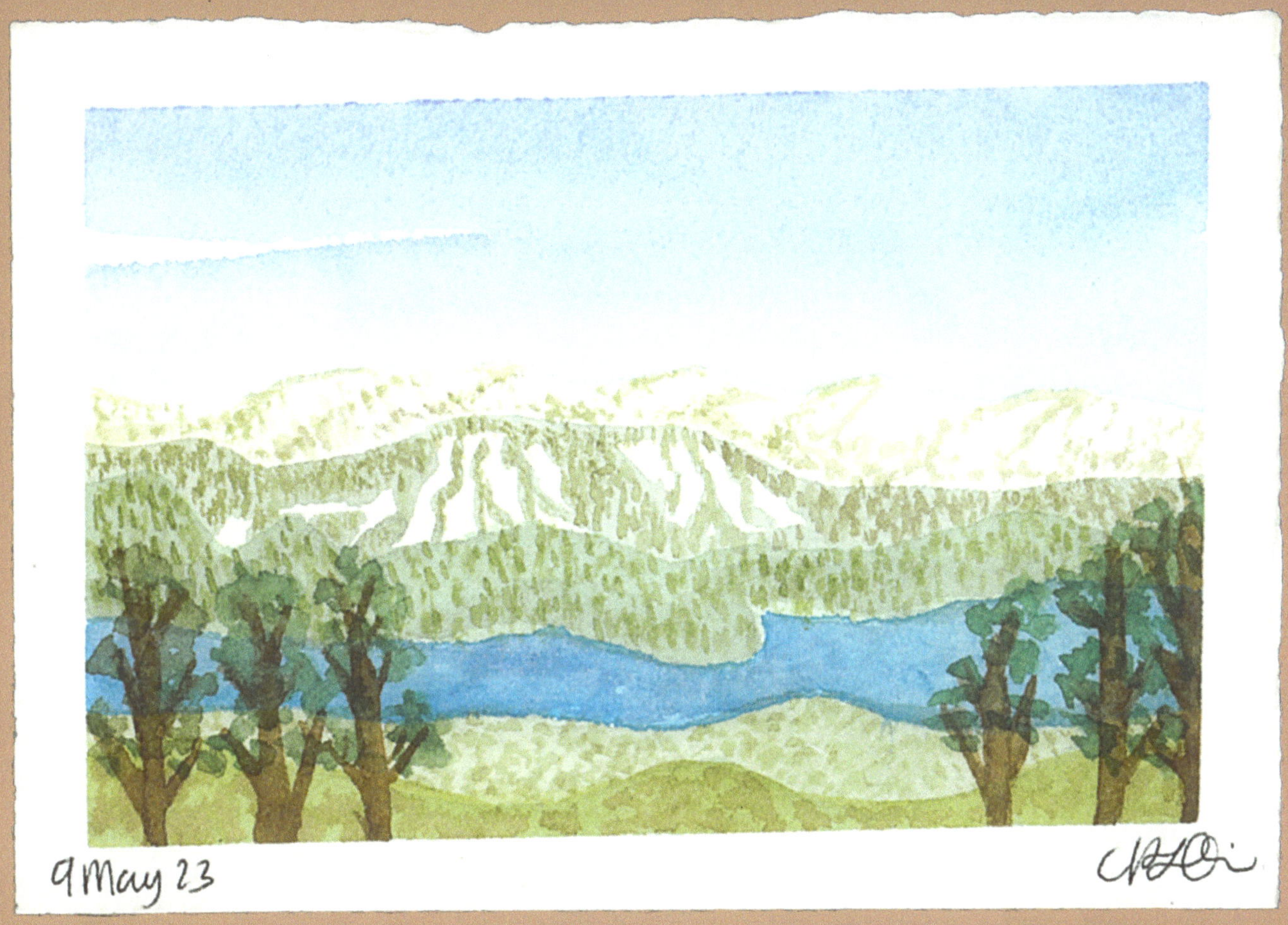

Highway 18 to Holcomb Creek

Trail day:	23	Ascent:	+2629'
Hiking day:	20	Descent:	-3344'
Trail miles:	266.1 - 289.9	Minimum elevation:	6096'
Hiking miles:	24.96	Maximum elevation:	7883'

Deep Creek Hot Springs

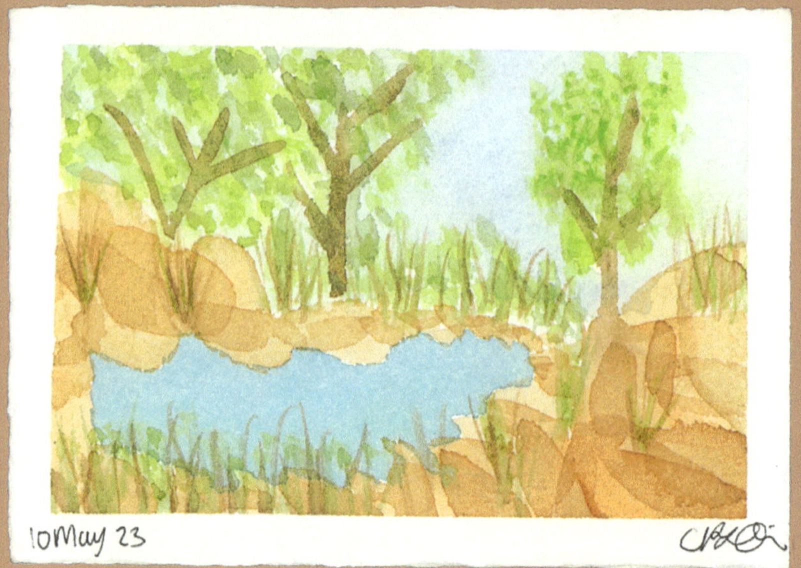

Holcomb Creek to Deep Creek

Trail day:	24
Hiking day:	21
Trail miles:	289.9 - 307.9
Hiking miles:	19.29
Ascent:	+1438'
Descent:	-3971'
Minimum elevation:	3486'
Maximum elevation:	6079'

You will get there if you keep going.

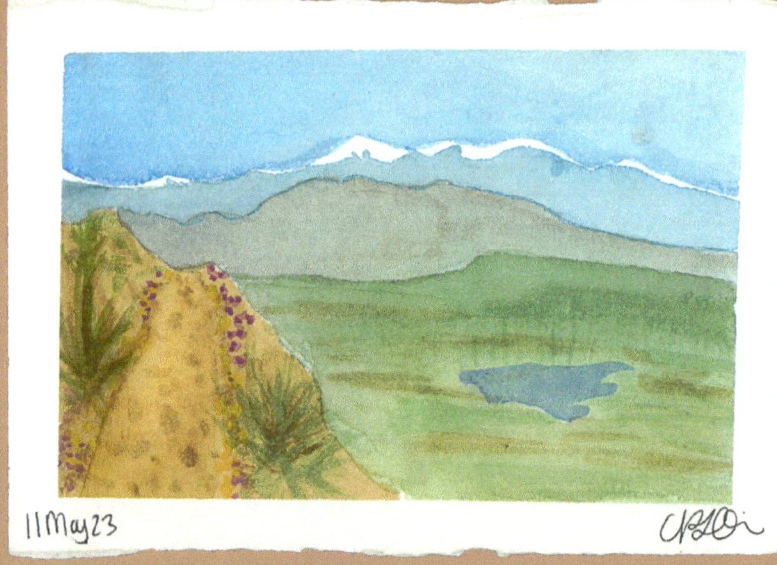

Deep Creek to Silverwood Lake

Trail day:	25
Hiking day:	22
Trail miles:	307.9 - 328.3
Hiking miles:	22.65
Ascent:	+2428'
Descent:	-2441'
Minimum elevation:	3007'
Maximum elevation:	3726'

Looking over the West Fork Mojave River Valley at the San Gabriel Mountains

Hiking past Railroad Tracks and Mormon Rocks after Crossing I-15

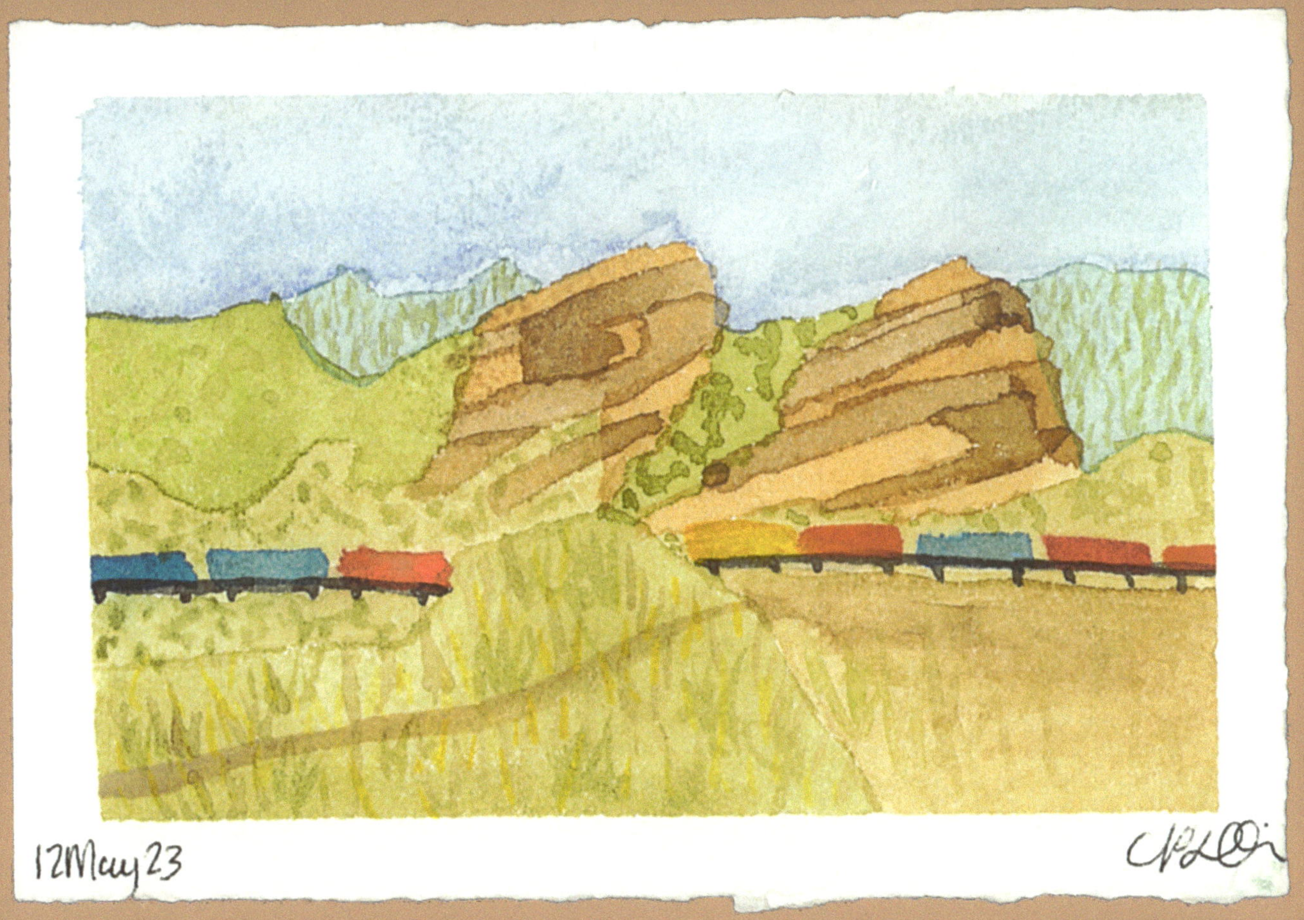

Silverwood Lake to Upper Lytle Creek Divide

Trail day:	26	Ascent:	+4497’
Hiking day:	23	Descent:	-2805’
Trail miles:	328.3 - 352.7	Minimum elevation:	2969’
Hiking miles:	25.33	Maximum elevation:	5192’

Ascending toward Wrightwood in the San Gabriel Mountains

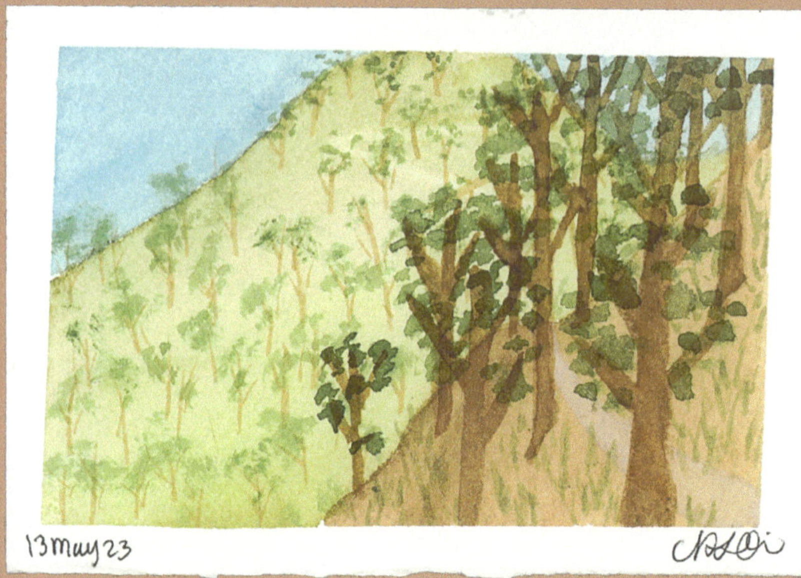

Upper Lytle Creek Divide to Wrightwood	
Trail day:	27
Hiking day:	24
Trail miles:	352.7 - 367.1
Hiking miles:	18.52
Ascent:	+3868’
Descent:	-2169’
Minimum elevation:	5177’
Maximum elevation:	8472’

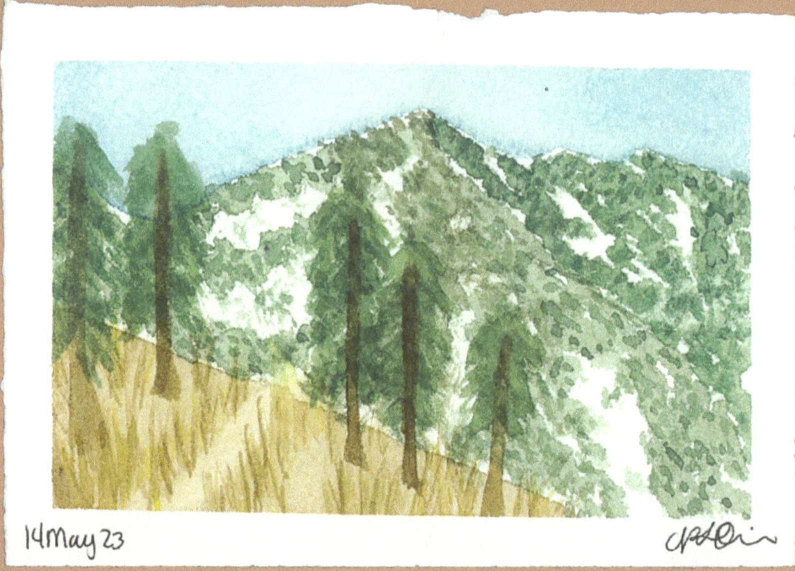

Wrightwood to Vincent Gap	
Trail day:	28
Hiking day:	25
Trail miles:	367.1 - 374.0
Hiking miles:	6.14
Ascent:	+1024’
Descent:	-1316’
Minimum elevation:	6635’
Maximum elevation:	7503’

Descending to Vincent Gap Approaching Mt Baden-Powell

Hiking through a Snowy Burn Area after Summiting Mt Baden-Powell

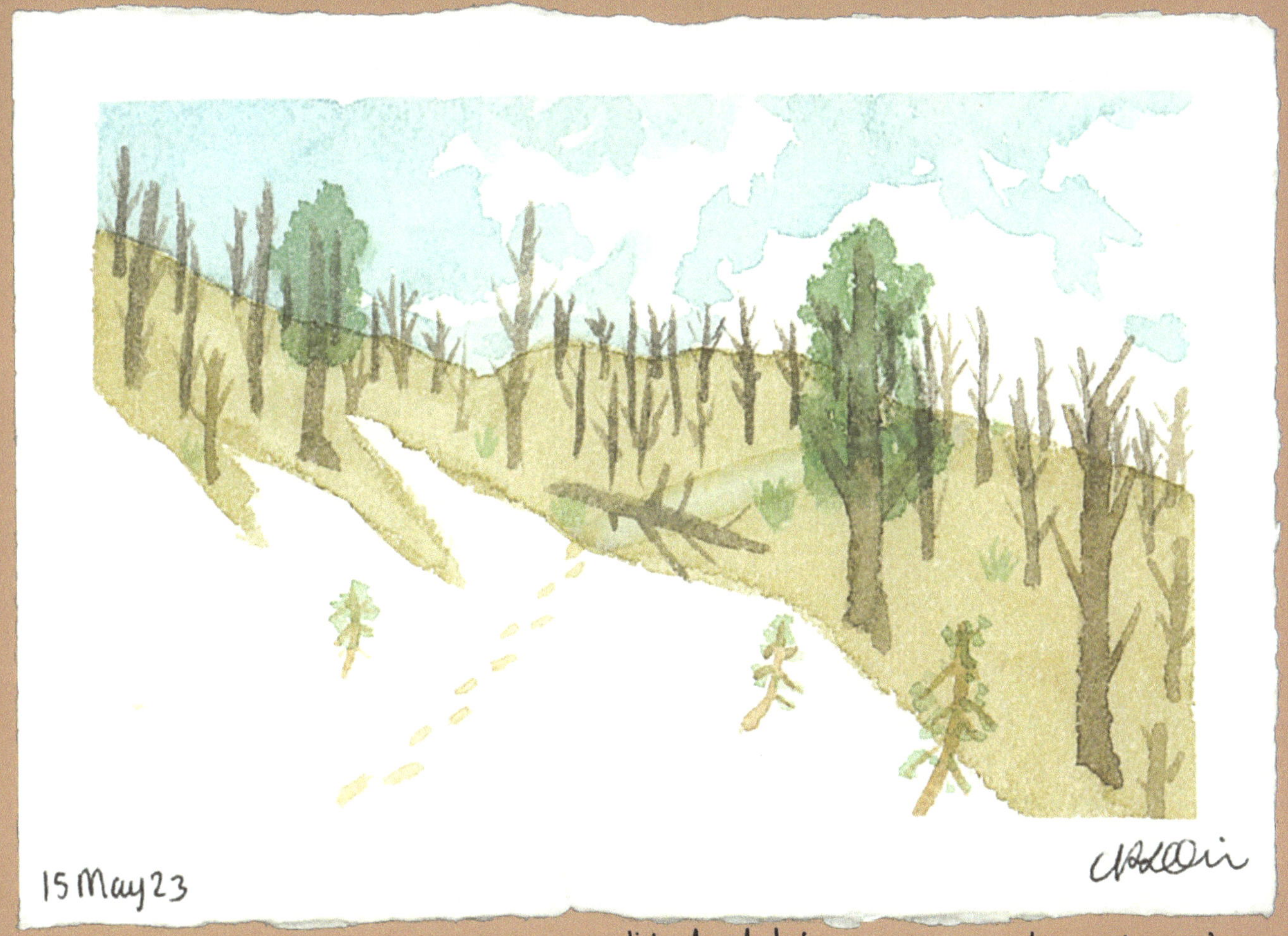

I've decided to prioritize painting over writing.

Vincent Gap to Cooper Canyon Trail Camp

Trail day:	29	Ascent:	+5226'
Hiking day:	26	Descent:	-5531'
Trail miles:	374.0 - 395.2	Minimum elevation:	5845'
Hiking miles:	20.22	Maximum elevation:	9365'

Sunset over Acton from the Ridge of Mt Gleason

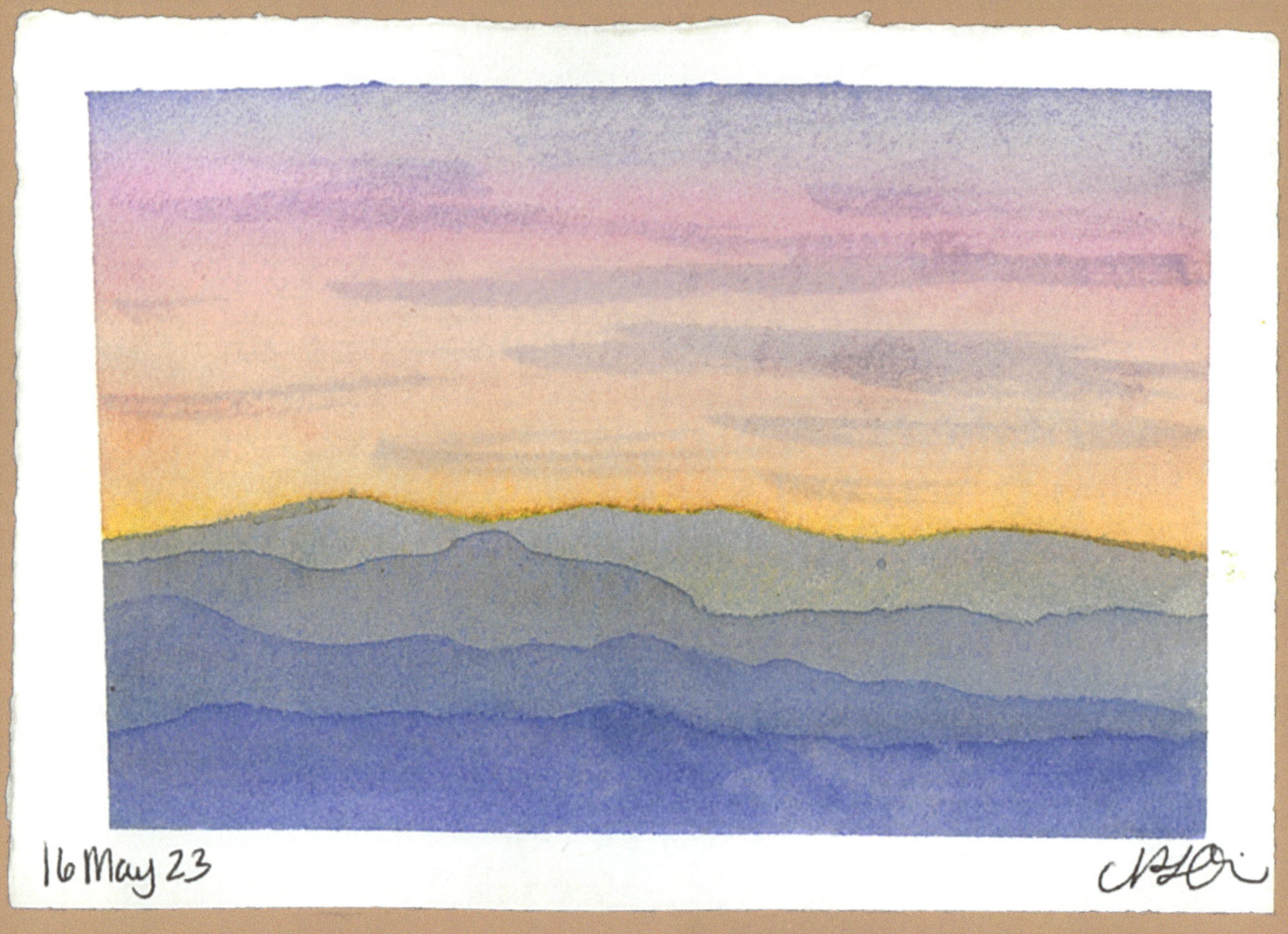

Cooper Canyon Trail Camp to Mill Creek

Trail day:	30	Ascent:	+3897’
Hiking day:	27	Descent:	-4554’
Trail miles:	395.2 - 420.8	Minimum elevation:	4944’
Hiking miles:	26.17	Maximum elevation:	7023’

Dropping into the Santa Clara River Valley Looking at Three Sisters Rocks

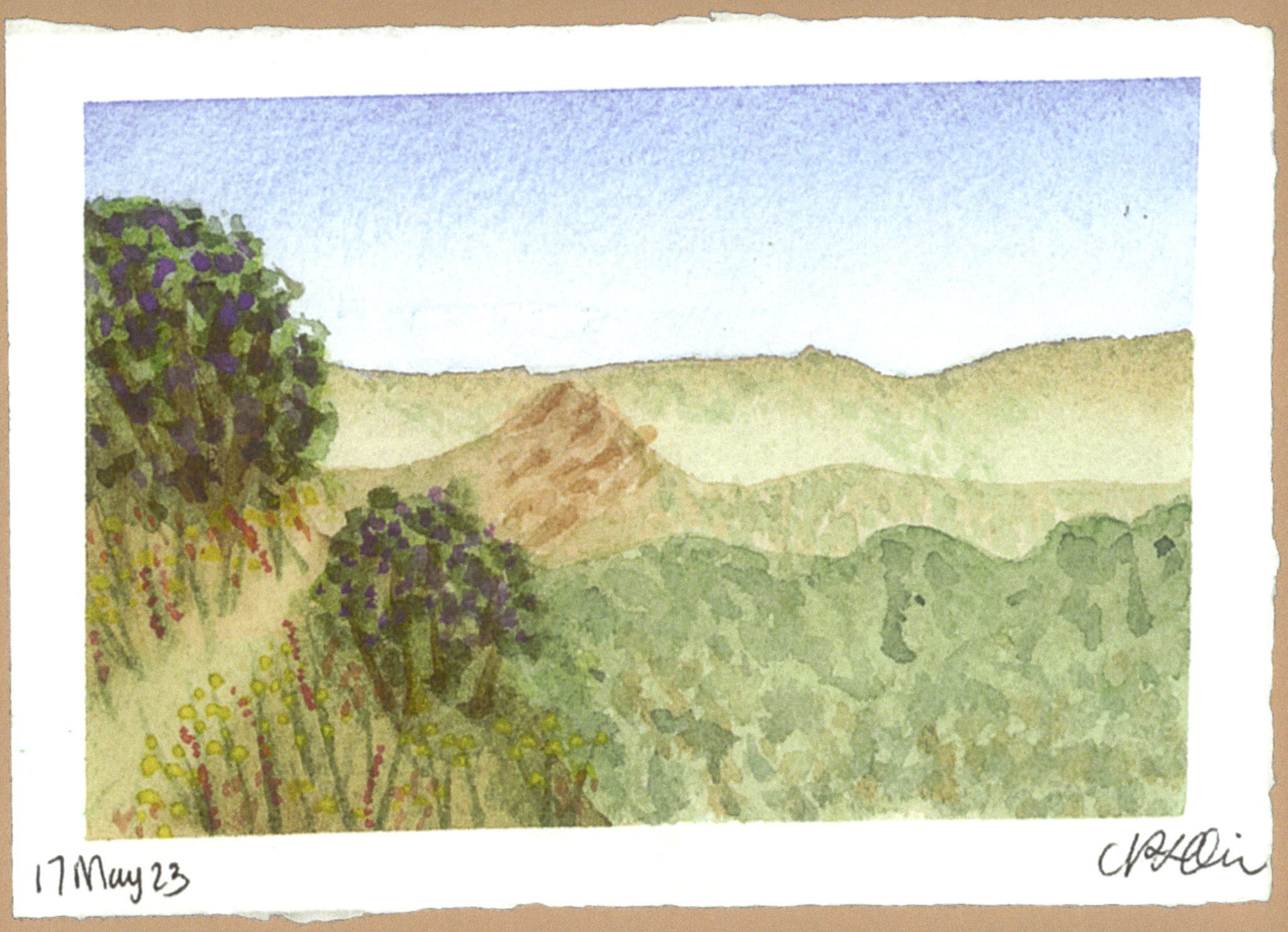

Mill Creek to Acton KOA

Trail day:	31	Ascent:	+2763'
Hiking day:	28	Descent:	-6150'
Trail miles:	420.8 - 444.3	Minimum elevation:	2238'
Hiking miles:	23.66	Maximum elevation:	6417'

Vasquez Rocks

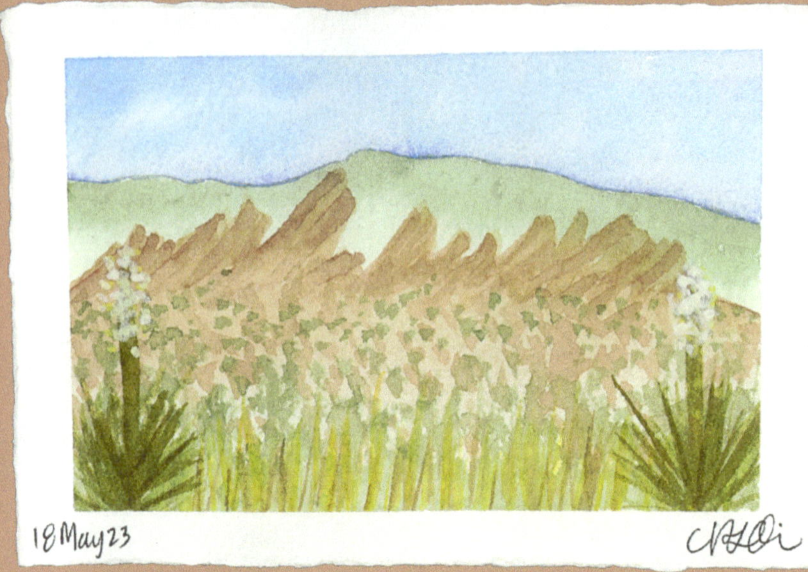

Acton KOA to Leona Divide

Trail day:	32
Hiking day:	29
Trail miles:	444.3 - 468.2
Hiking miles:	24.89
Ascent:	+5170’
Descent:	-3463’
Minimum elevation:	2220’
Maximum elevation:	4623’

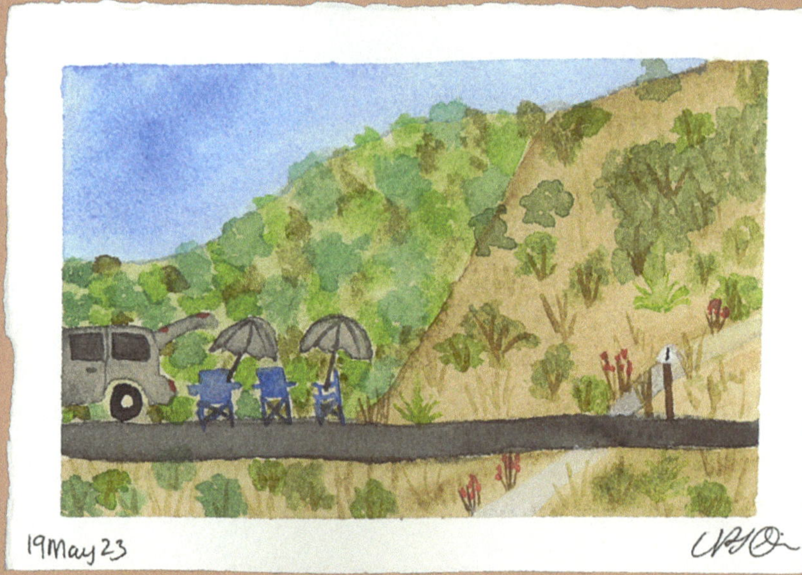

Trail Magic on Lake Hughes Road

Leona Divide to Lake Hughes Road

Trail day:	33
Hiking day:	30
Trail miles:	468.2 - 485.5
Hiking miles:	18.07
Ascent:	+2047’
Descent:	-2969’
Minimum elevation:	3016’
Maximum elevation:	4304’

Copious Poodle Dog Bush in a Burn Area

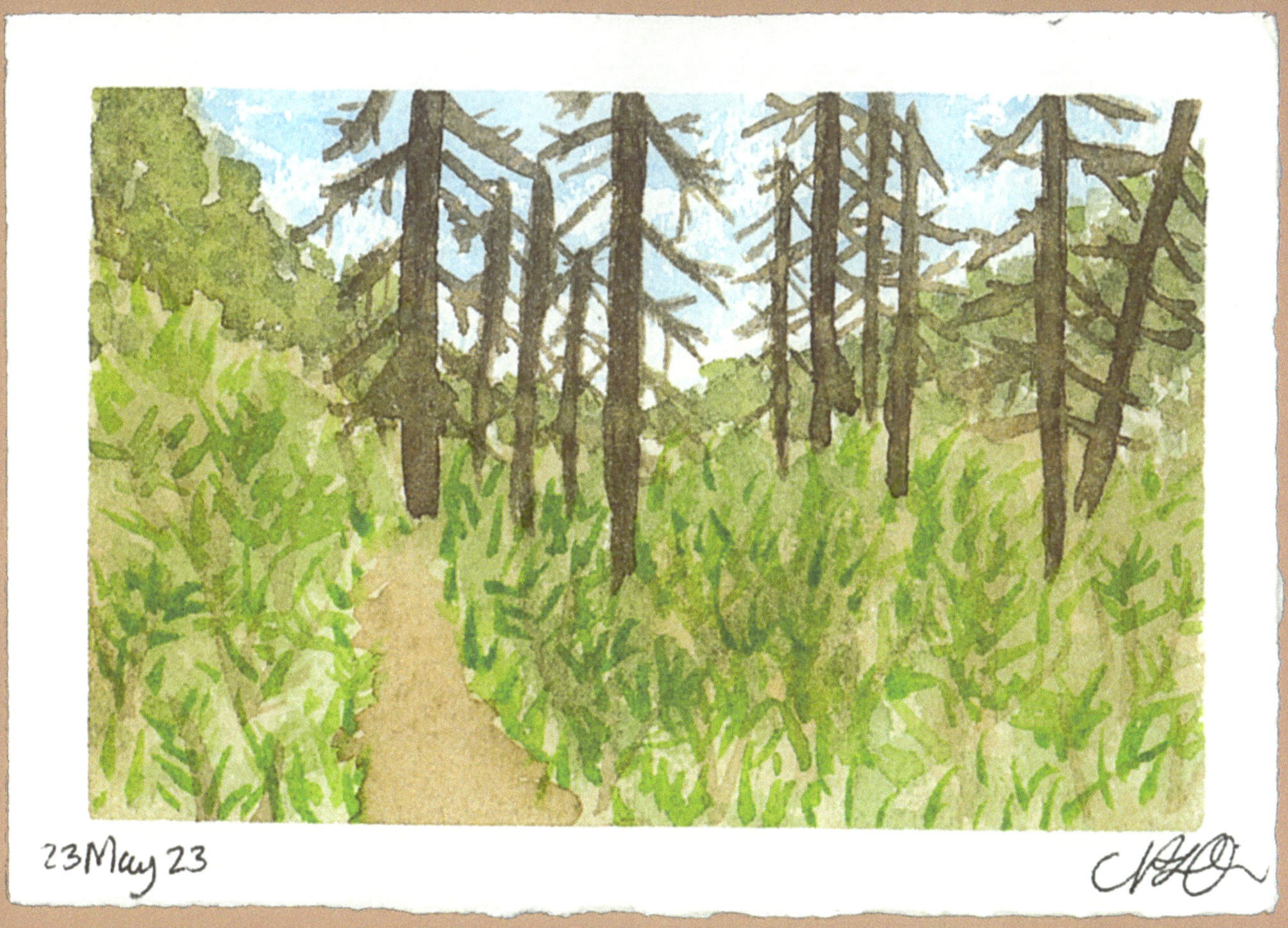

Lake Hughes Road to Sawmill Camp

Trail day:	37	Ascent:	+3297’
Hiking day:	31	Descent:	-1159’
Trail miles:	485.5 - 498.2	Minimum elevation:	3369’
Hiking miles:	12.42	Maximum elevation:	5624’

Los Angeles Aqueduct

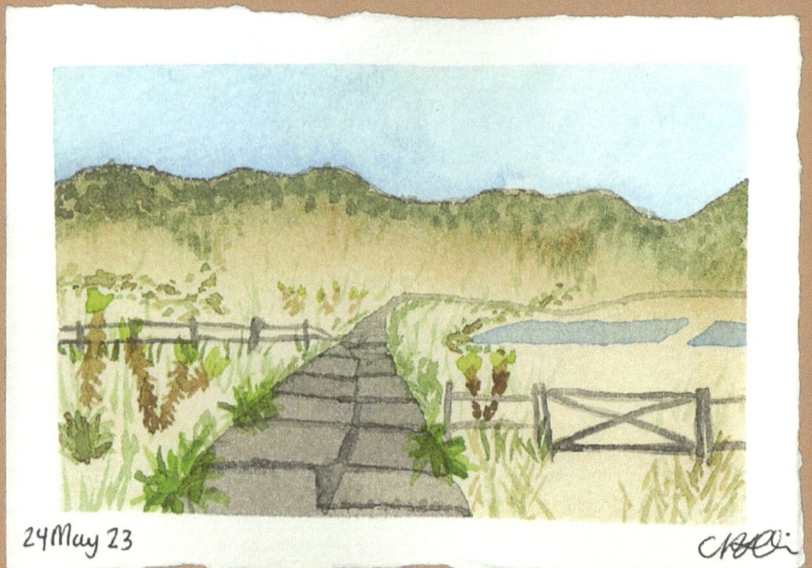

I decided to hike further to put miles in the bank.

Sawmill Camp to Los Angeles Aqueduct

Trail day:	38
Hiking day:	32
Trail miles:	498.2 - 529.4
Hiking miles:	31.84
Ascent:	+3029'
Descent:	-5154'
Minimum elevation:	2869'
Maximum elevation:	5751'

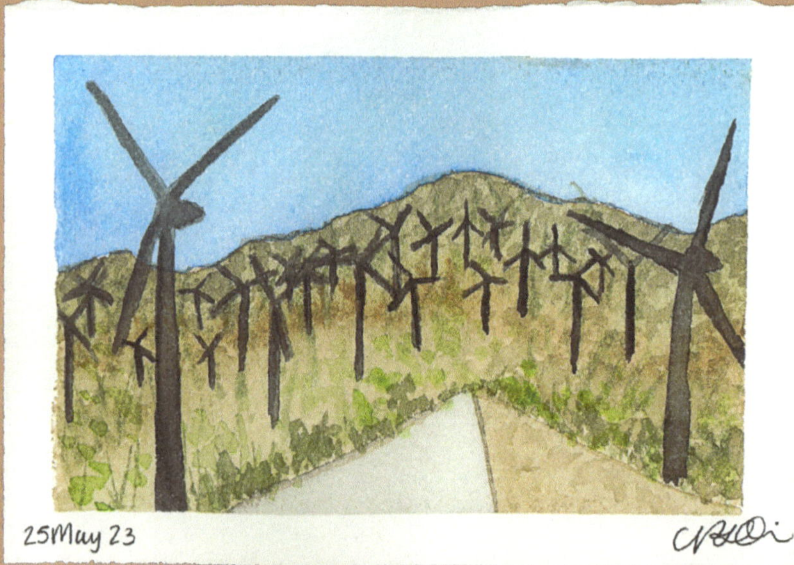

Wind Farm along the Los Angeles Aqueduct

Los Angeles Aqueduct to Cameron Ridge

Trail day:	39
Hiking day:	33
Trail miles:	529.4 - 549.7
Hiking miles:	20.65
Ascent:	+4513'
Descent:	-1431'
Minimum elevation:	2858'
Maximum elevation:	6298'

Sunrise over a Wind Farm Descending to Tehachapi

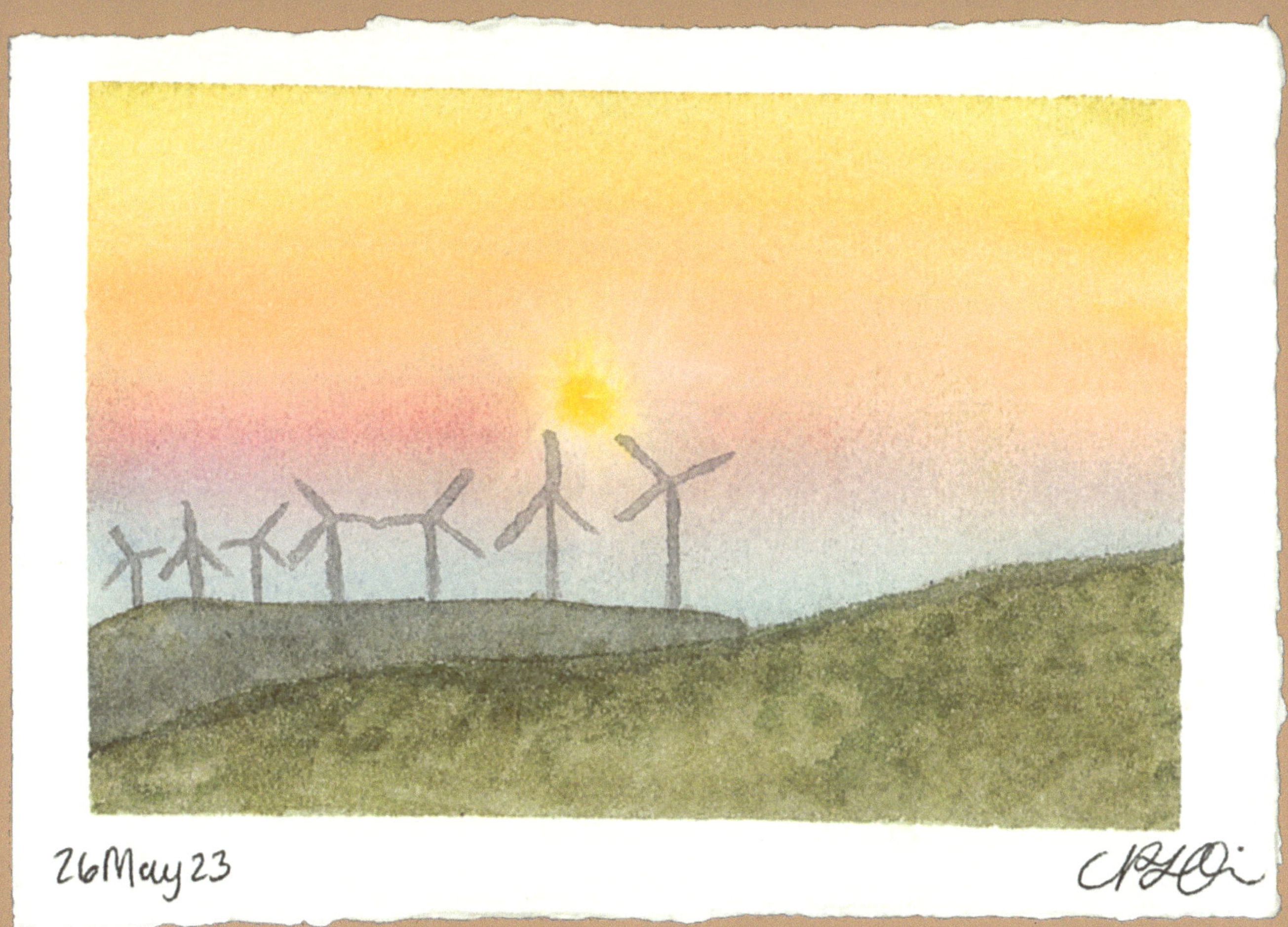

Cameron Ridge to Highway 58

Trail day:	40	Ascent:	+2030’
Hiking day:	34	Descent:	-4385’
Trail miles:	549.7 - 566.1	Minimum elevation:	3805’
Hiking miles:	17.26	Maximum elevation:	6247’

Climbing North from Highway 58

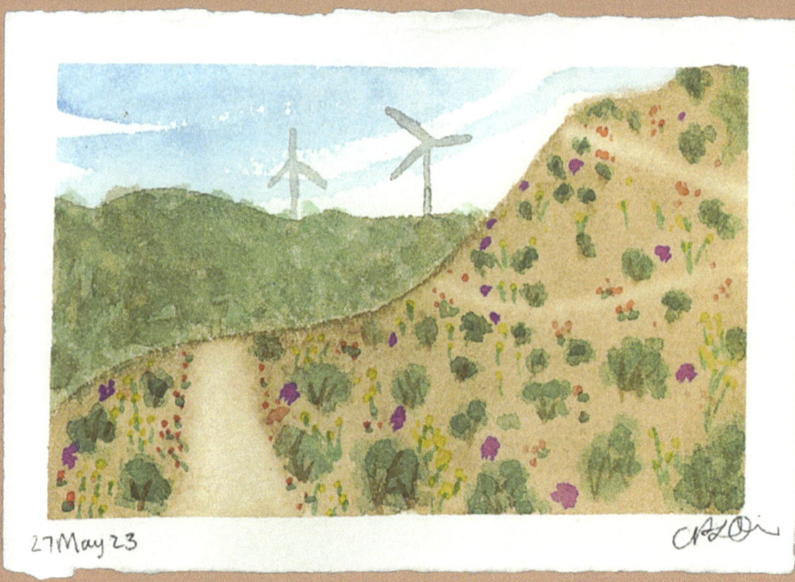

Highway 58 to Golden Oak Spring

Trail day:	41
Hiking day:	35
Trail miles:	566.1 - 583.3
Hiking miles:	15.20
Ascent:	+4006’
Descent:	-2382’
Minimum elevation:	3785’
Maximum elevation:	6301’

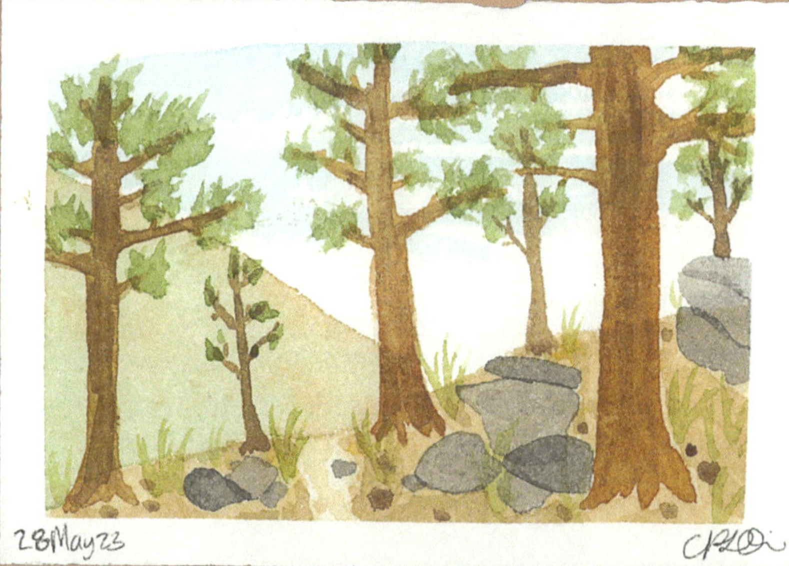

Golden Oak Spring to Landers Creek

Trail day:	42
Hiking day:	36
Trail miles:	583.3 - 607.5
Hiking miles:	24.65
Ascent:	+4895’
Descent:	-3914’
Minimum elevation:	4688’
Maximum elevation:	6816’

Walking through a Pine Forest near Landers Creek

Water Cache at Kelso Road

Landers Creek to Bird Spring Pass

Trail day:	43
Hiking day:	37
Trail miles:	607.5 - 632.0
Hiking miles:	24.91
Ascent:	+3665'
Descent:	-4803'
Minimum elevation:	4551'
Maximum elevation:	6700'

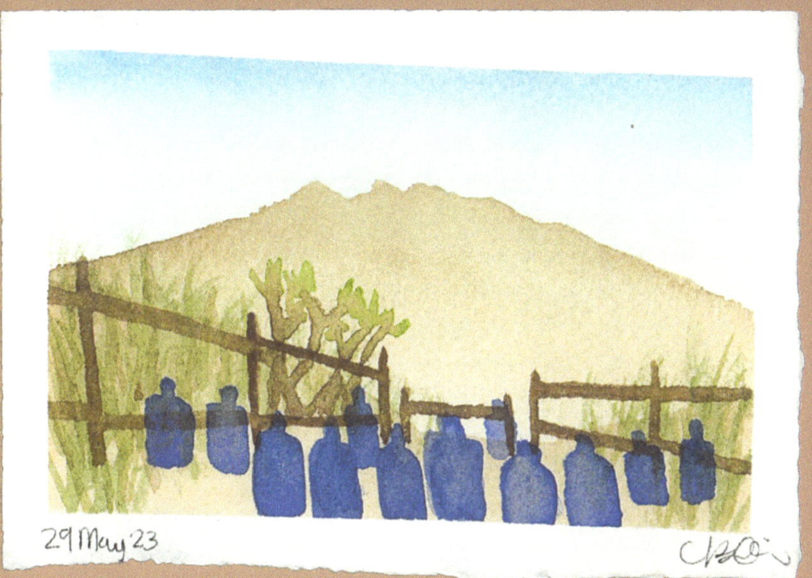

Bird Spring Pass to Walker Pass

Trail day:	44
Hiking day:	38
Trail miles:	632.0 - 652.5
Hiking miles:	20.99
Ascent:	+3304'
Descent:	-3632'
Minimum elevation:	5040'
Maximum elevation:	6977'

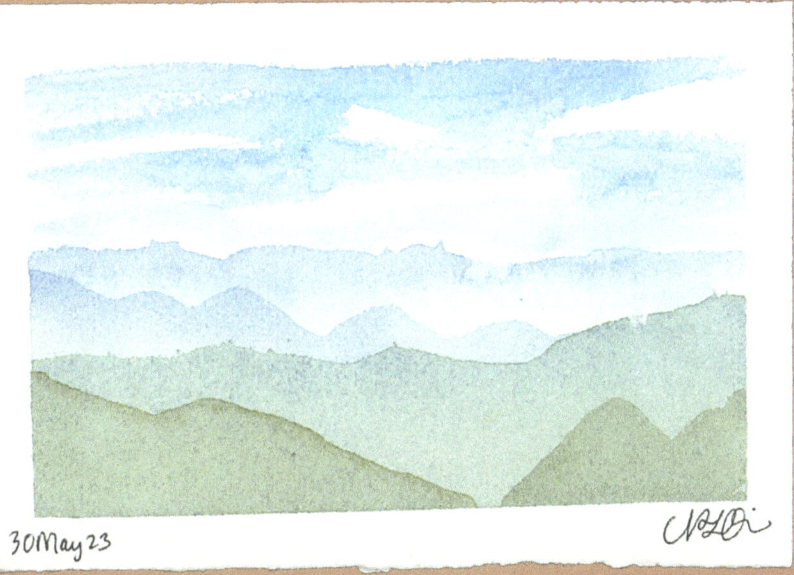

Is It the Sierra or Is It Clouds?

Climbing up Scree Approaching the South Ridge of Owens Peak

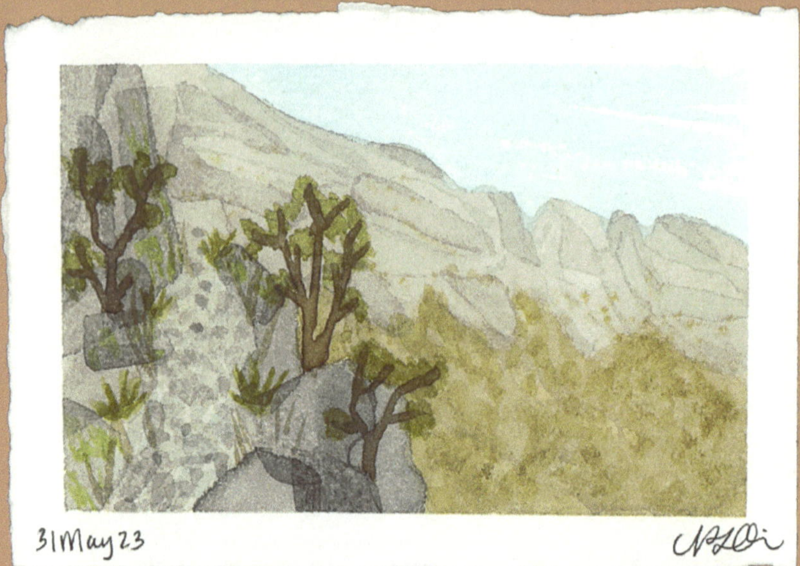

Freedom is getting to choose what you struggle with.

Walker Pass to Lamont Peak

Trail day:	45
Hiking day:	39
Trail miles:	652.5 - 674.0
Hiking miles:	21.66
Ascent:	+4787’
Descent:	-3612’
Minimum elevation:	5044’
Maximum elevation:	7294’

1June23

Lamont Peak to Manter Creek

Trail day:	46
Hiking day:	40
Trail miles:	674.0 - 694.7
Hiking miles:	21.41
Ascent:	+3337’
Descent:	-4209’
Minimum elevation:	5558’
Maximum elevation:	8002’

Descending into the Kern River Valley

Hiking along the South Fork of the Kern River

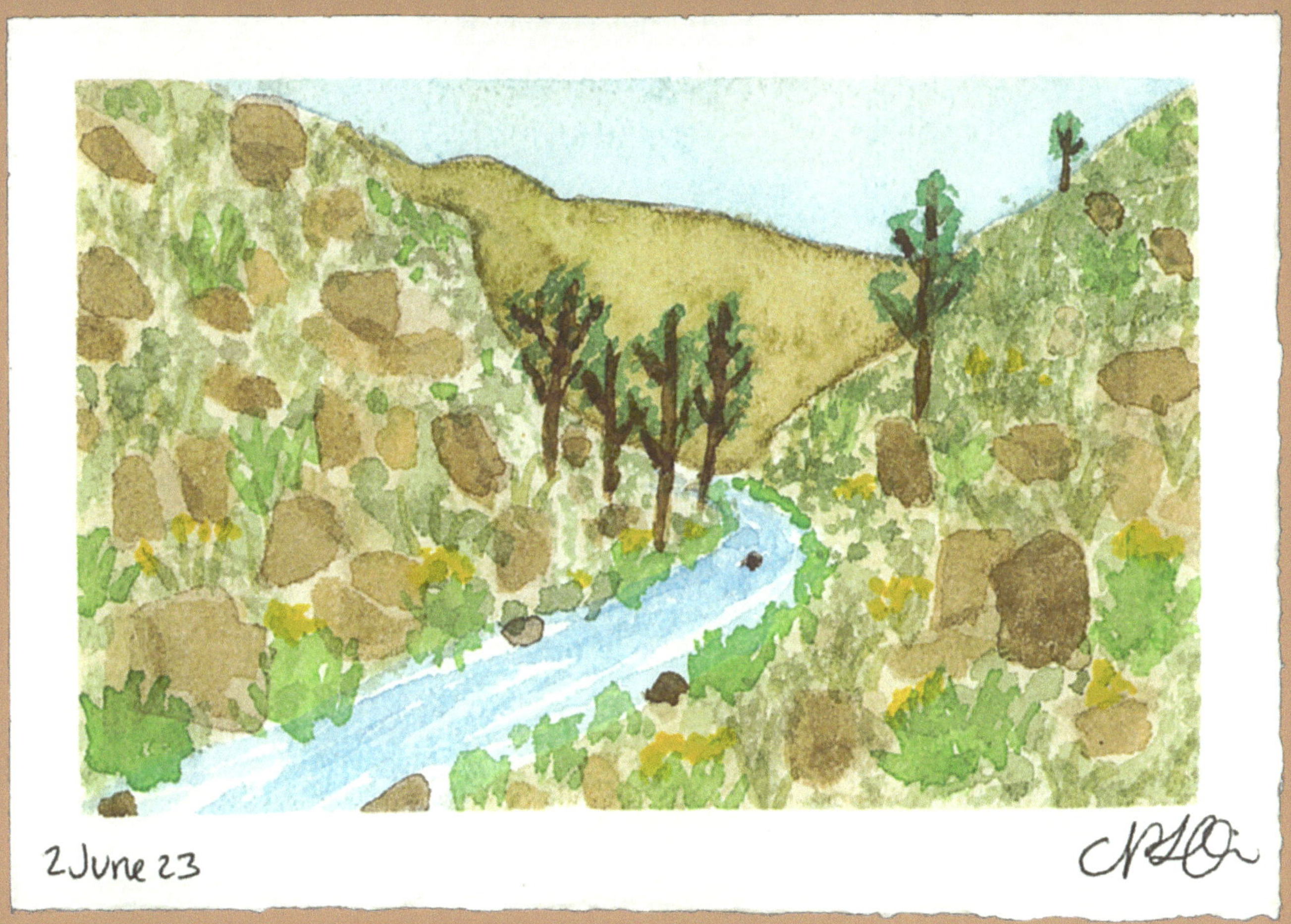

Manter Creek to Kennedy Meadows South

Trail day:	47	Ascent:	+1142'
Hiking day:	41	Descent:	-988'
Trail miles:	694.7 - 703.4	Minimum elevation:	5749'
Hiking miles:	8.94	Maximum elevation:	6087'

Northern California

NorCal

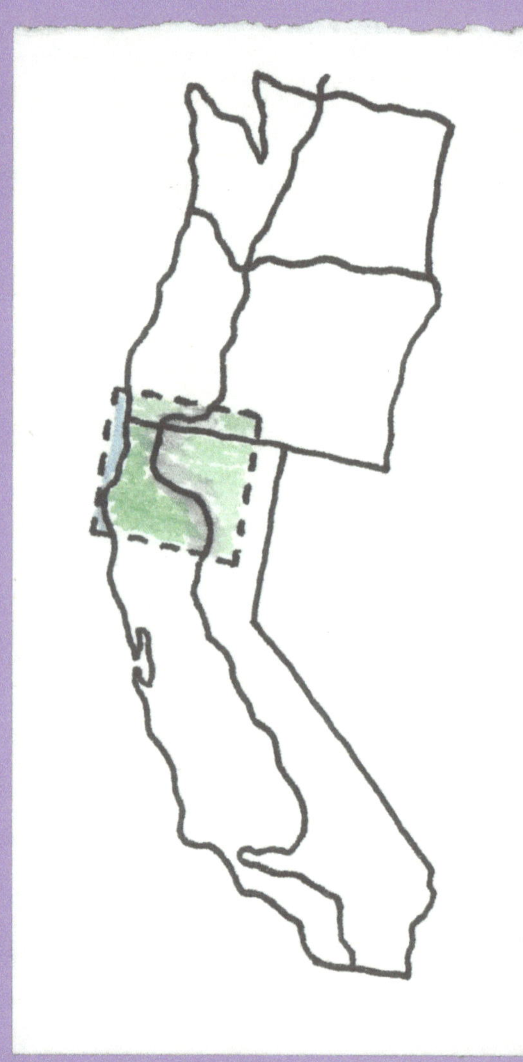

Northbound: Chester, CA to Ashland, OR

June 12 to July 2, 2023

Trail days:	21
Hiking days:	21
Trail miles:	1332.4 - 1718.1
Average miles per hiking day:	18.4
Fewest miles per hiking day:	3.07
Most miles per hiking day:	25.45

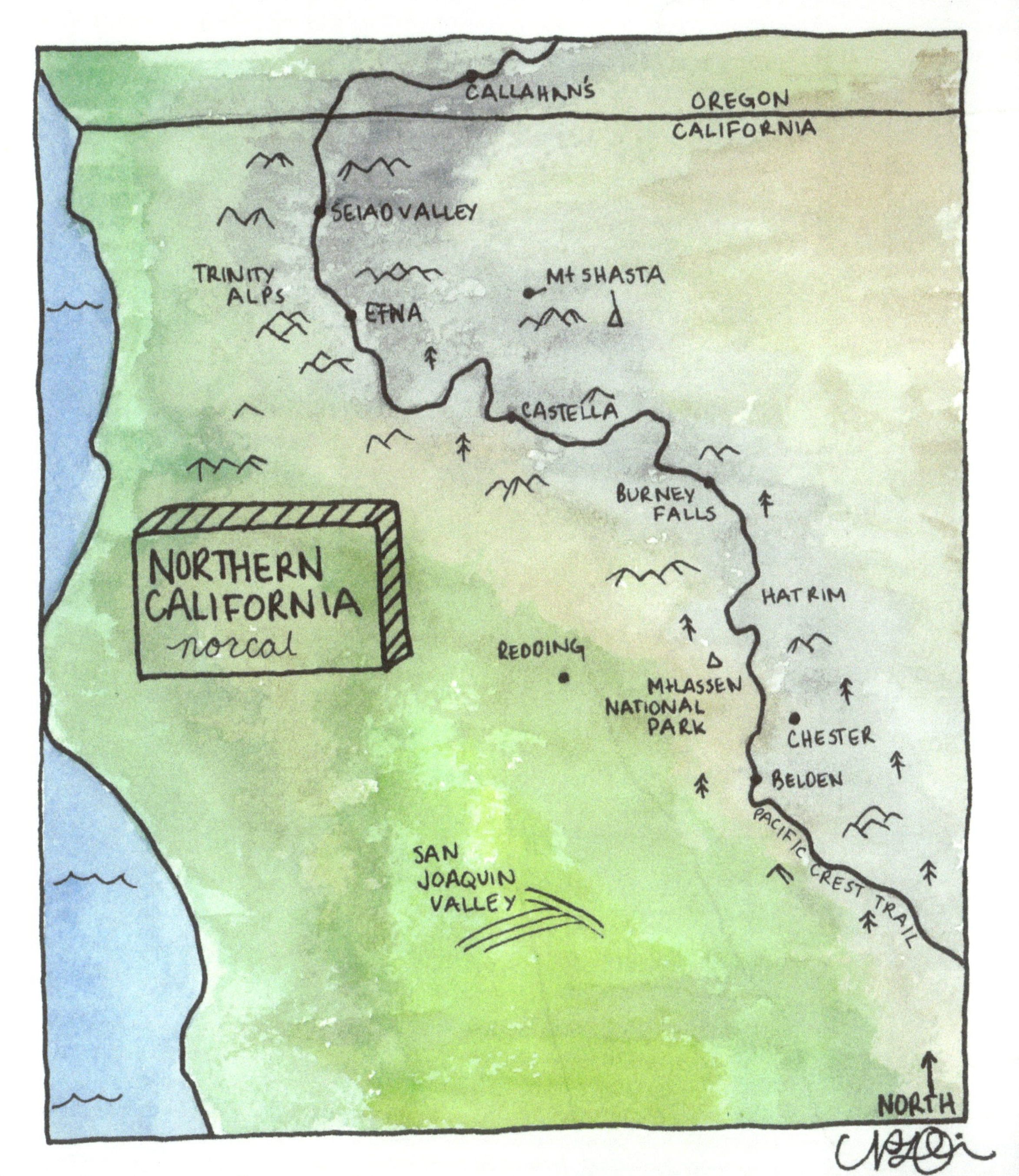
CALLAHAN'S
OREGON
CALIFORNIA
SEIAD VALLEY
TRINITY ALPS
Mt SHASTA
ETNA
CASTELLA
BURNEY FALLS
NORTHERN CALIFORNIA
norcal
HAT RIM
REDDING
Mt LASSEN NATIONAL PARK
CHESTER
BELDEN
PACIFIC CREST TRAIL
SAN JOAQUIN VALLEY
NORTH

Boiling Spring Lake in Lassen Volcanic National Park

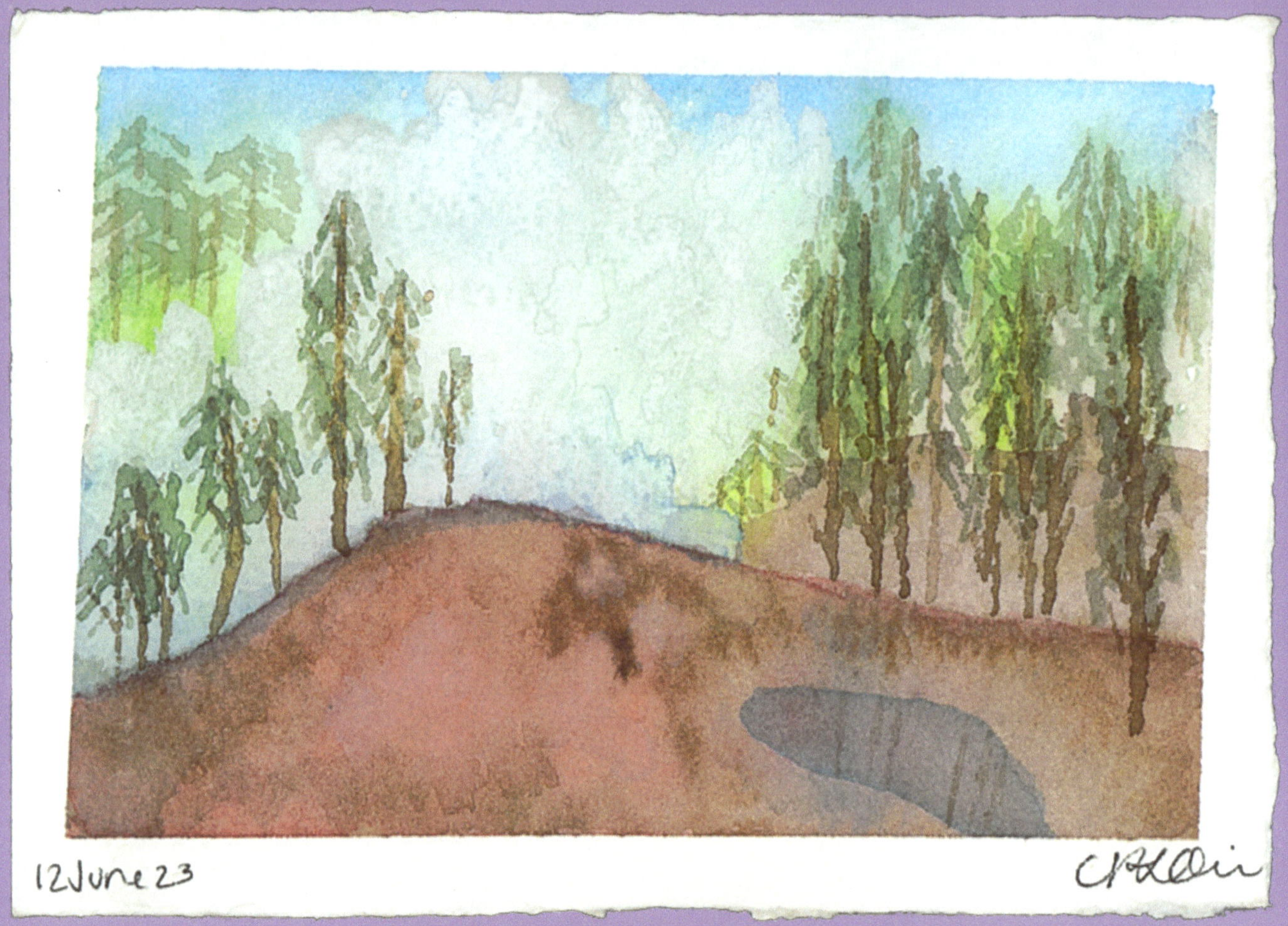

Chester, CA to Lassen Volcanic National Park

Trail day:	57	Ascent:	+3281'
Hiking day:	42	Descent:	-2439'
Trail miles:	1332.4 - 1349.9	Minimum elevation:	5027'
Hiking miles:	19.00	Maximum elevation:	6316'

View of Lassen Peak from Soap Lake

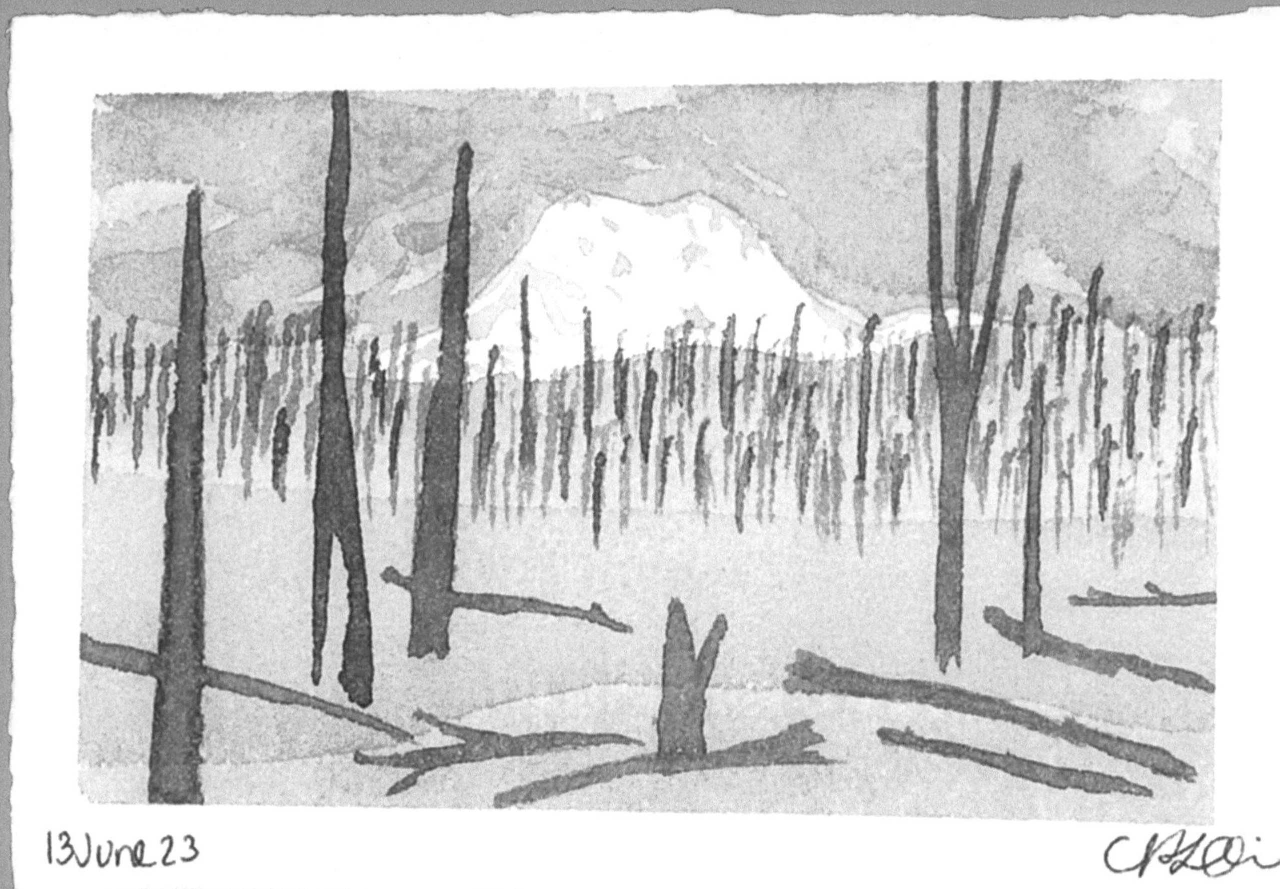

burn burn burn. so many dead trees.

Lassen Volcanic National Park to Hat Creek RV

Trail day:	58	Ascent:	+2070’
Hiking day:	43	Descent:	-3480’
Trail miles:	1349.9 - 1374.5	Minimum elevation:	4564’
Hiking miles:	26.89	Maximum elevation:	6737

Mt Shasta from Hat Creek Rim

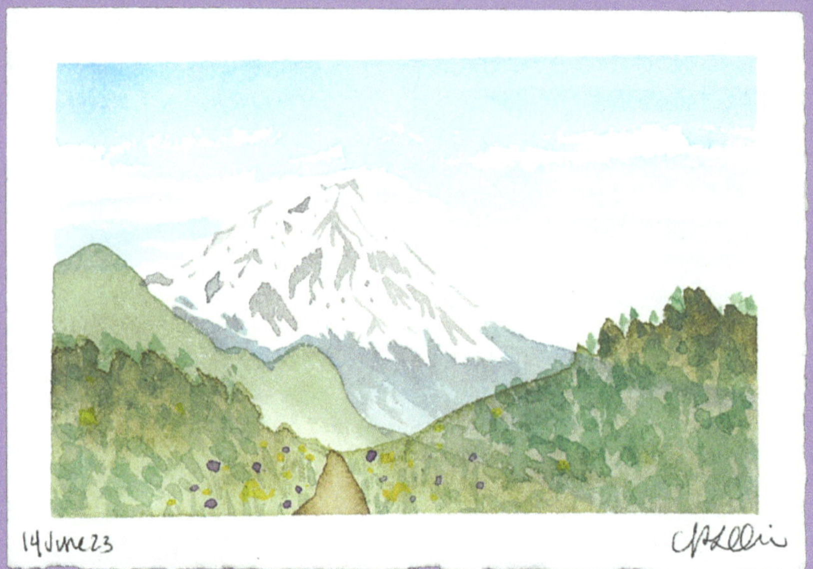

Difficult day questioning why I am out here.

Hat Creek RV to Lost Creek

Trail day:	59
Hiking day:	44
Trail miles:	1374.5 - 1387.6
Hiking miles:	14.76
Ascent:	+1433'
Descent:	-1155'
Minimum elevation:	4333'
Maximum elevation:	4903'

15 June 23

Lost Creek to Baum Lake

Trail day:	60
Hiking day:	45
Trail miles:	1387.6 - 1409.5
Hiking miles:	22.73
Ascent:	+1079'
Descent:	-2936'
Minimum elevation:	2971'
Maximum elevation:	5115'

Baum Lake

My Favorite Flower So Far

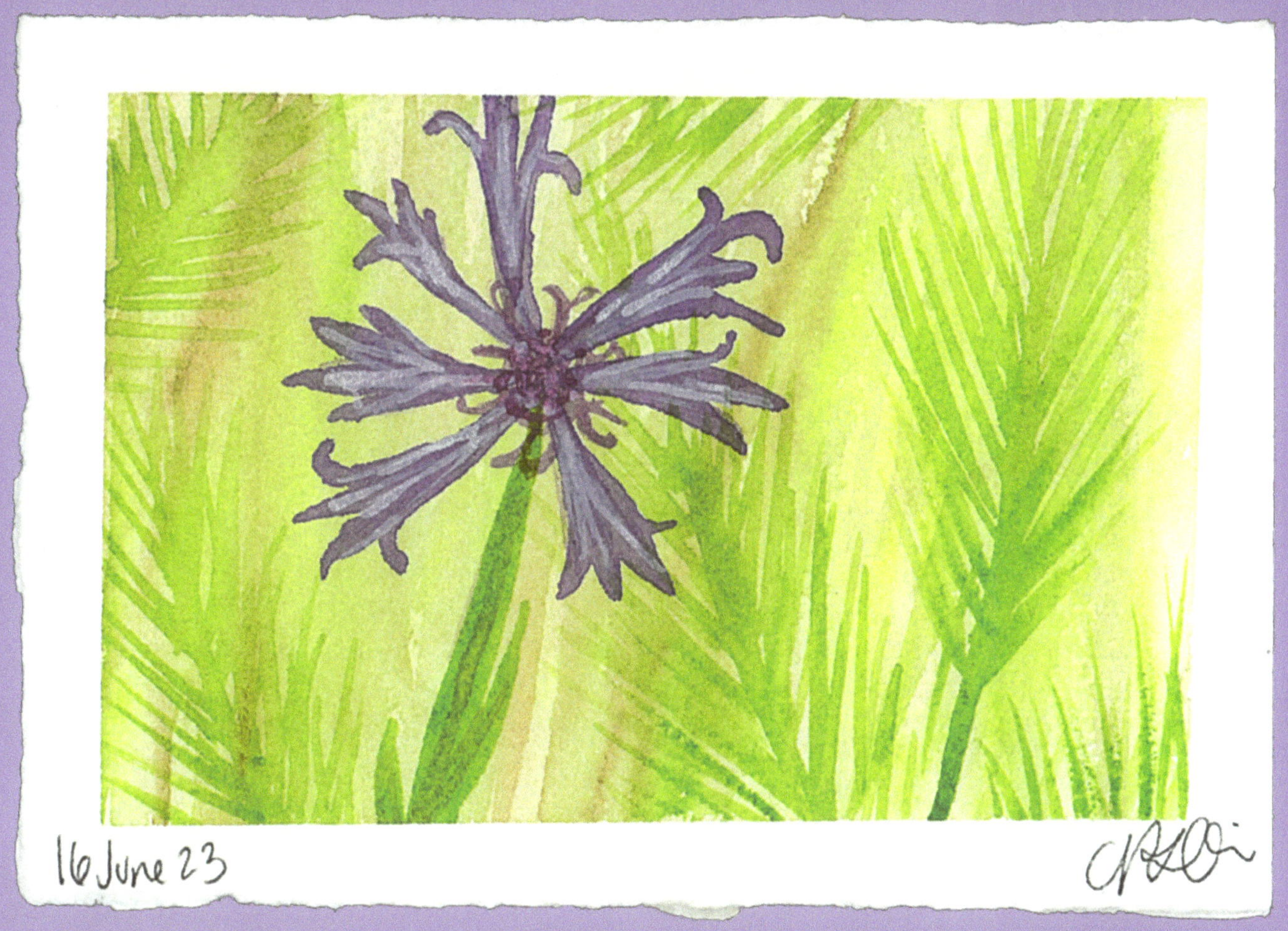

Baum Lake to Burney

Trail day:	61	Ascent:	+318’
Hiking day:	46	Descent:	-249’
Trail miles:	1409.5 - 1412.4	Minimum elevation:	3030’
Hiking miles:	3.07	Maximum elevation:	3319’

Burney Falls

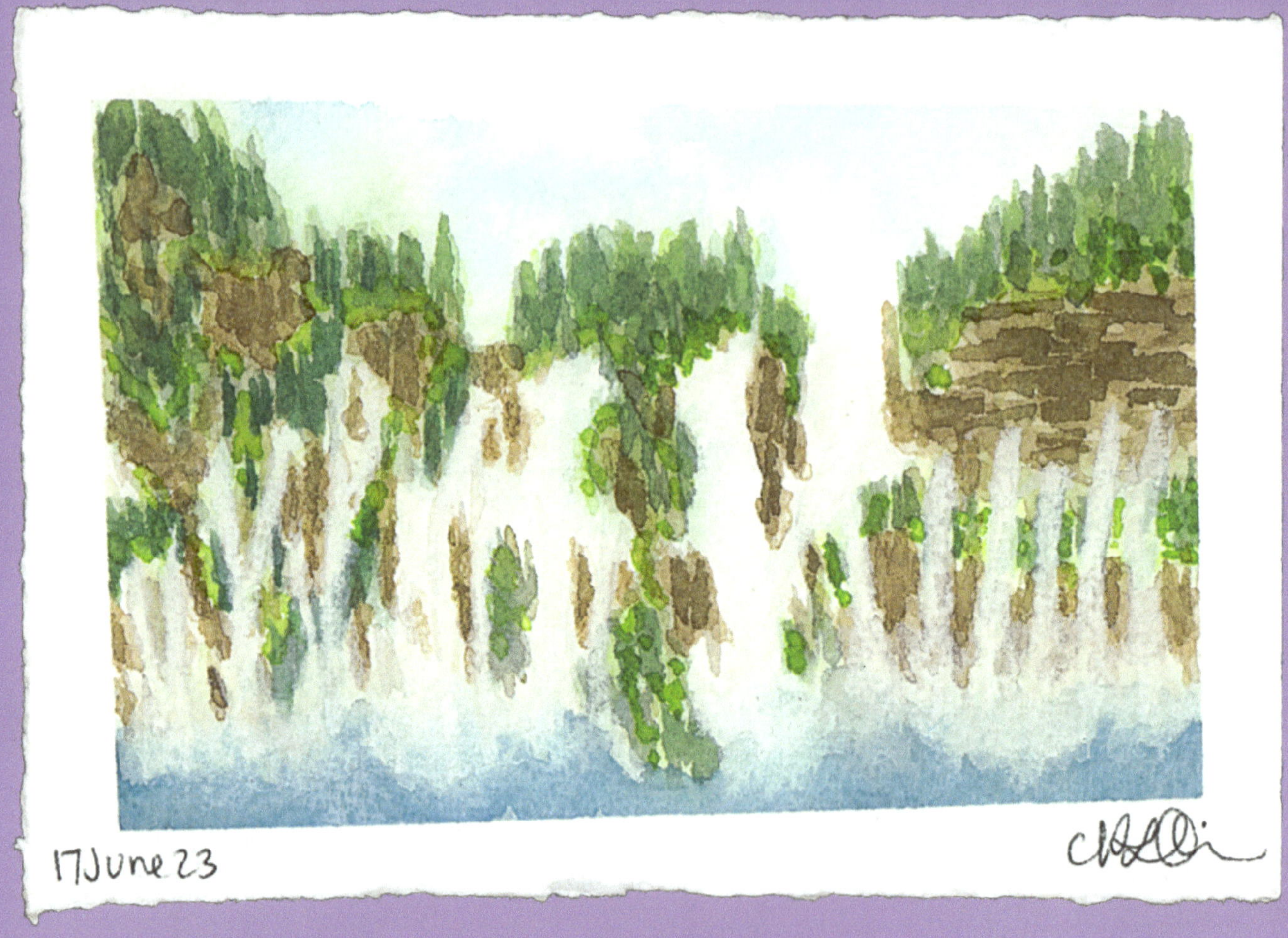

Burney to Rock Creek Falls

Trail day:	62	Ascent:	+1624’
Hiking day:	47	Descent:	-1398’
Trail miles:	1412.4 - 1426.6	Minimum elevation:	2804’
Hiking miles:	16.47	Maximum elevation:	3390’

View of Mt Shasta on the Way to Bartle Gap

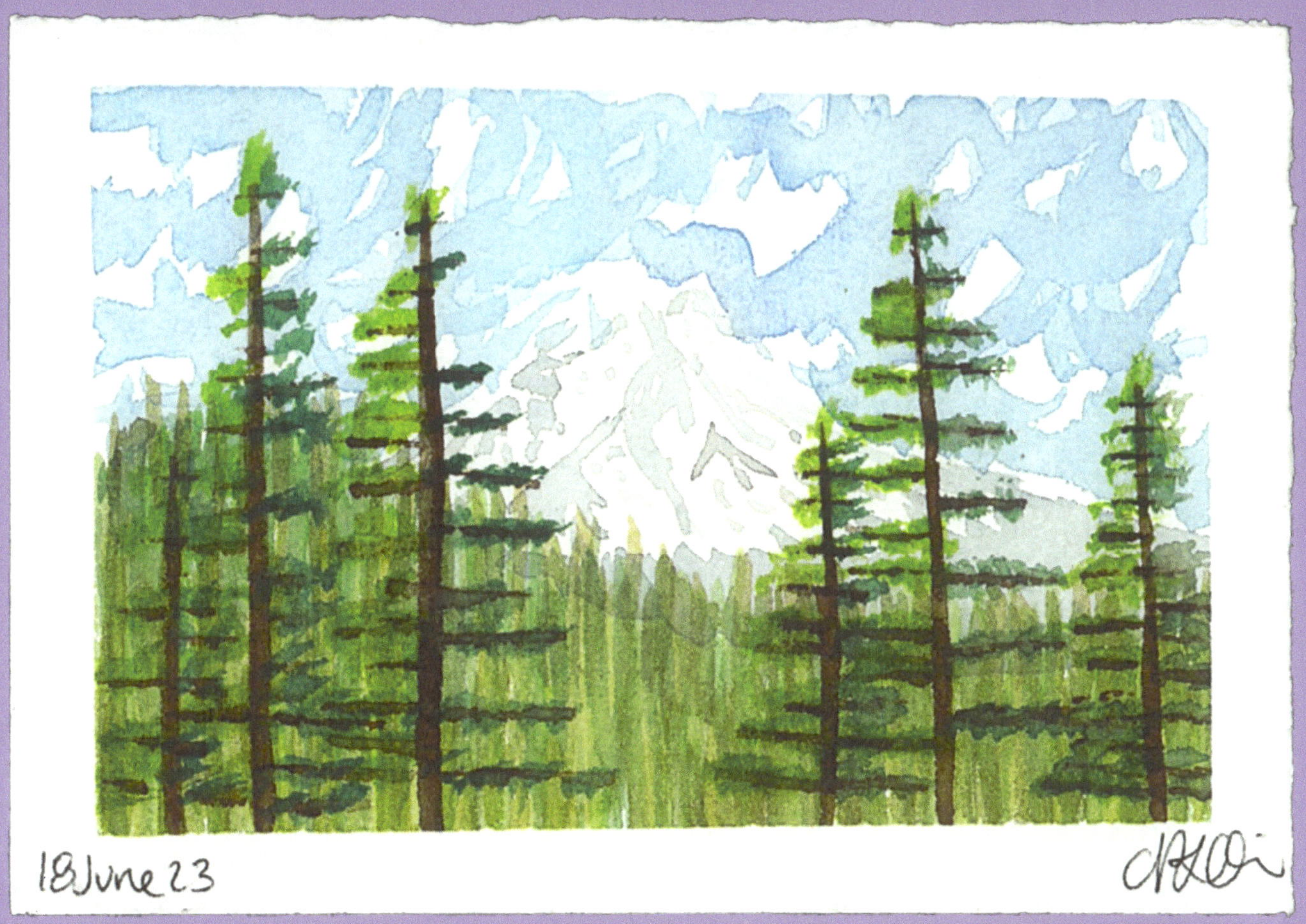

Rock Creek Falls to Bartle Gap

Trail day:	63	Ascent:	+4108’
Hiking day:	48	Descent:	-2303’
Trail miles:	1426.6 - 1447.1	Minimum elevation:	3323’
Hiking miles:	21.19	Maximum elevation:	5505’

Traversing a Snowy Ridge near Pigeon Hill

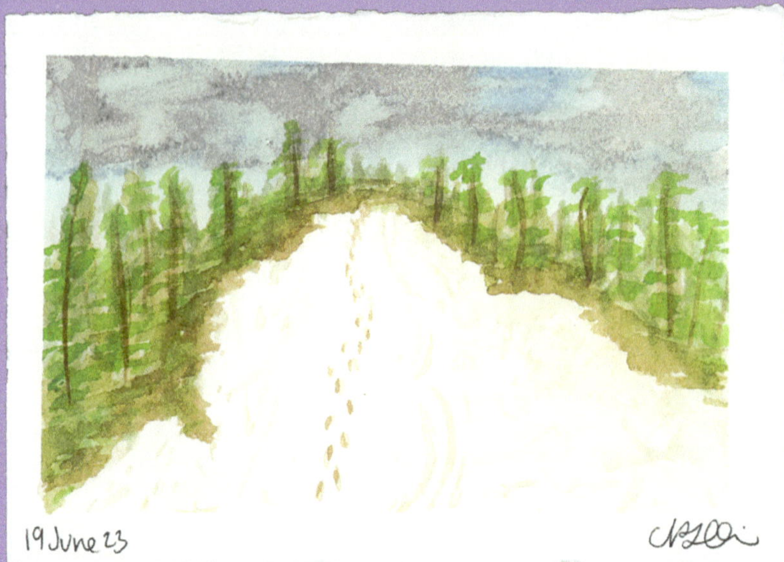

You get what you get and you don't throw a fit.

Bartle Gap to Butcherknife Creek

Trail day:	64
Hiking day:	49
Trail miles:	1447.1 - 1468.1
Hiking miles:	22.14
Ascent:	+3160'
Descent:	-4500'
Minimum elevation:	3335'
Maximum elevation:	6161'

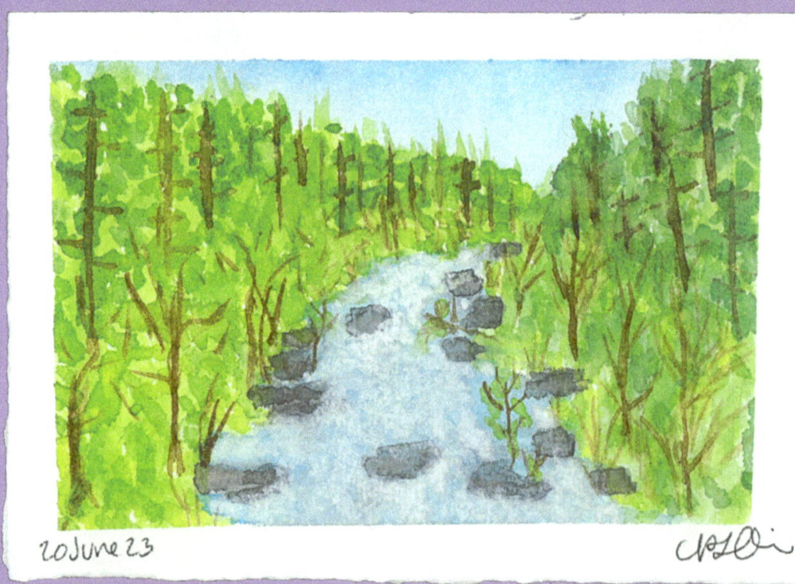

Butcherknife Creek to Ash Camp

Trail day:	65
Hiking day:	50
Trail miles:	1468.1 - 1490.5
Hiking miles:	21.71
Ascent:	+4269'
Descent:	-3240'
Minimum elevation:	2277'
Maximum elevation:	4509'

McCloud River at Ash Camp

Mt Shasta and Castle Crags at Sunrise

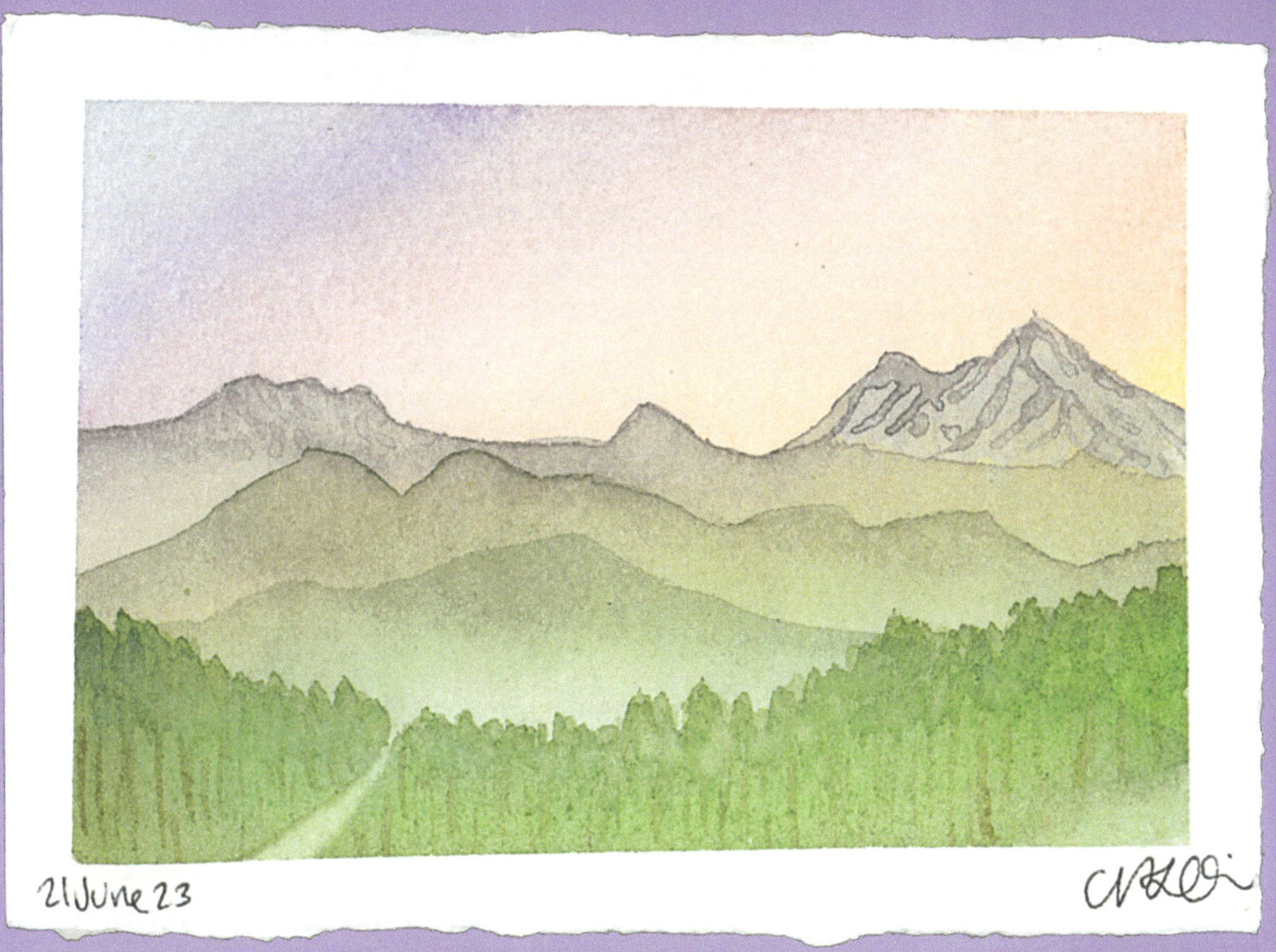

Ash Camp to I-5

Trail day:	66	Ascent:	+348’
Hiking day:	51	Descent:	-2760’
Trail miles:	1490.5 - 1502.3	Minimum elevation:	2009’
Hiking miles:	8.75	Maximum elevation:	4682’

Ascending to Castle Crags

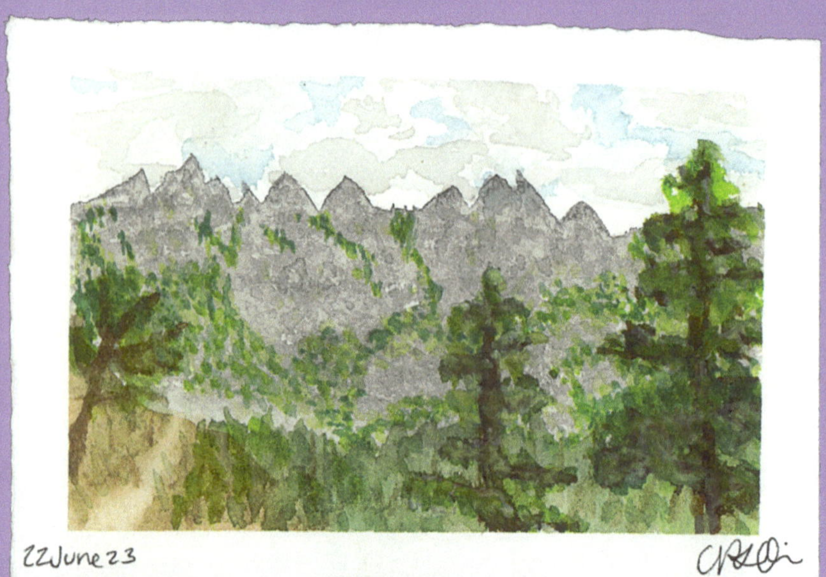

I-5 to Boulder Peak	
Trail day:	67
Hiking day:	52
Trail miles:	1502.3 - 1522.2
Hiking miles:	21.21
Ascent:	+5863’
Descent:	-1539’
Minimum elevation:	1995’
Maximum elevation:	6696’

Be gentle.

Beat the rain to camp!

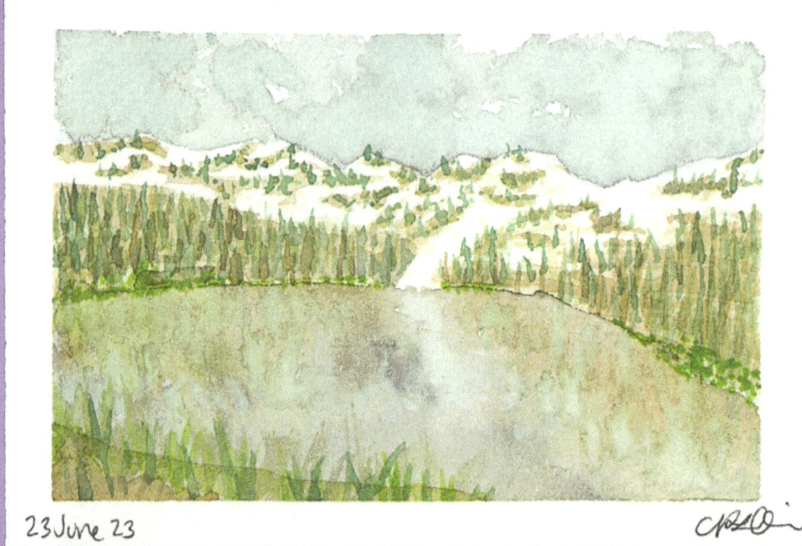

Boulder Creek to Bluff Lake	
Trail day:	68
Hiking day:	53
Trail miles:	1522.2 - 1545.3
Hiking miles:	24.25
Ascent:	+2486’
Descent:	-2316’
Minimum elevation:	6461’
Maximum elevation:	7717’

Deadfall Lake

Trinity Alps at Sunset with Storm Clouds

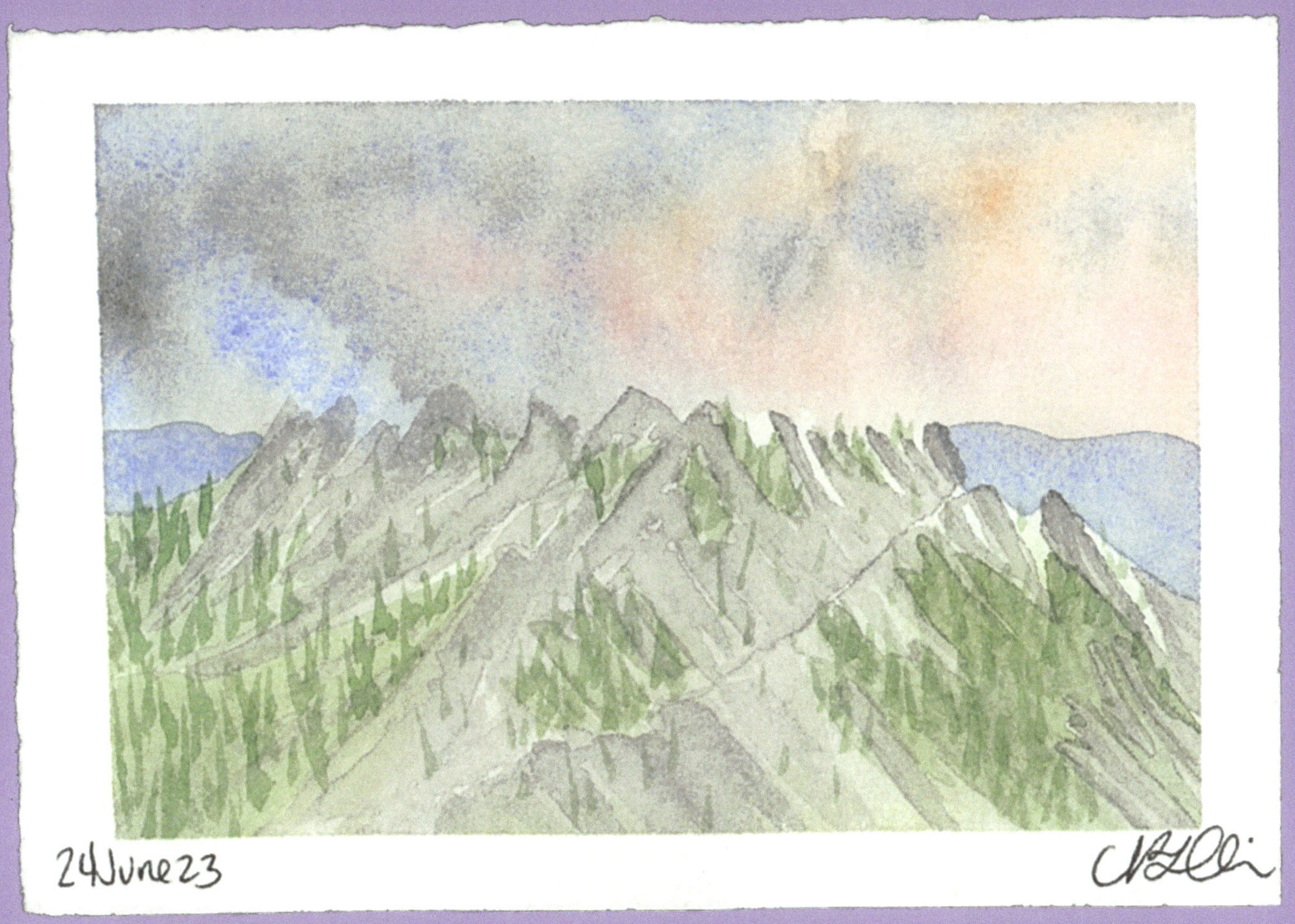

Bluff Lake to Eagle Peak

Trail day:	69	Ascent:	+3379’
Hiking day:	54	Descent:	-2713’
Trail miles:	1545.3 - 1569.9	Minimum elevation:	5409’
Hiking miles:	25.45	Maximum elevation:	7125’

Entering the Russian Wilderness

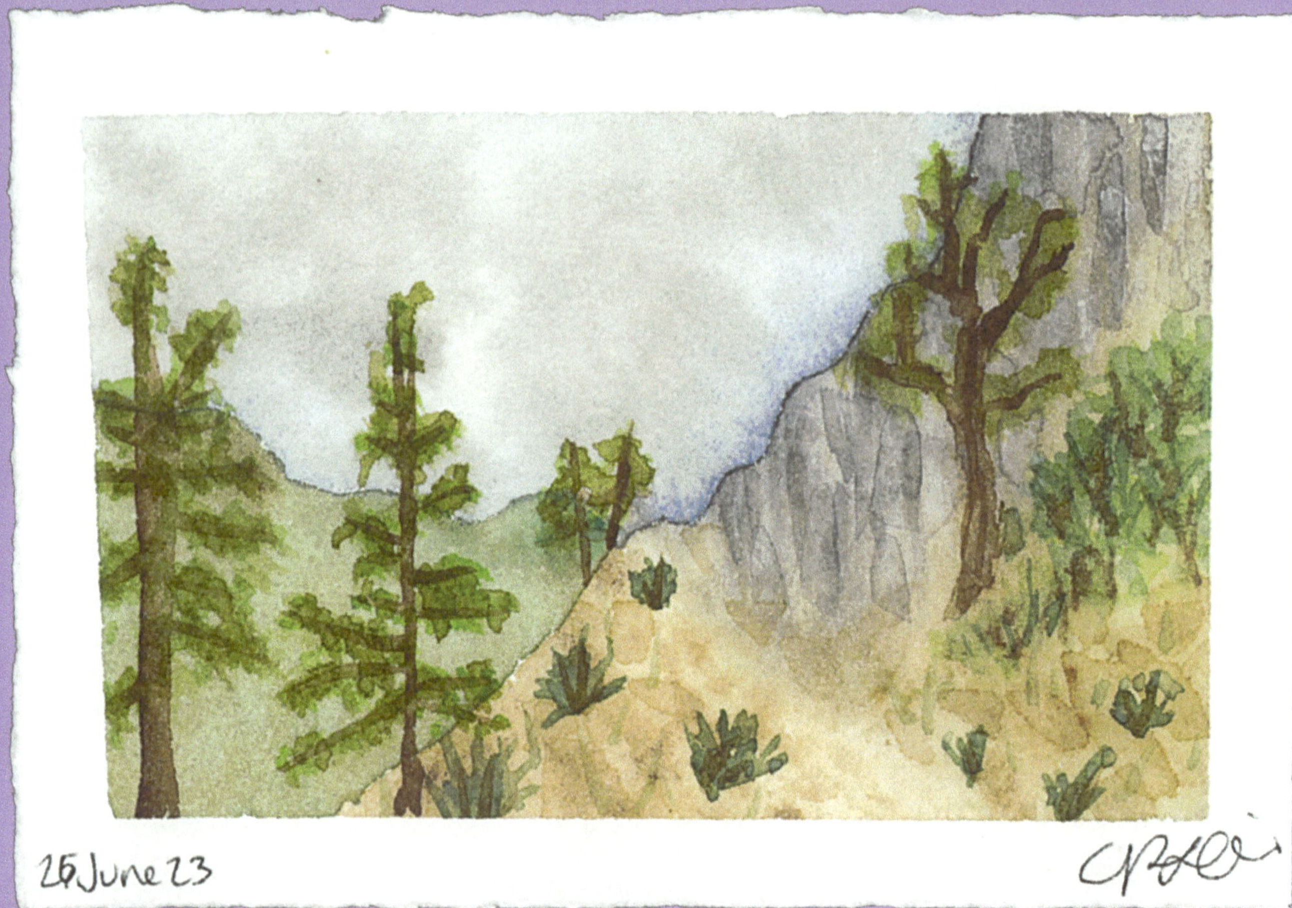

Nature eats babies all the time.

Eagle Peak to Russian Wilderness

Trail day:	70	Ascent:	+4019’
Hiking day:	55	Descent:	-4170’
Trail miles:	1569.9 - 1591.9	Minimum elevation:	5866’
Hiking miles:	23.90	Maximum elevation:	7413’

Dotty's in Etna, CA

Russian Wilderness to Etna Summit

Trail day:	71
Hiking day:	56
Trail miles:	1591.9 - 1600.8
Hiking miles:	9.12
Ascent:	+1366'
Descent:	-2360'
Minimum elevation:	5951'
Maximum elevation:	7364'

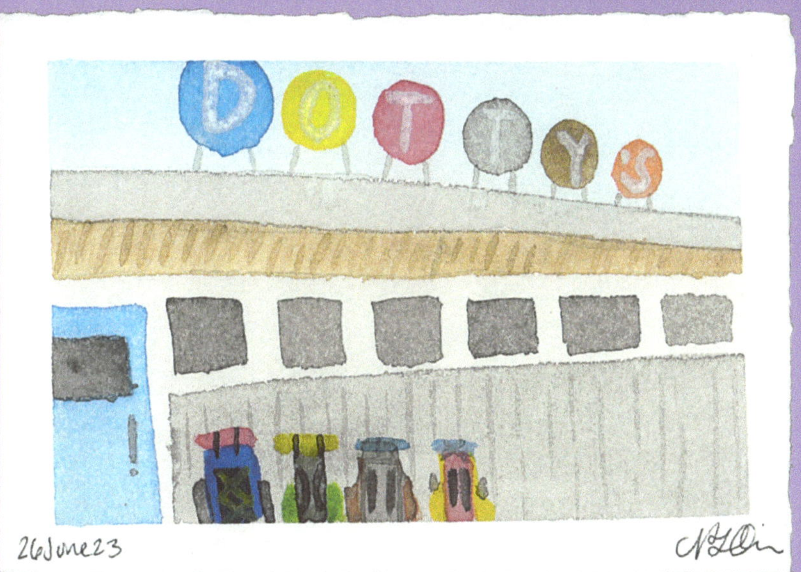

Recovery is part of the big adventure.

Etna Summit to Marten Lake

Trail day:	72
Hiking day:	57
Trail miles:	1600.8 - 1614.8
Hiking miles:	14.62
Ascent:	+2329'
Descent:	-2060'
Minimum elevation:	5956'
Maximum elevation:	6743'

Marten Lake

A Black Bear Running Away from Me above Upper Sky High Lake

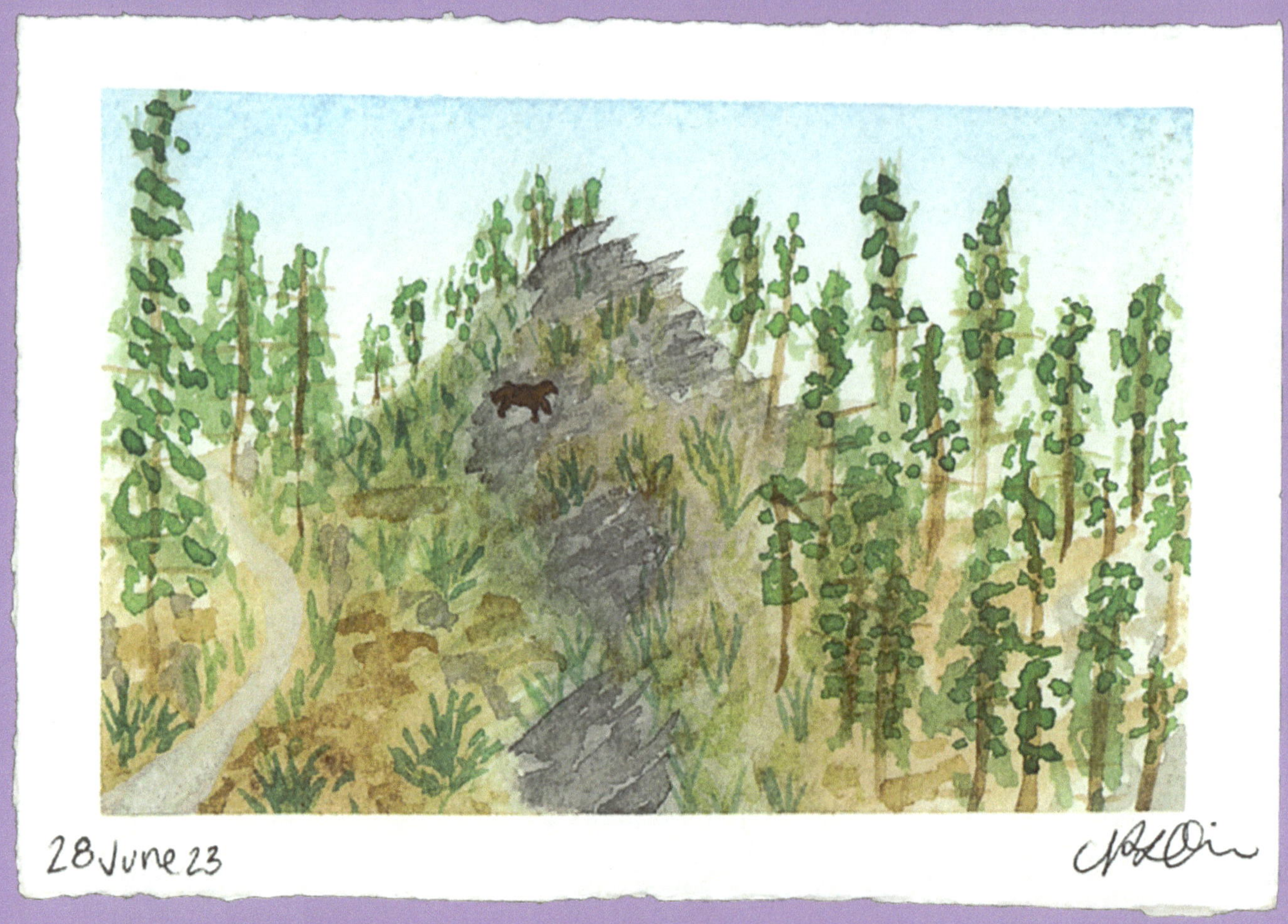

Marten Lake to Cold Spring Trailhead

Trail day:	73	Ascent:	+4715’
Hiking day:	58	Descent:	-5684’
Trail miles:	1614.8 - 1638.5	Minimum elevation:	5356’
Hiking miles:	25.11	Maximum elevation:	7115’

Road Walking the Klamath River Bridge into Seiad Valley

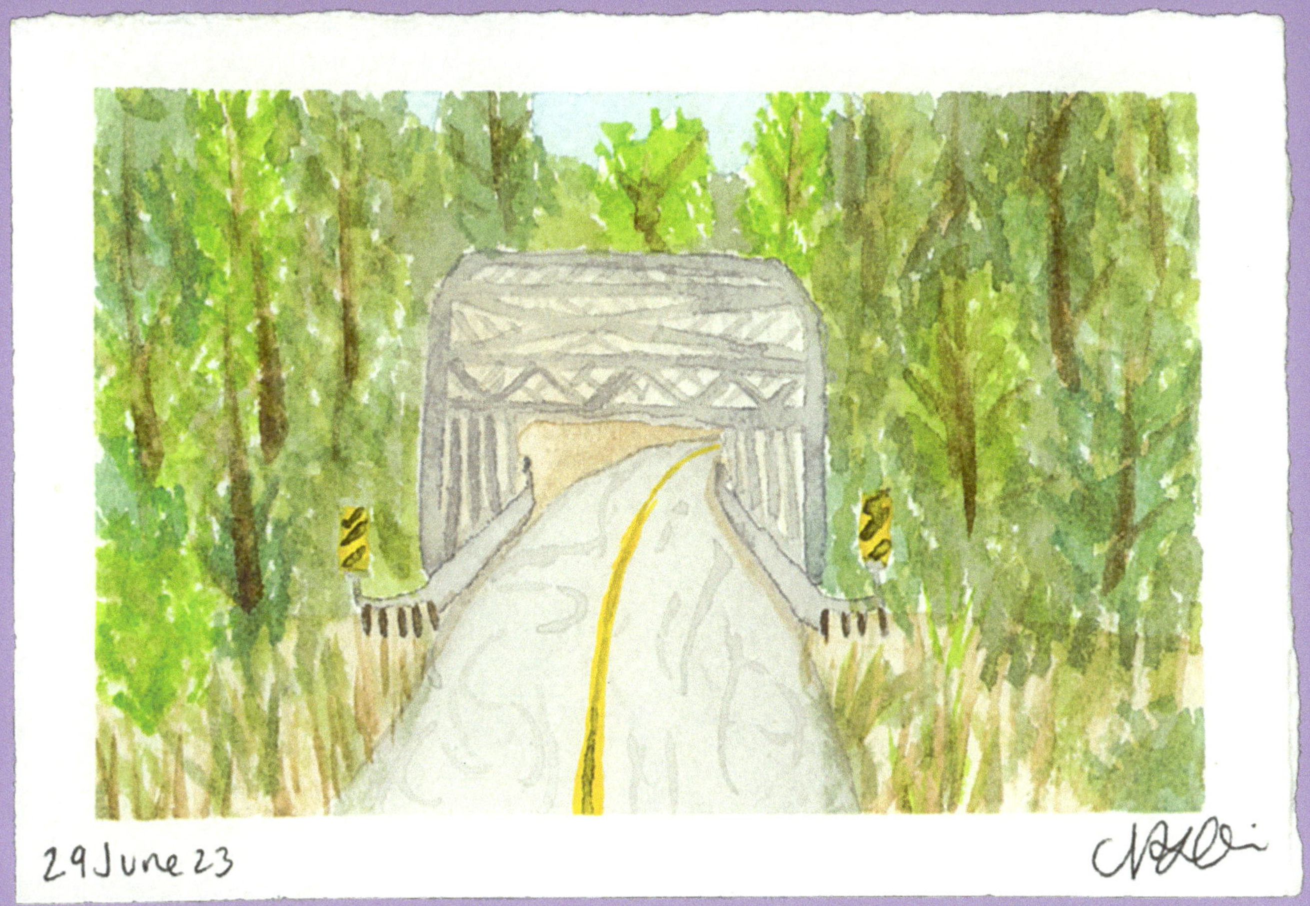

Cold Spring Trailhead to Seiad Valley

Trail day:	74	Ascent:	+781’
Hiking day:	59	Descent:	-4732’
Trail miles:	1638.5 - 1657.8	Minimum elevation:	1385’
Hiking miles:	17.90	Maximum elevation:	5355’

Blowdowns near Copper Butte

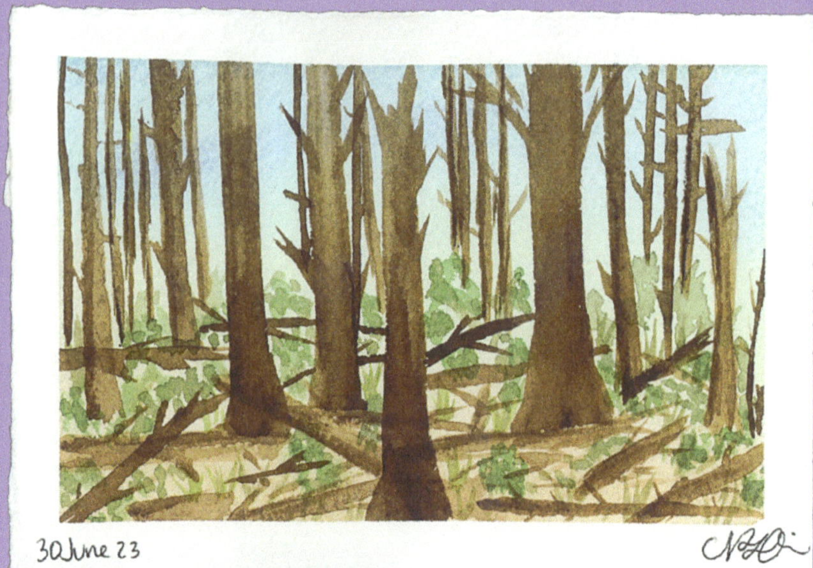

Seiad Valley to Copper Butte

Trail day:	75
Hiking day:	60
Trail miles:	1657.8 - 1676.3
Hiking miles:	21.55
Ascent:	+6901'
Descent:	-2247'
Minimum elevation:	1407'
Maximum elevation:	6119'

lunch @ Donomore Cabin → found dad's logbook entry!

Copper Butte to Wrangle Gap

Trail day:	76
Hiking day:	61
Trail miles:	1676.3 - 1699.1
Hiking miles:	25.20
Ascent:	+4198'
Descent:	-3716'
Minimum elevation:	5359'
Maximum elevation:	7324'

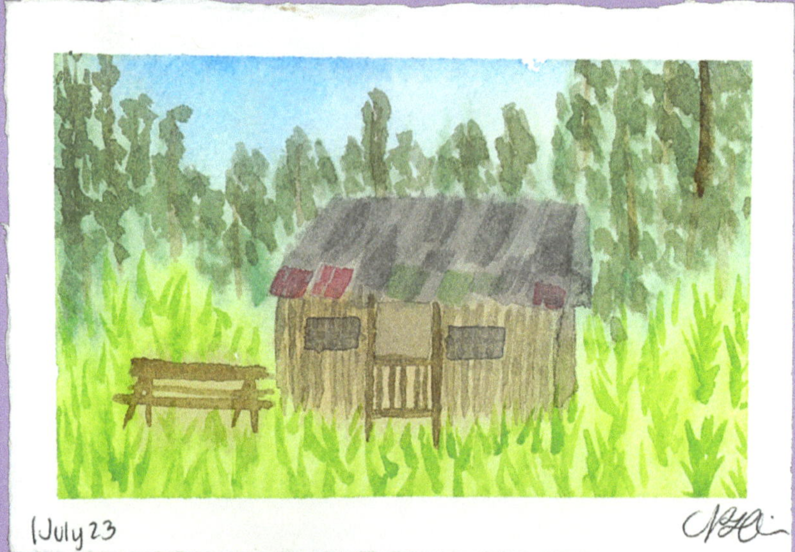

Donomore Cabin

Sunrise on Big Red Mountain

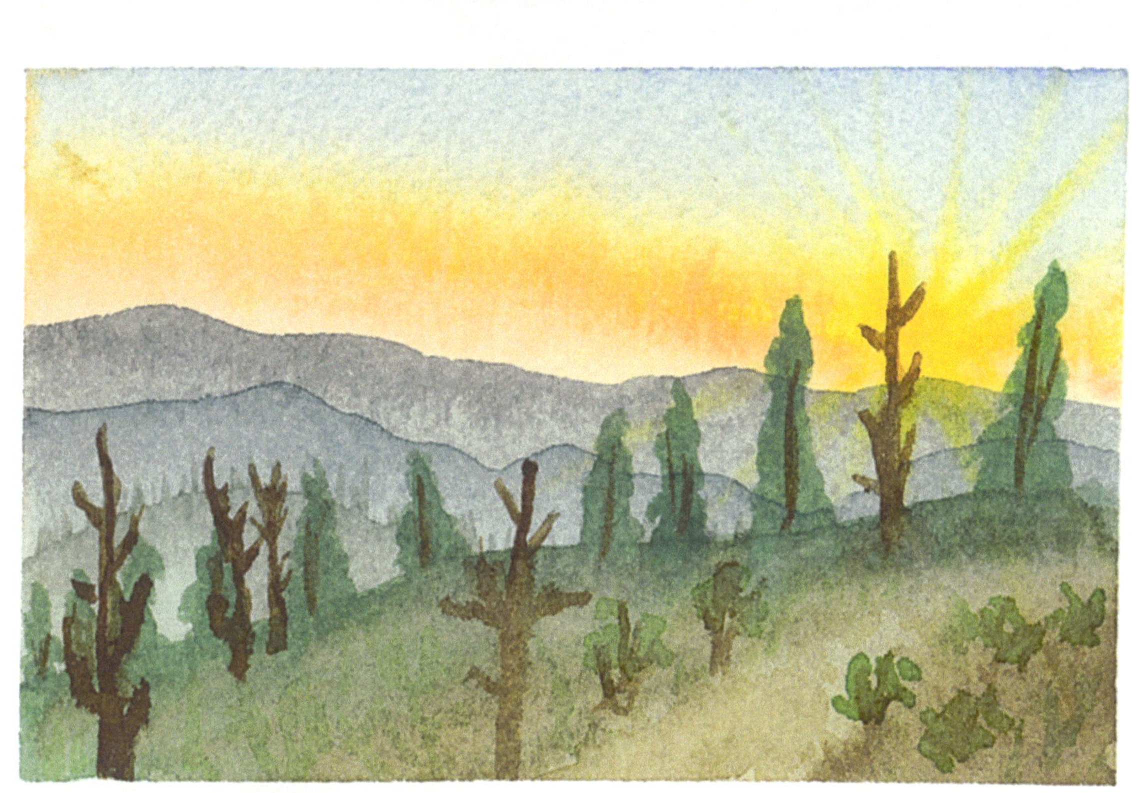

Wrangle Gap to I-5 in Ashland, OR

Trail day:	77	Ascent:	+2406’
Hiking day:	62	Descent:	-4867’
Trail miles:	1699.1 - 1718.1	Minimum elevation:	4041’
Hiking miles:	20.36	Maximum elevation:	7022’

Oregon

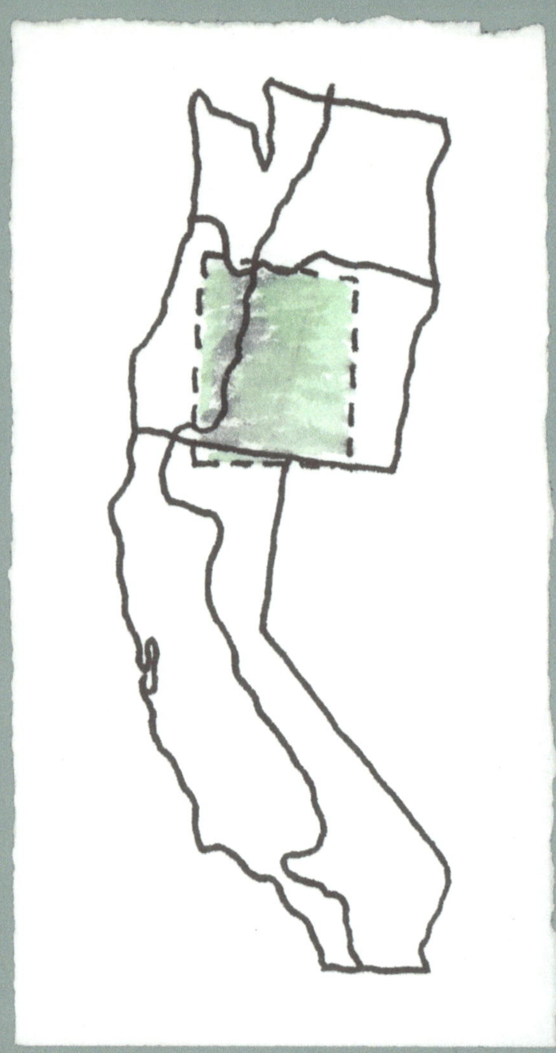

Northbound: Ashland, OR to Cascade Locks, OR

July 5 to 28, 2023

Trail days:	24
Hiking days:	24
Trail miles:	1718.8 - 2155.7
Average miles per hiking day:	17.96
Fewest miles per hiking day:	3.12
Most miles per hiking day:	25.71

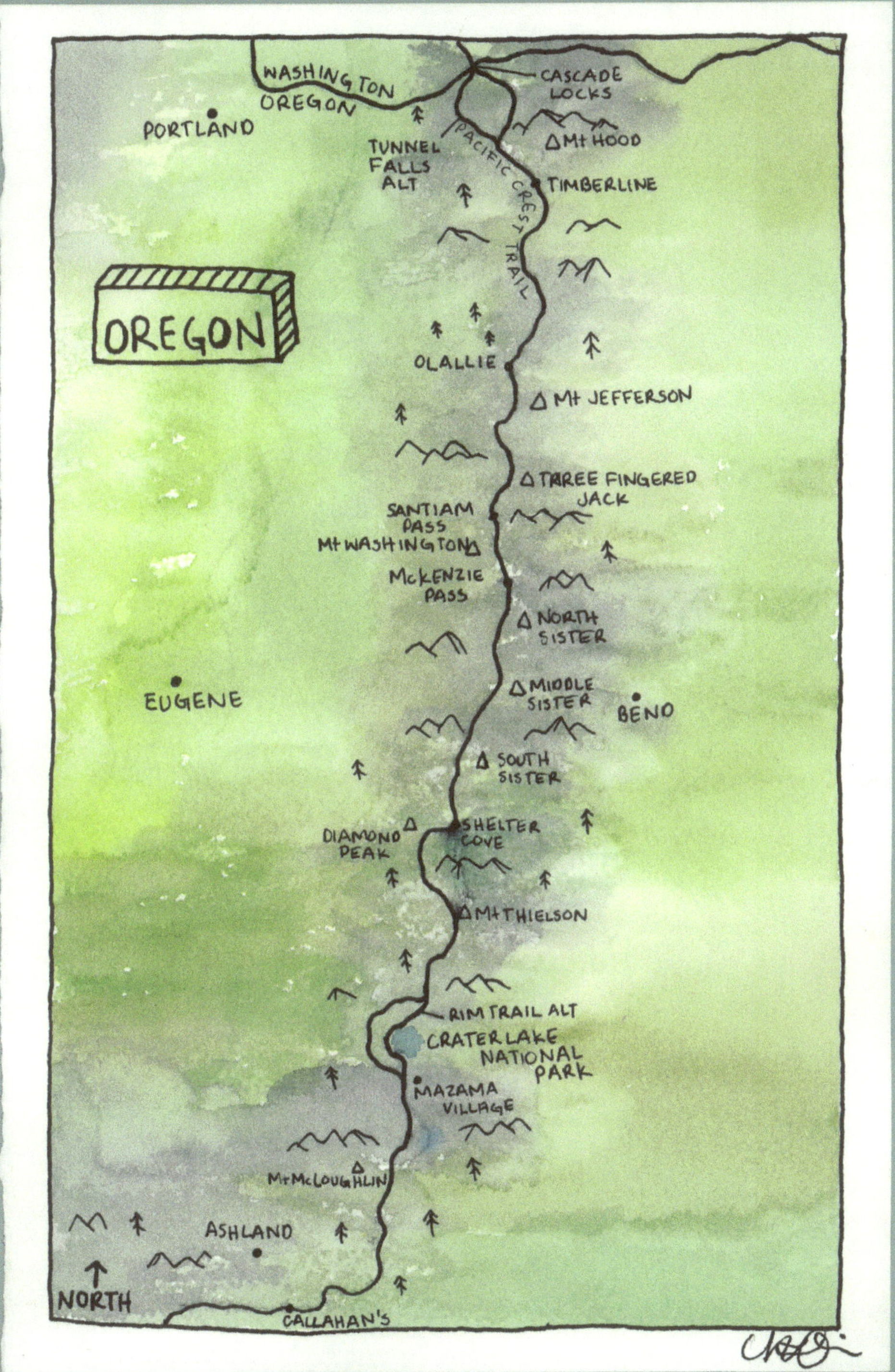
WASHINGTON
OREGON
CASCADE LOCKS
PORTLAND
TUNNEL FALLS ALT
PACIFIC CREST TRAIL
Mt HOOD
TIMBERLINE
OREGON
OLALLIE
Mt JEFFERSON
THREE FINGERED JACK
SANTIAM PASS
Mt WASHINGTON
McKENZIE PASS
NORTH SISTER
MIDDLE SISTER
BEND
EUGENE
SOUTH SISTER
SHELTER COVE
DIAMOND PEAK
Mt THIELSON
RIM TRAIL ALT
CRATER LAKE NATIONAL PARK
MAZAMA VILLAGE
Mt McLOUGHLIN
ASHLAND
NORTH
CALLAHAN'S

Pilot Rock

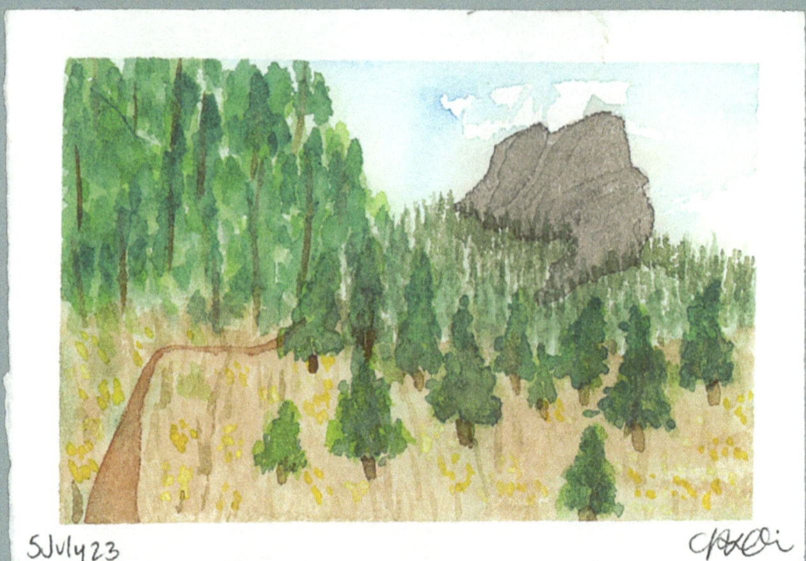

Ashland to Soda Mountain Wilderness

Trail day:	80
Hiking day:	63
Trail miles:	1718.8 - 1729.1
Hiking miles:	10.75
Ascent:	+2484’
Descent:	-1063’
Minimum elevation:	3918’
Maximum elevation:	5436’

hike hike hike

animal in the night... with a shreek!

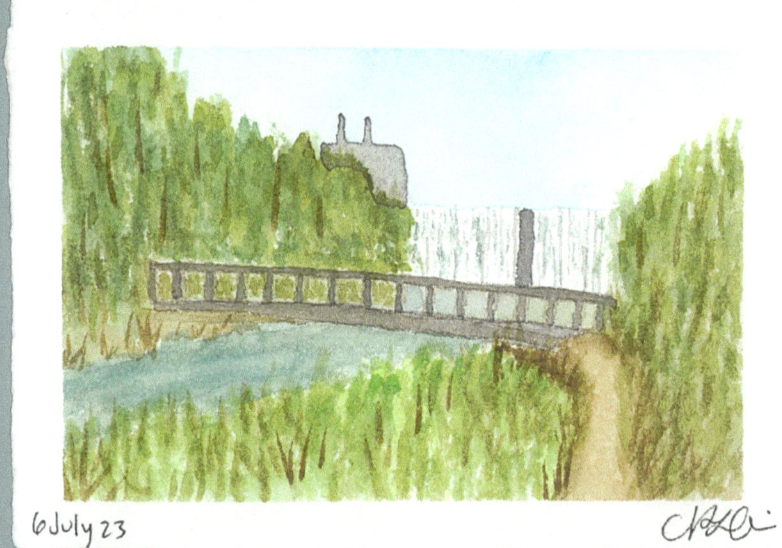

Soda Mountain Wilderness to Hyatt Lake

Trail day:	81
Hiking day:	64
Trail miles:	1729.1 - 1743.7
Hiking miles:	15.56
Ascent:	+2288’
Descent:	-2518’
Minimum elevation:	4526’
Maximum elevation:	5587’

Bridge over Keene Creek from Little Hyatt Reservoir

A Walk in the Woods

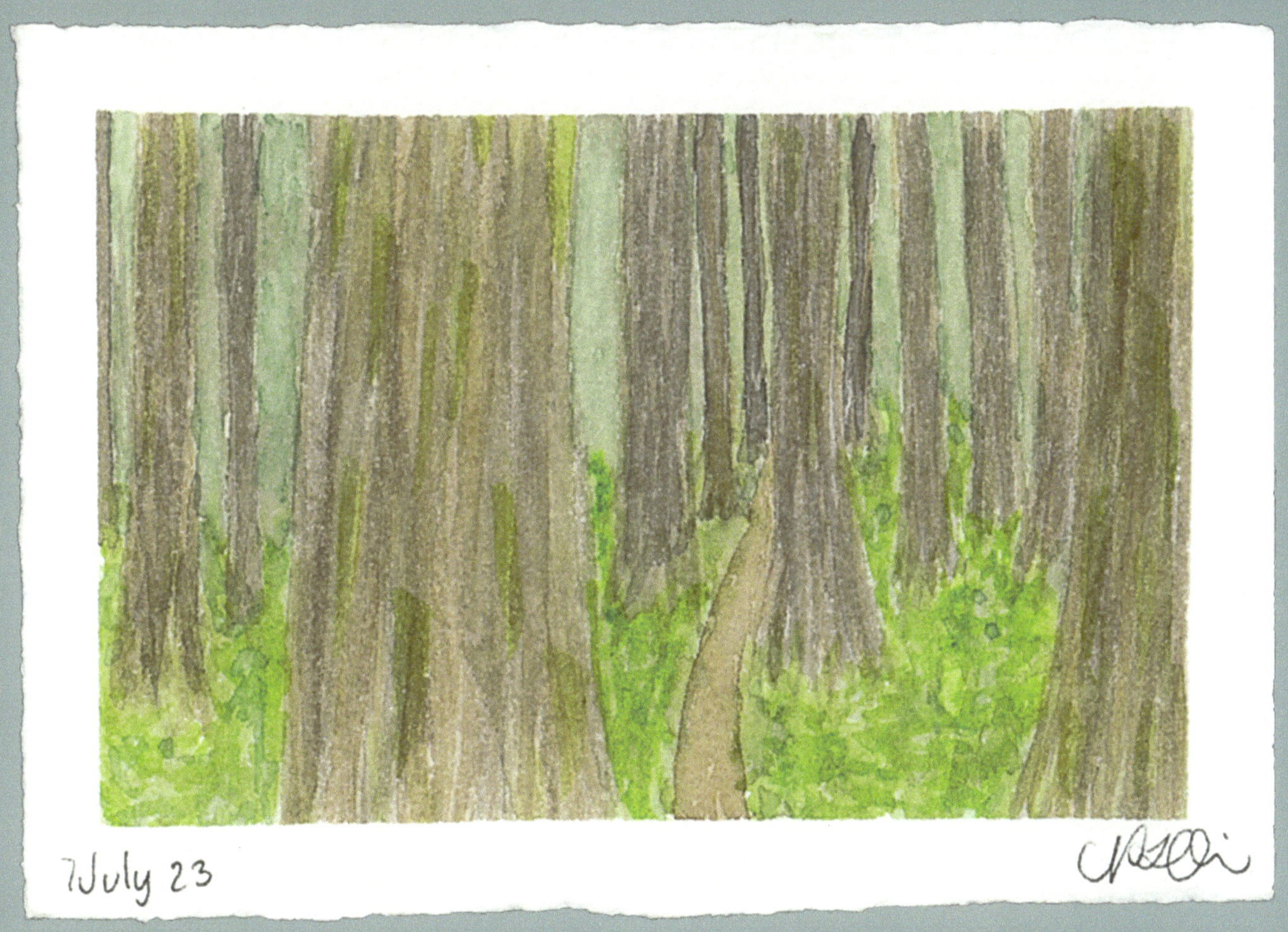

Hyatt Lake to South Brown Mountain Shelter

Trail day:	82	Ascent:	+3071’
Hiking day:	65	Descent:	-2752’
Trail miles:	1743.7 - 1764.3	Minimum elevation:	4534’
Hiking miles:	21.15	Maximum elevation:	6206’

Looking at Mt McLoughlin from the Lava Rocks on Brown Mountain

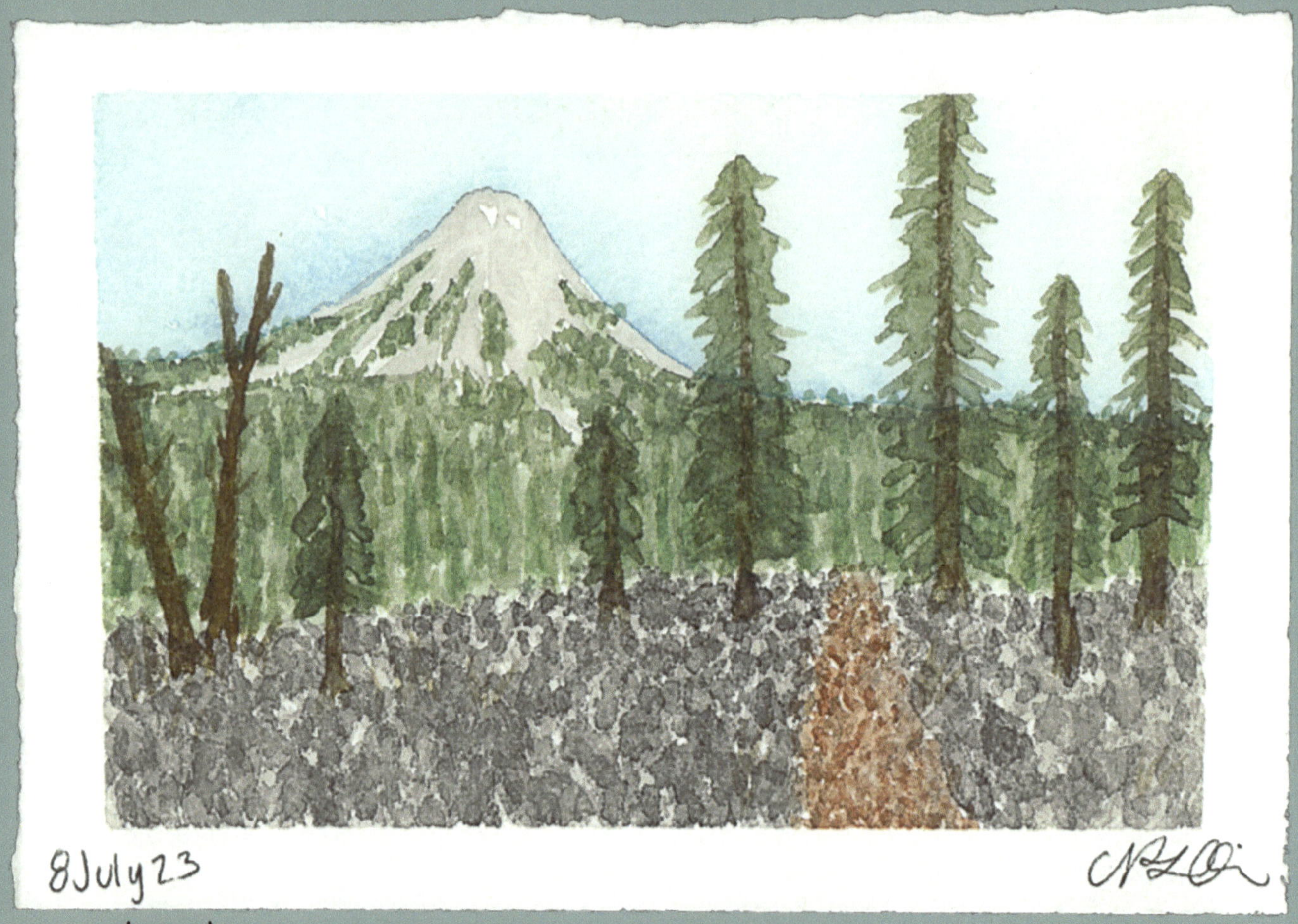

Mosquito hell.

South Brown Mountain Shelter to Island Lake

Trail day:	83	Ascent:	+2999'
Hiking day:	66	Descent:	-2438'
Trail miles:	1764.3 - 1787.8	Minimum elevation:	4975'
Hiking miles:	25.22	Maximum elevation:	6351'

Seven Lakes Trail Junction

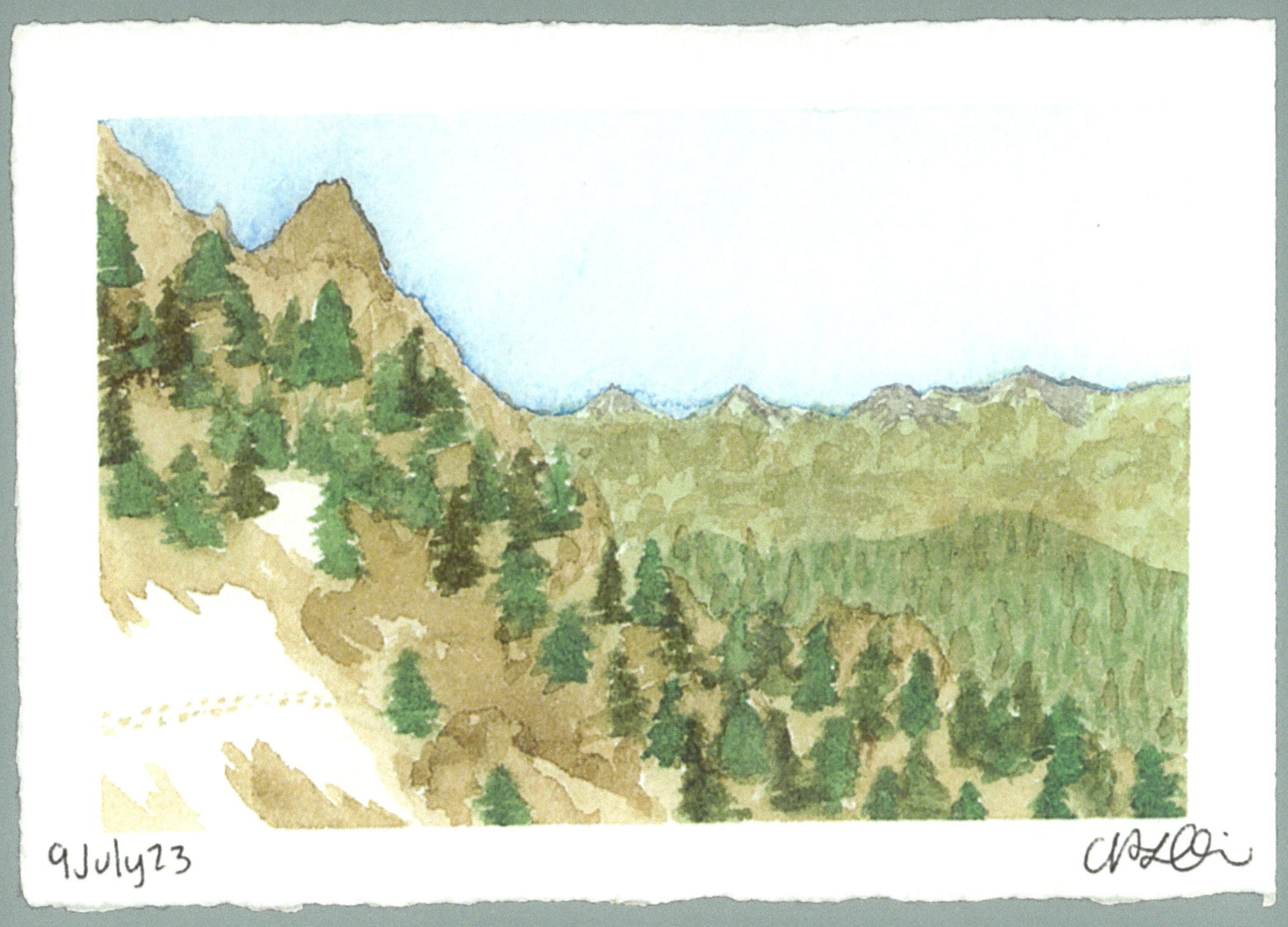

Island Lake to Seven Mile Trail Junction

Trail day:	84	Ascent:	+2405’
Hiking day:	67	Descent:	-2569’
Trail miles:	1787.8 - 1805.3	Minimum elevation:	5770’
Hiking miles:	20.74	Maximum elevation:	7331’

Walking through a Burn Area South of Crater Lake

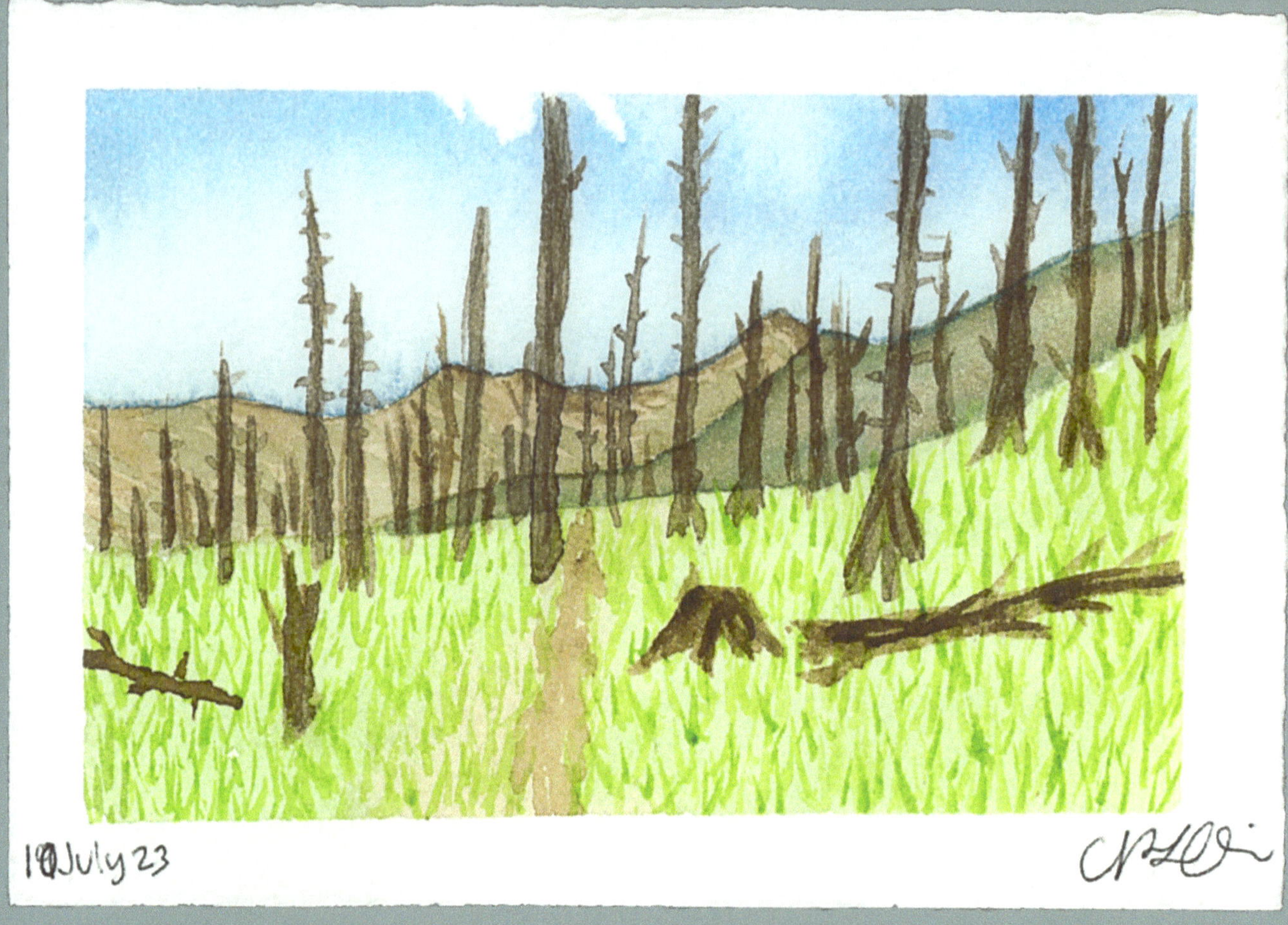

Seven Mile Trail Junction to Mazama Village

Trail day:	85	Ascent:	+2448’
Hiking day:	68	Descent:	-2182’
Trail miles:	1805.3 - 1821.9	Minimum elevation:	5780’
Hiking miles:	19.38	Maximum elevation:	6770’

Crater Lake during the Day

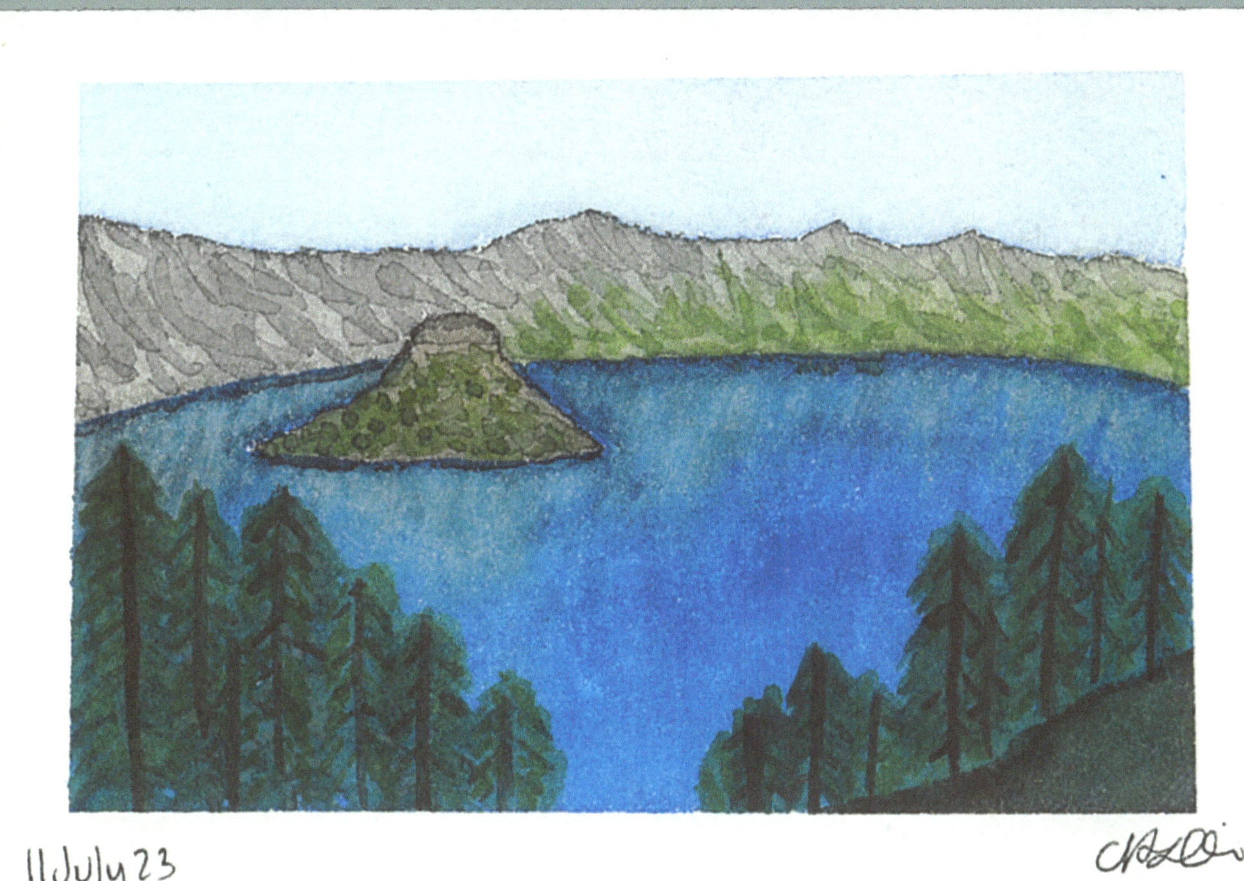

talk to tourists. pet dogs. paint.

Mazama Village to Lightning Spring

Trail day:	86	Ascent:	+472’
Hiking day:	69	Descent:	-751’
Trail miles:	1821.9 - Crater Lake Rim Trail	Minimum elevation:	6837’
Hiking miles:	3.20	Maximum elevation:	7273’

Crater Lake at Sunrise

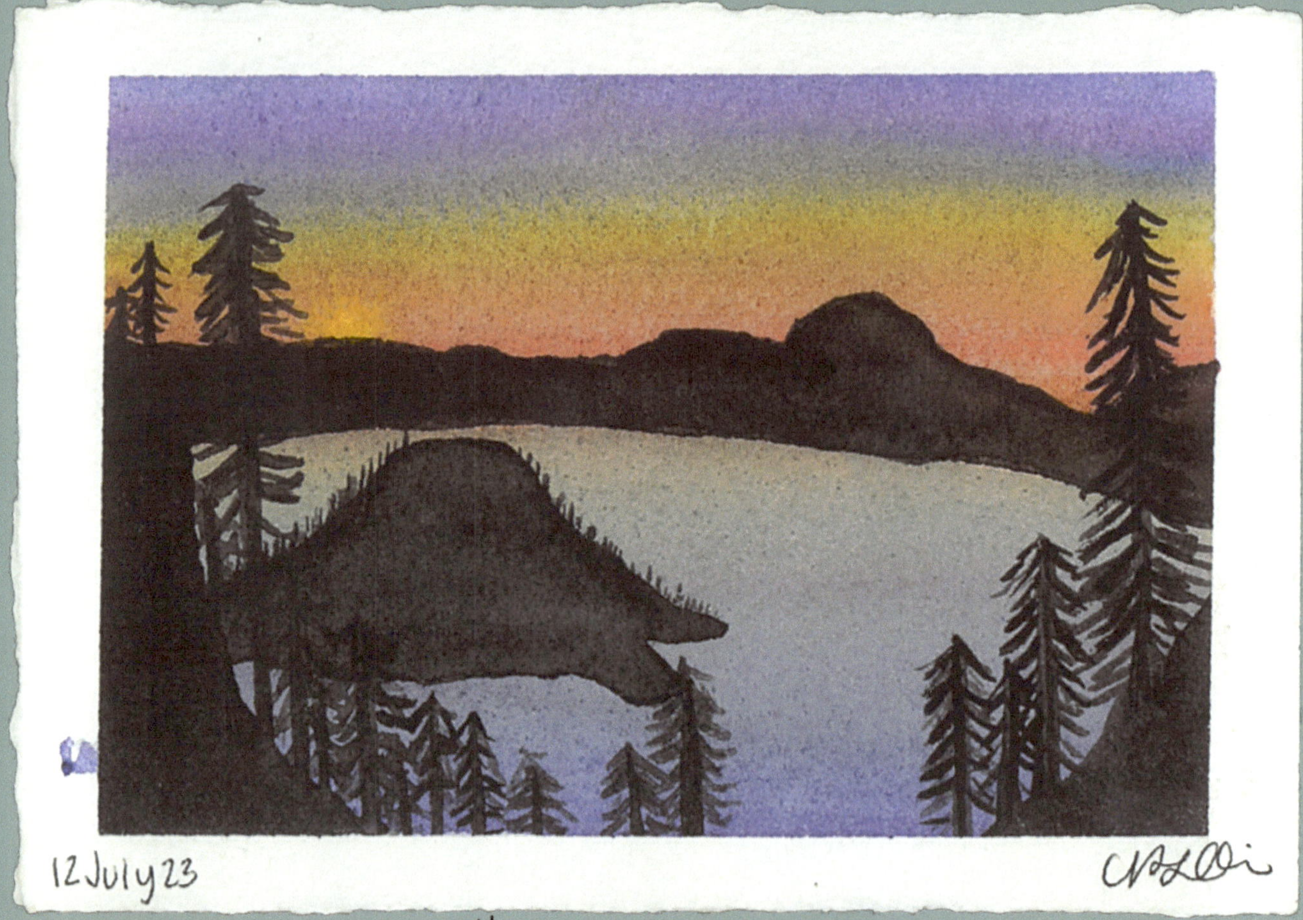

Chipmunk crawled on my lap!!!

Lightning Spring to Mt Theilson

Trail day:	87	Ascent:	+3000’
Hiking day:	70	Descent:	-2478’
Trail miles:	Crater Lake Rim Trail - 1854.9	Minimum elevation:	5920’
Hiking miles:	23.73	Maximum elevation:	7712’

Camping under Mt Theilson

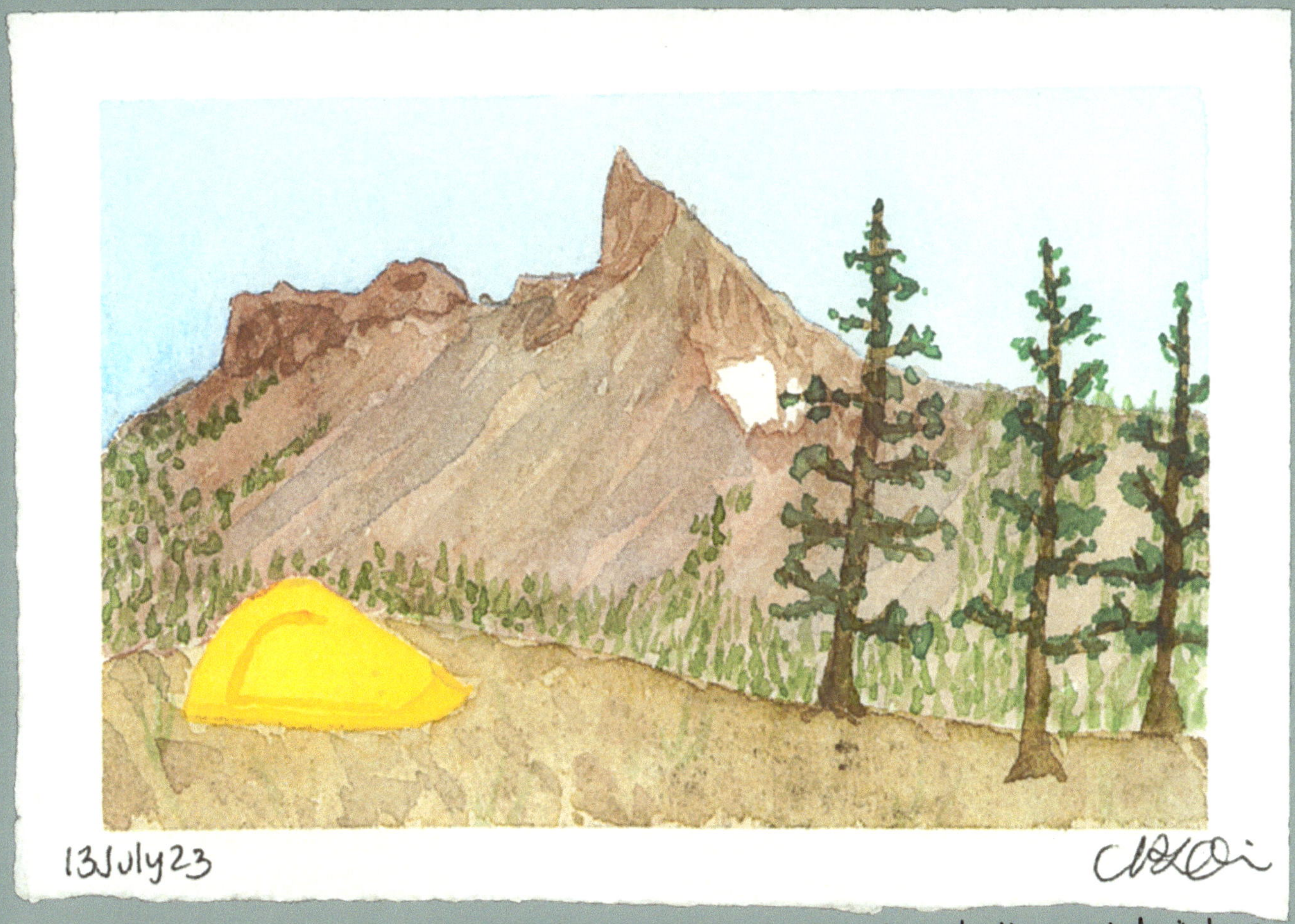

The best way to be successful is to make it so you don't have another option.

Mt Theilson to Bradley Creek Trail Junction

Trail day:	88	Ascent:	+2555'
Hiking day:	71	Descent:	-3255'
Trail miles:	1854.9 - 1875.2	Minimum elevation:	5962'
Hiking miles:	23.24	Maximum elevation:	7573'

The First View of Mt Hood

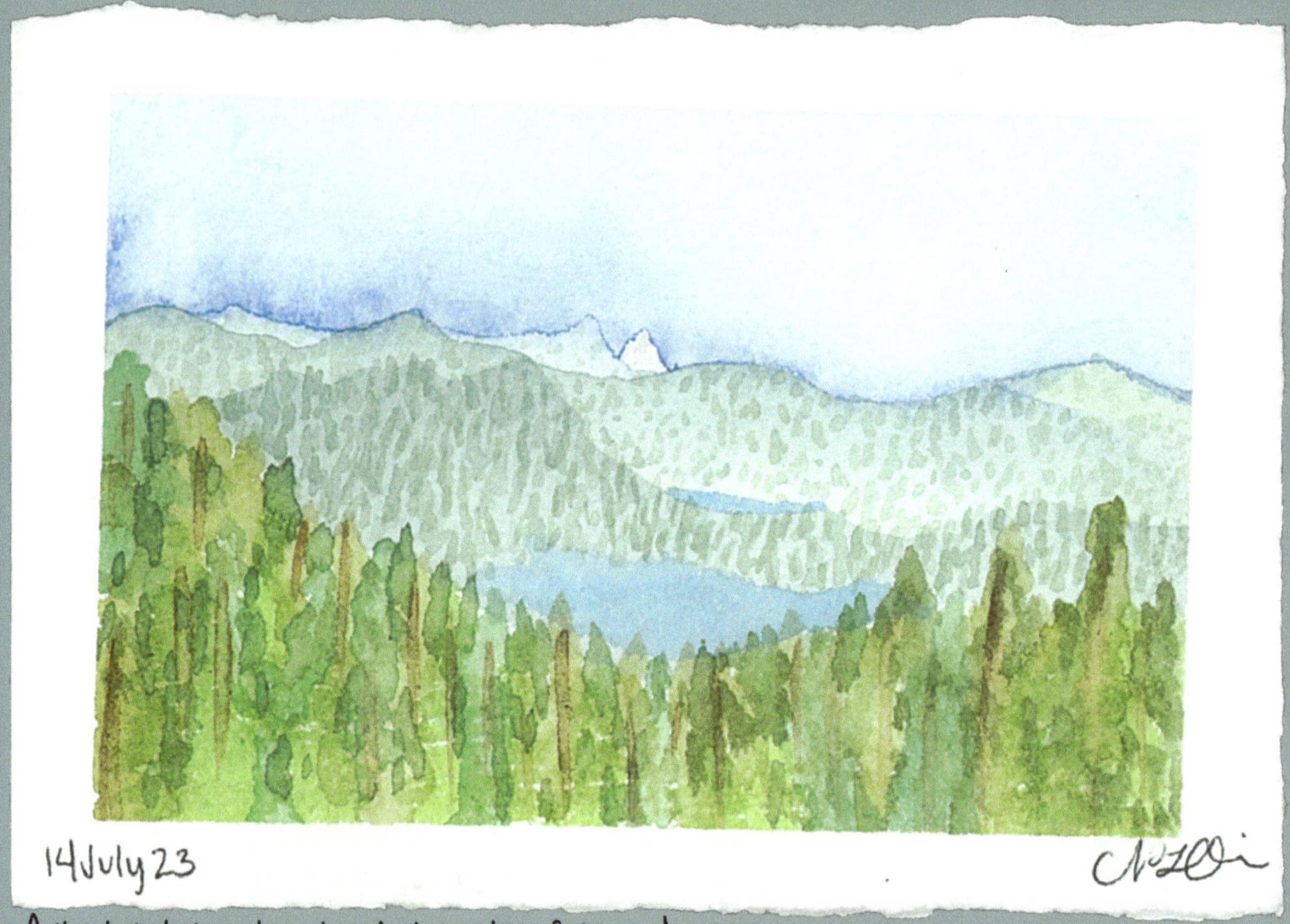

full pit toilet. cat in truck. hoards of blue dragons.

Bradley Creek Trail Junction to Rock Pile and Marie Lakes Junction

Trail day:	89	Ascent:	+2533’
Hiking day:	72	Descent:	-2956’
Trail miles:	1875.2 - 1894.7	Minimum elevation:	5591’
Hiking miles:	21.08	Maximum elevation:	7160’

Diamond Peak Wilderness

Rock Pile and Marie Lakes Junction to Shelter Cove	
Trail day:	90
Hiking day:	73
Trail miles:	1894.7 - 1907.2
Hiking miles:	13.63
Ascent:	+1230'
Descent:	-2562'
Minimum elevation:	4843'
Maximum elevation:	7031'

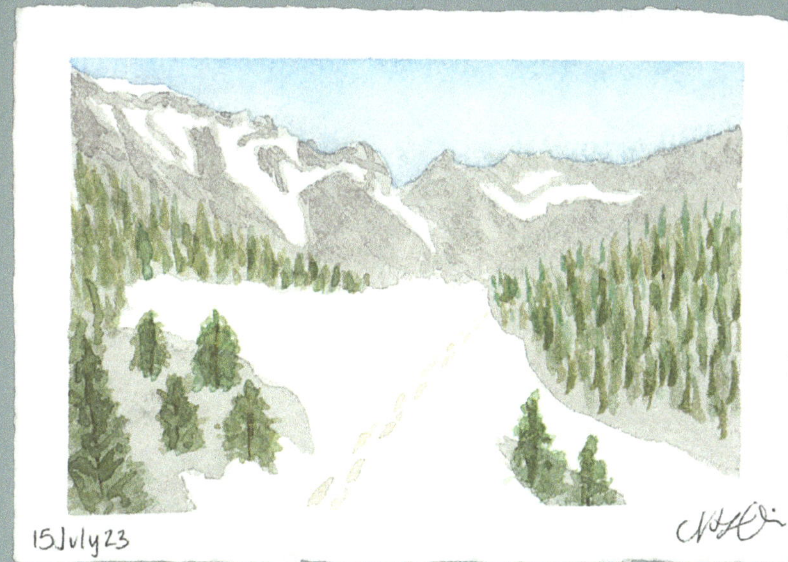

All is the price of all.

cotton candy colored skies

Shelter Cove to Charlton Lake	
Trail day:	91
Hiking day:	74
Trail miles:	1907.2 - 1926.1
Hiking miles:	20.88
Ascent:	+3064'
Descent:	-2162'
Minimum elevation:	4858'
Maximum elevation:	6585'

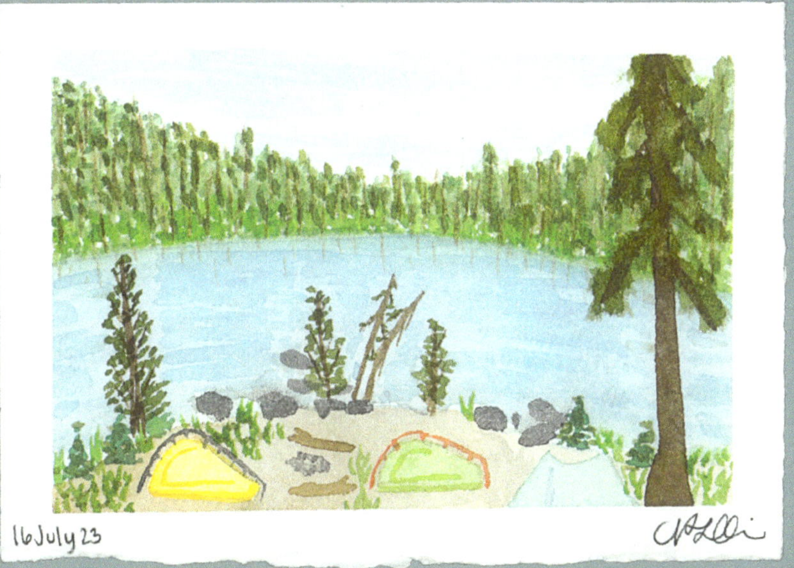

Charlton Lakeside Camping

Walking through a Burn Area in the Morning Mist

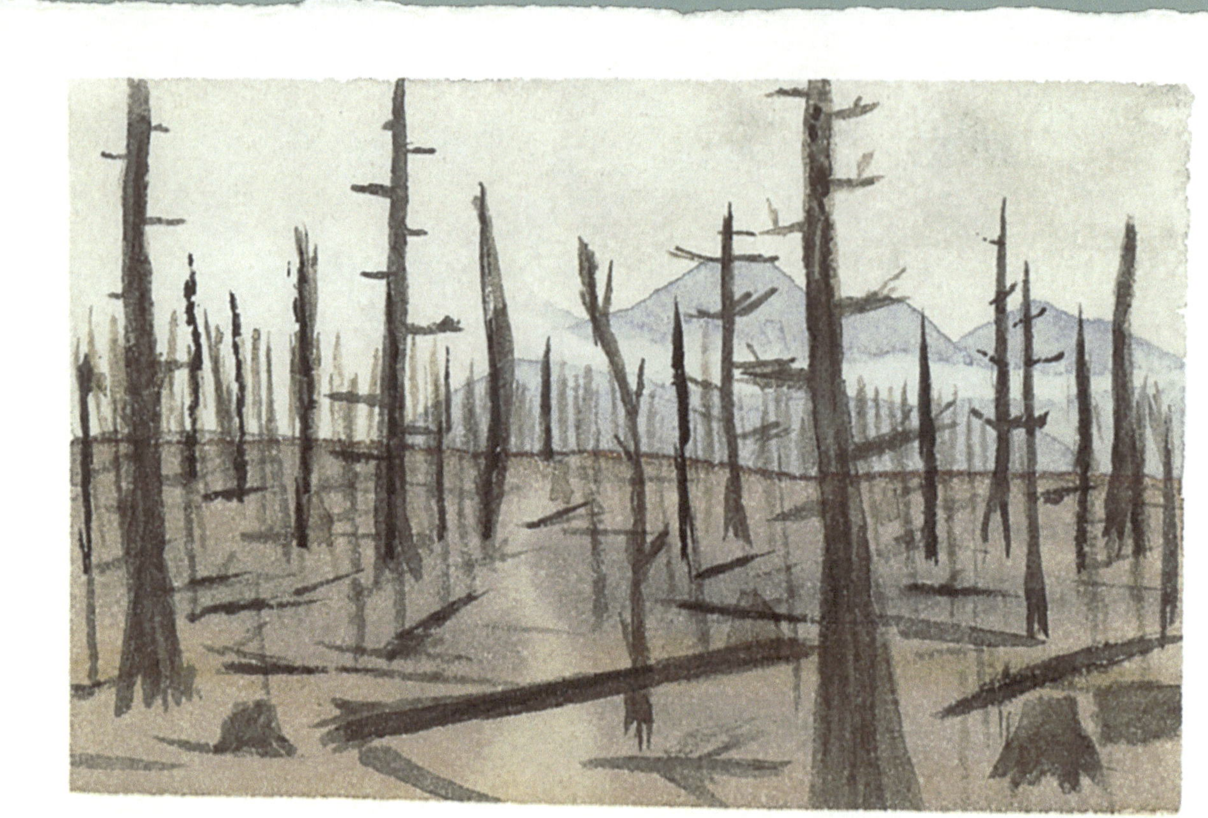

Charlton Lake to Dumbbell Lake

Trail day:	92	Ascent:	+2316’
Hiking day:	75	Descent:	-2493’
Trail miles:	1926.1 - 1948.2	Minimum elevation:	5075’
Hiking miles:	23.07	Maximum elevation:	6120’

Crossing a Meadow Looking at South and Middle Sisters

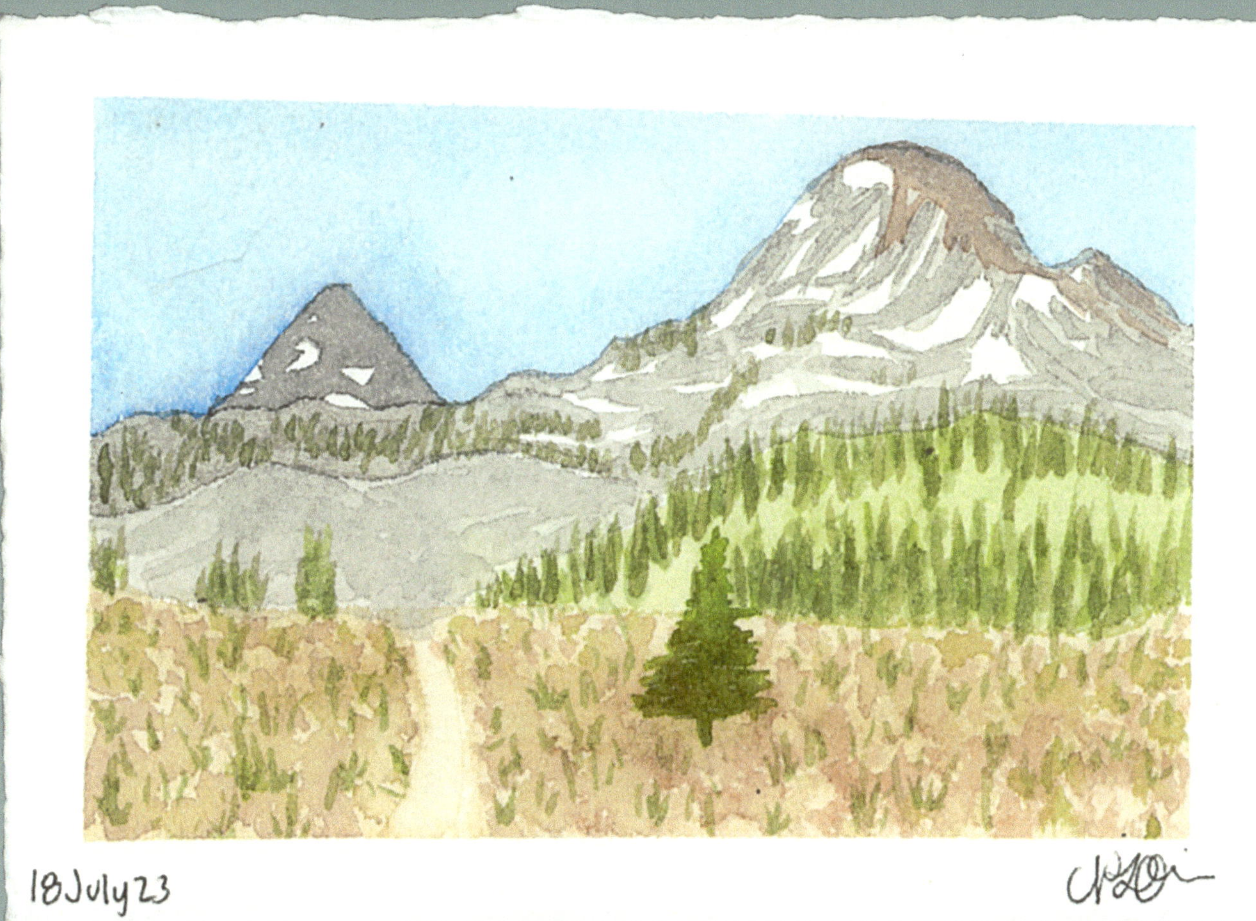

Do what you can with what you have.

Dumbbell Lake to Pond near Separation Creek

Trail day:	93	Ascent:	+3041'
Hiking day:	76	Descent:	-2126'
Trail miles:	1948.2 - 1967.5	Minimum elevation:	5241'
Hiking miles:	21.15	Maximum elevation:	6462'

Passing by a Single Tree in a Field of Lava on Little Belknap

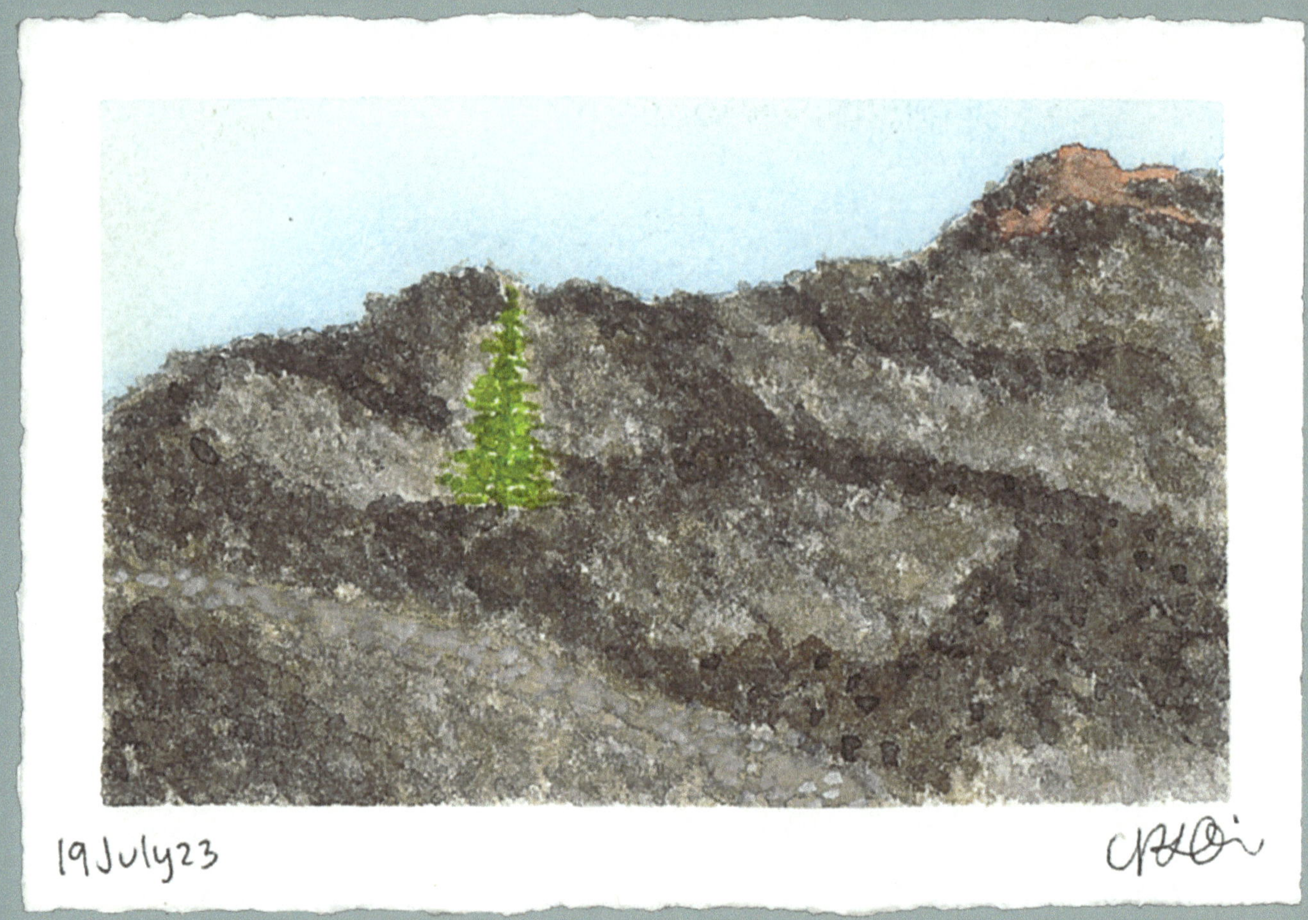

lava rocks. exhausting + miserable. hot. difficult walking.

Separation Creek to Little Belknap

Trail day:	94	Ascent:	+3553’
Hiking day:	77	Descent:	-4683’
Trail miles:	1967.5 - 1989.7	Minimum elevation:	5192’
Hiking miles:	24.16	Maximum elevation:	7146’

Waiting for a Hitch from Santiam Pass into Bend on Highway 20

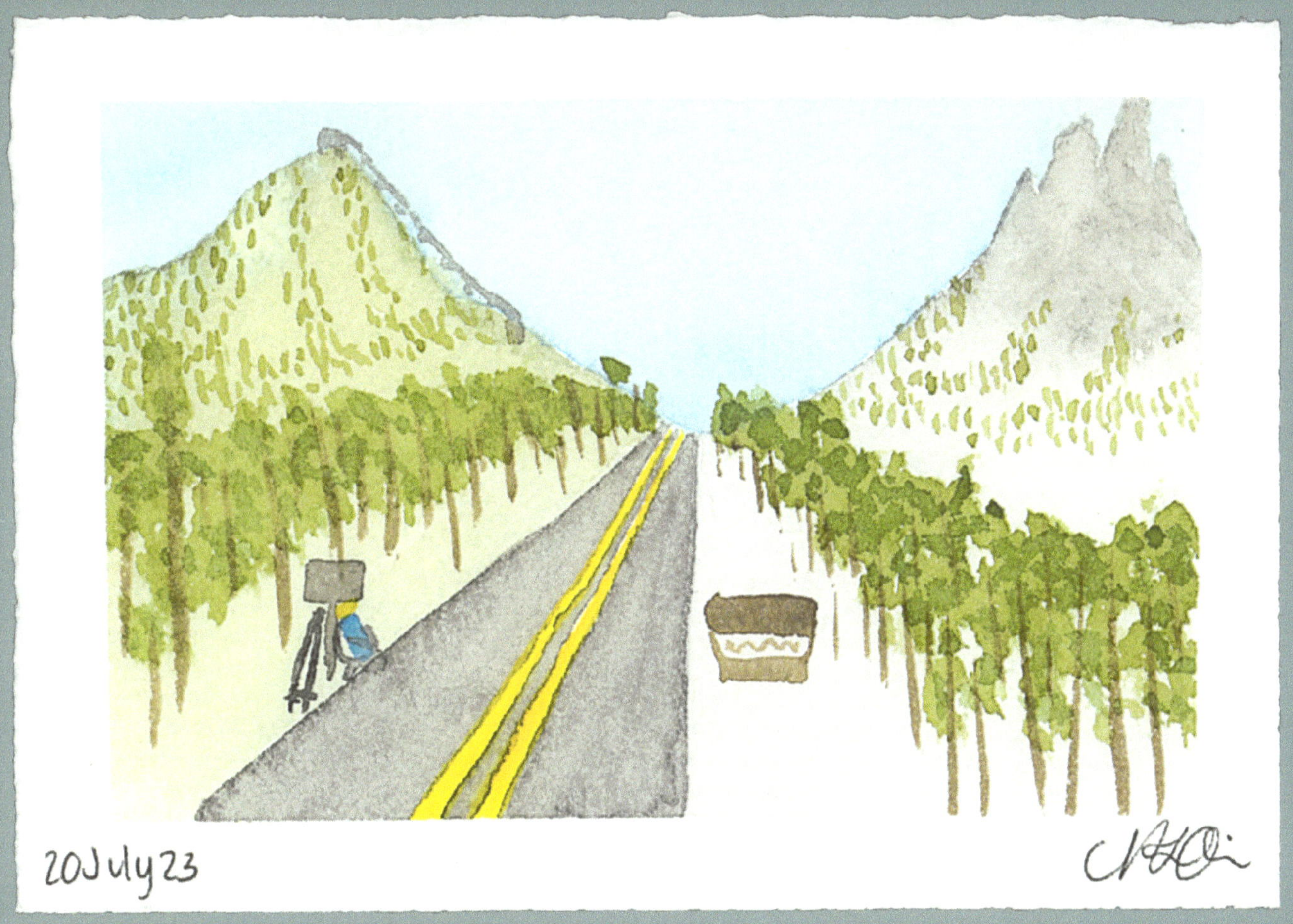

Little Belknap to Highway 20

Trail day:	95	Ascent:	+1030’
Hiking day:	78	Descent:	-1572’
Trail miles:	1989.7 - 2002.0	Minimum elevation:	4684’
Hiking miles:	12.52	Maximum elevation:	5877’

Three Finger Jack

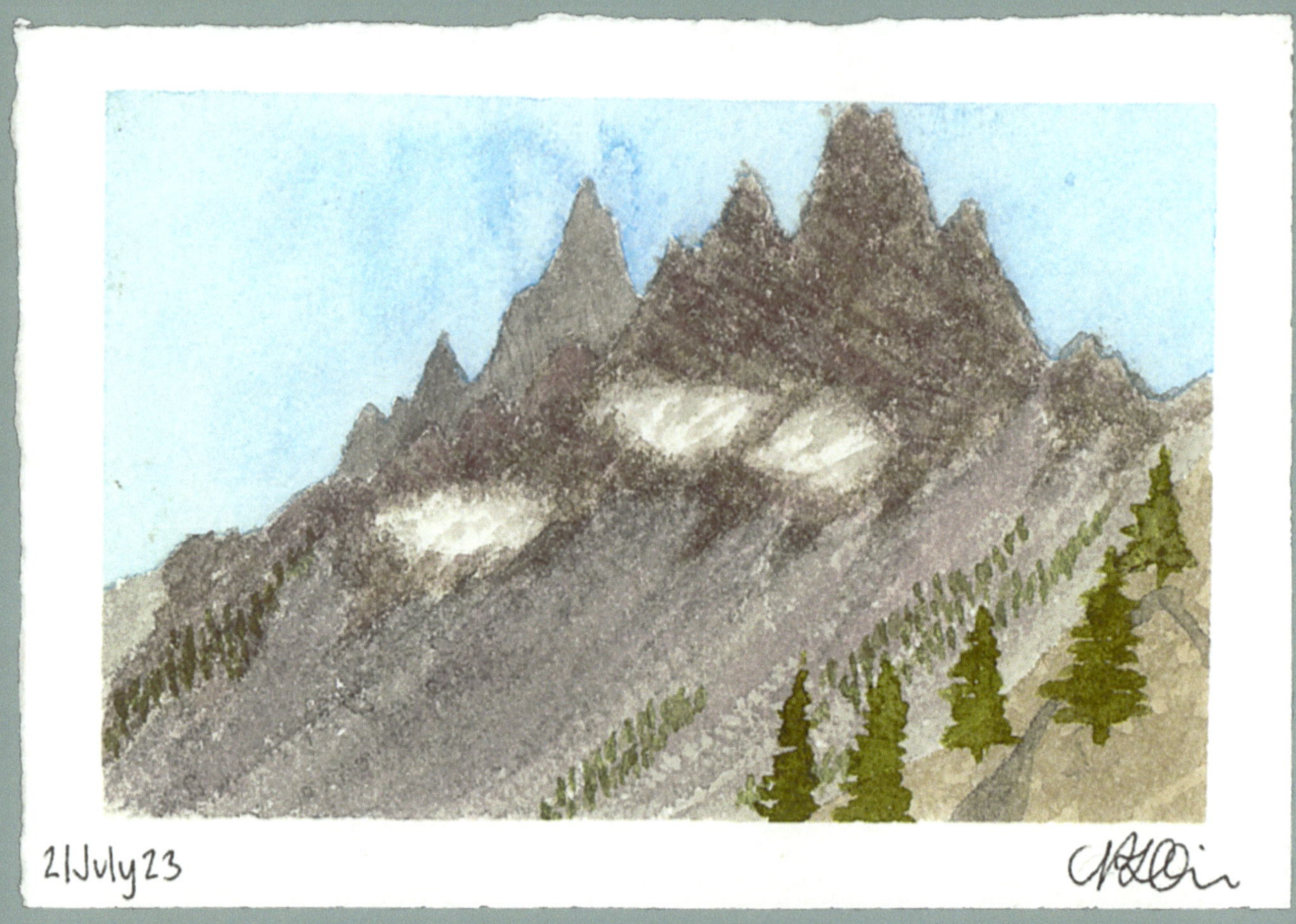

Highway 20 to Rockpile Lake

Trail day:	96	Ascent:	+2821’
Hiking day:	79	Descent:	-1415’
Trail miles:	2002.0 - 2016.4	Minimum elevation:	4862’
Hiking miles:	15.71	Maximum elevation:	6509’

Mt Jefferson from Park Ridge

Rockpile Lake to Park Ridge in Mt Hood Wilderness

Trail day:	97
Hiking day:	80
Trail miles:	2016.4 - 2038.4
Hiking miles:	23.16
Ascent:	+3997'
Descent:	-3415'
Minimum elevation:	4367'
Maximum elevation:	6889'

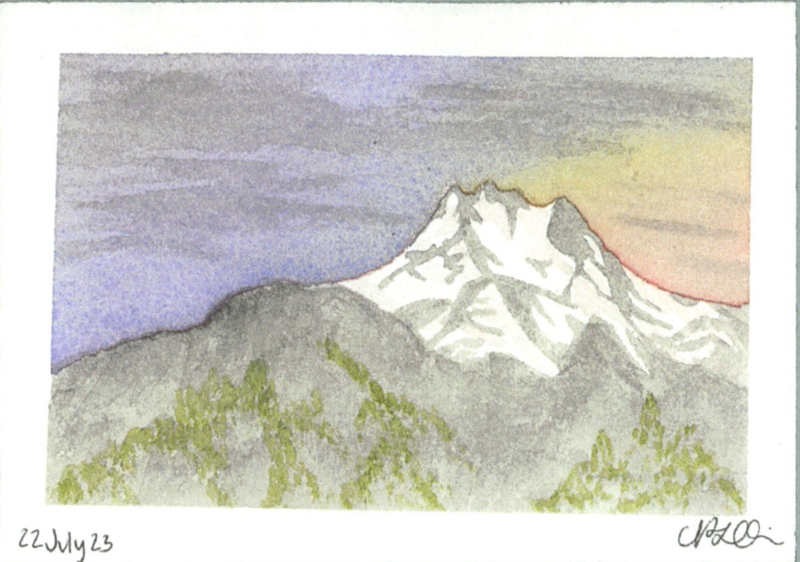

Milky streams

Park Ridge to Pinhead Saddle

Trail day:	98
Hiking day:	81
Trail miles:	2038.4 - 2060.9
Hiking miles:	23.82
Ascent:	+2188'
Descent:	-4065'
Minimum elevation:	4391'
Maximum elevation:	6868'

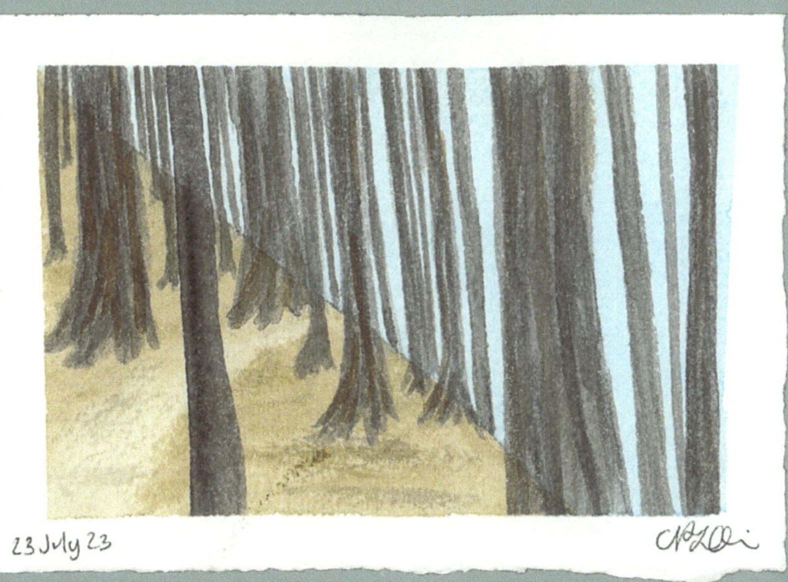

Walking through the Newly Opened Lionhead Burn Area

PCT Sign at Forest Road 42

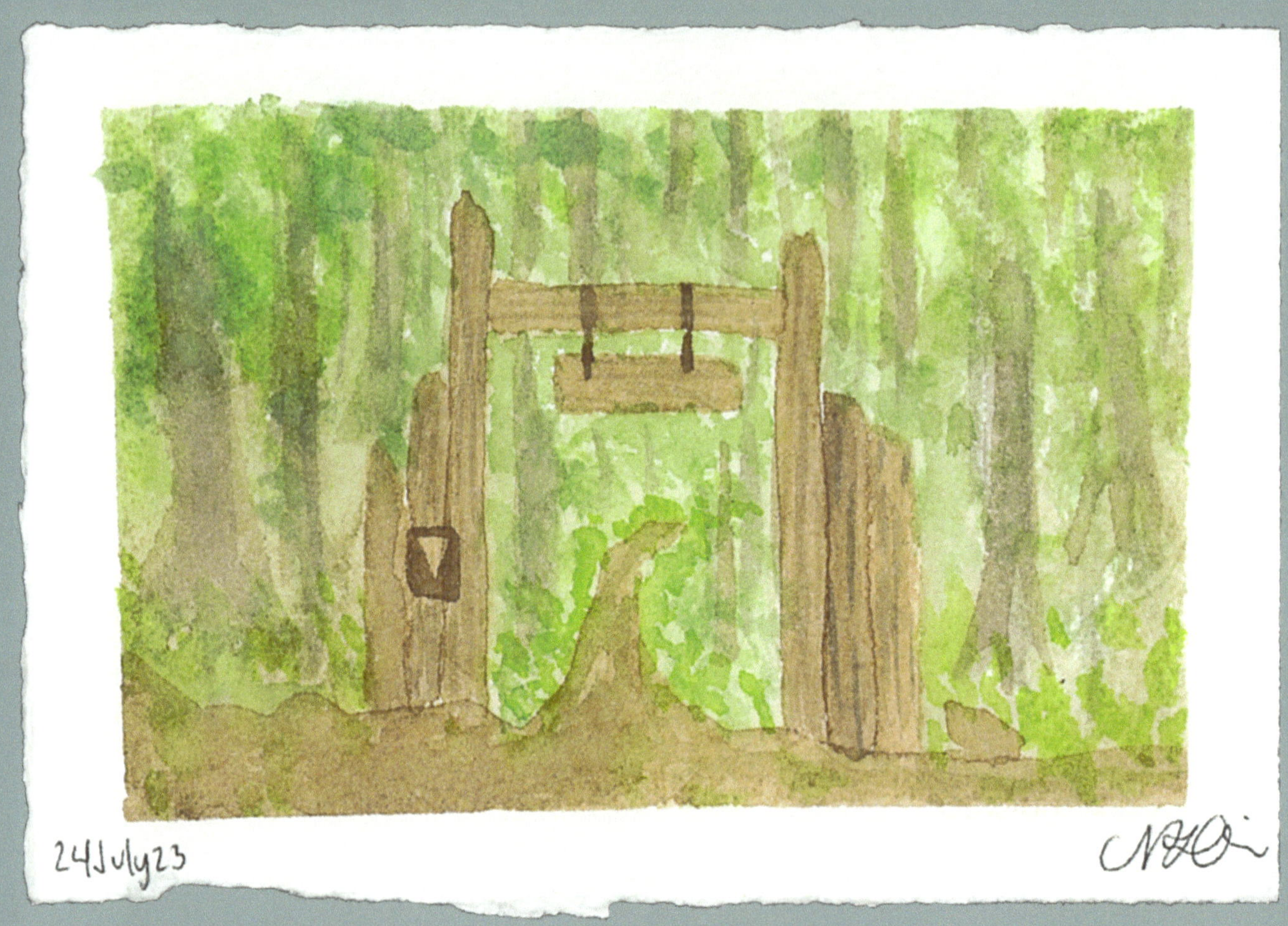

Pinhead Saddle to Spring in Mt Hood Wilderness

Trail day:	99	Ascent:	+2527’
Hiking day:	82	Descent:	-3590’
Trail miles:	2060.9 - 2085.4	Minimum elevation:	3263’
Hiking miles:	25.71	Maximum elevation:	5079’

Mt Hood

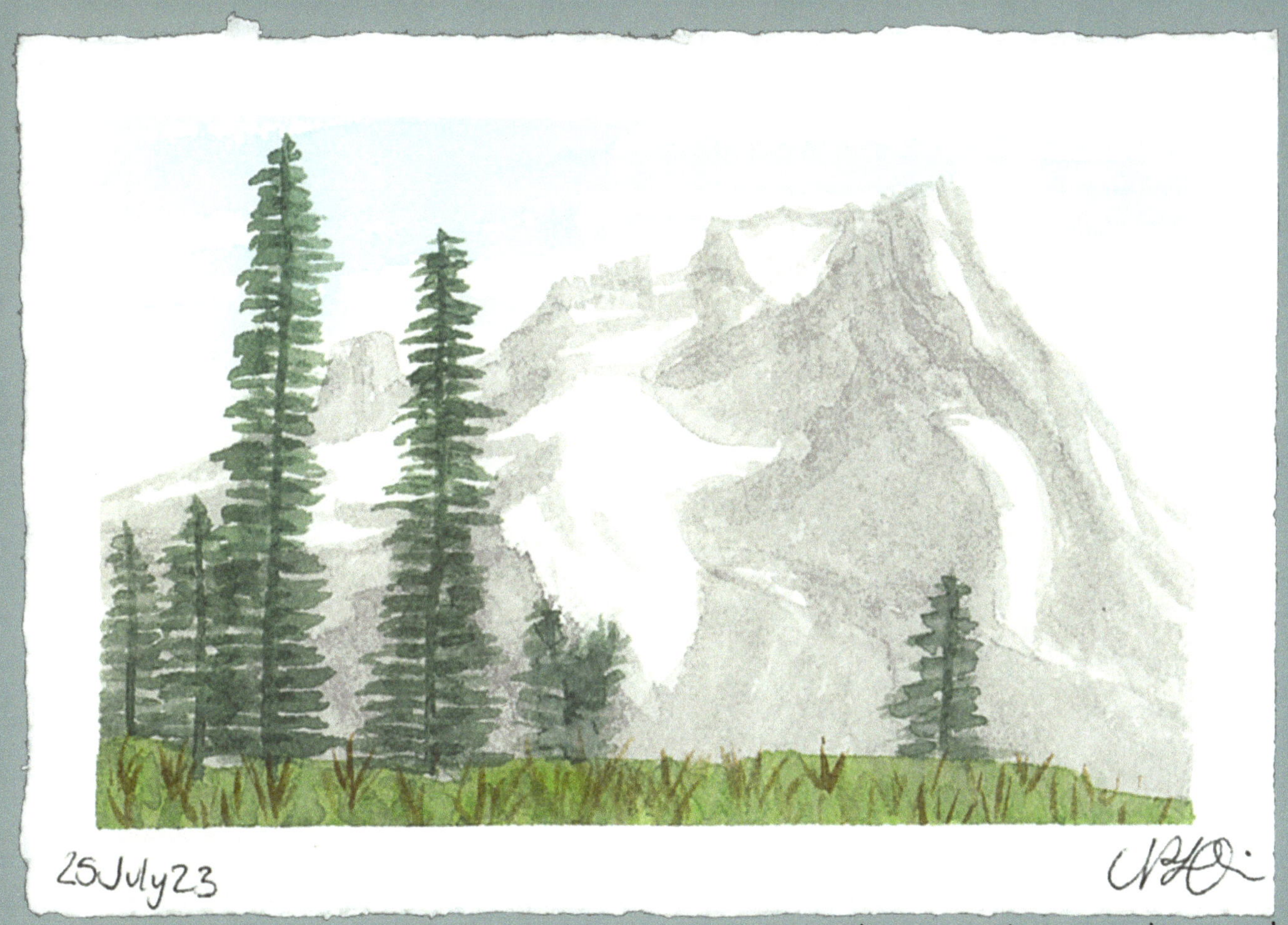

walking uphill on sand is hard

Mt Hood Wilderness to Timberline Lodge

Trail day:	100	Ascent:	+3182’
Hiking day:	83	Descent:	-1191’
Trail miles:	2085.4 - 2099.7	Minimum elevation:	3944’
Hiking miles:	15.25	Maximum elevation:	6019’

Paradise Park Loop Alternate

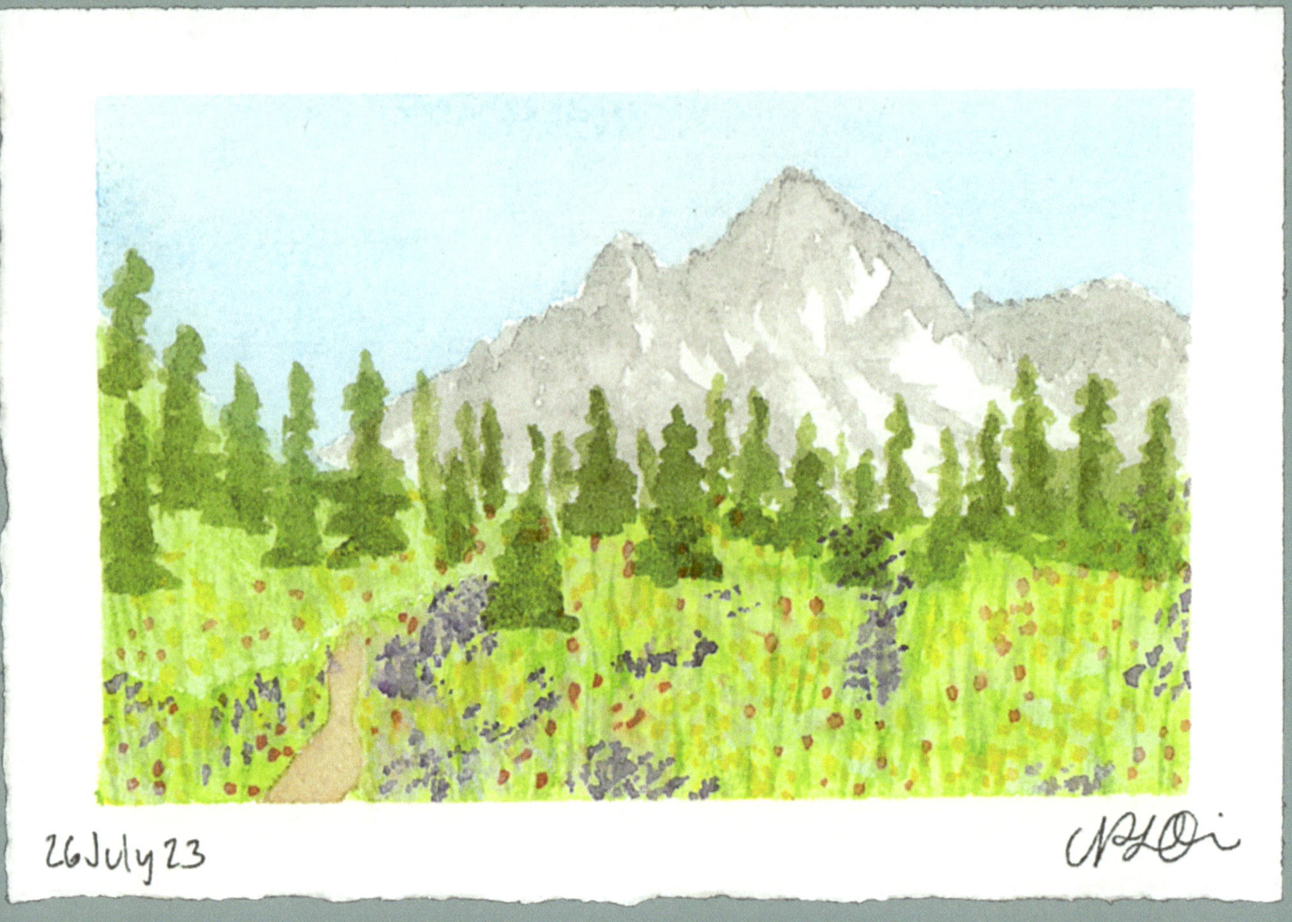

Timberline Lodge to Lolo Pass

Trail day:	101	Ascent:	+3261’
Hiking day:	84	Descent:	-5784’
Trail miles:	2099.7 - 2116.9	Minimum elevation:	2862’
Hiking miles:	18.57	Maximum elevation:	6089’

Tunnel Falls

Lolo Pass to 7.8 of Tunnel Falls Alternate

Trail day:	102
Hiking day:	85
Trail miles:	2116.9 - 2130.3 (+7.8)
Hiking miles:	23.31
Ascent:	+2398'
Descent:	-5020'
Minimum elevation:	816'
Maximum elevation:	4505'

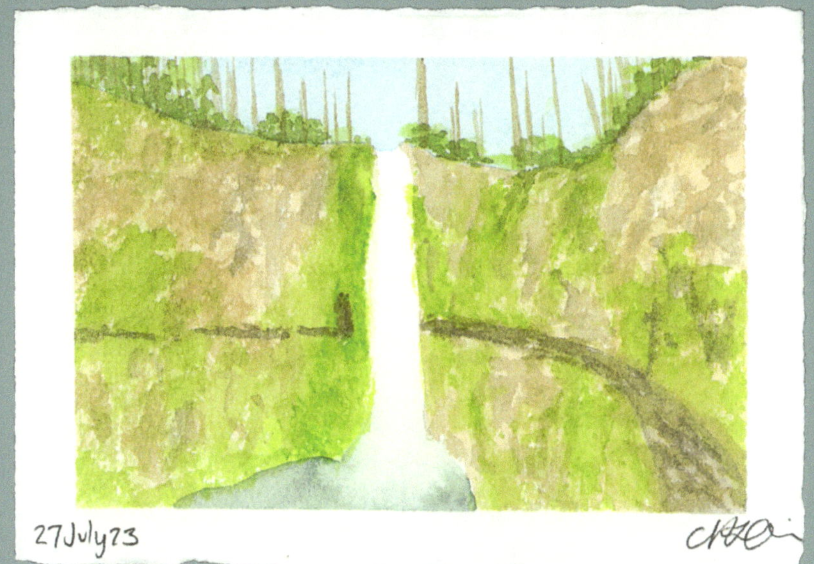

tiny spot... squeezed 5 tents.

Mile 7.8 of Tunnel Falls Alternate to Table Mountain

Trail day:	103
Hiking day:	86
Trail miles:	2130.3 (+7.8) - 2155.7
Hiking miles:	14.10
Ascent:	+1837'
Descent:	-1841'
Minimum elevation:	142'
Maximum elevation:	851'

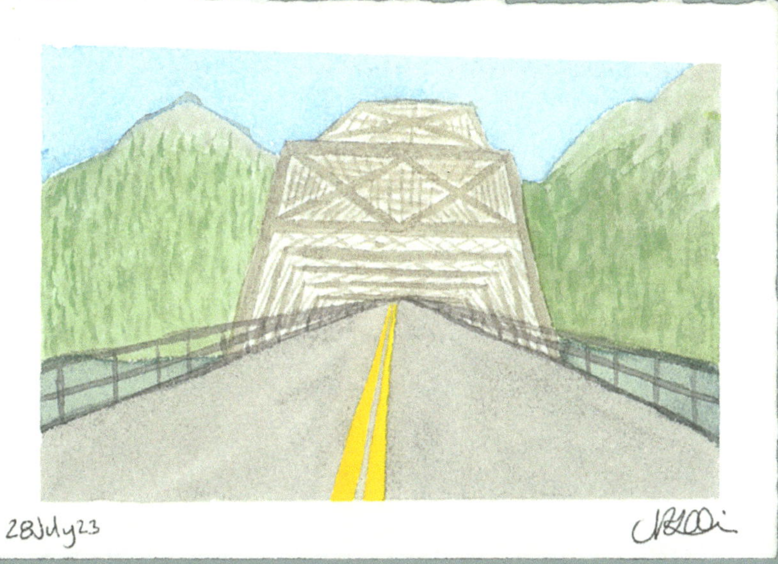

Bridge of the Gods over the Columbia River

Southern Washington

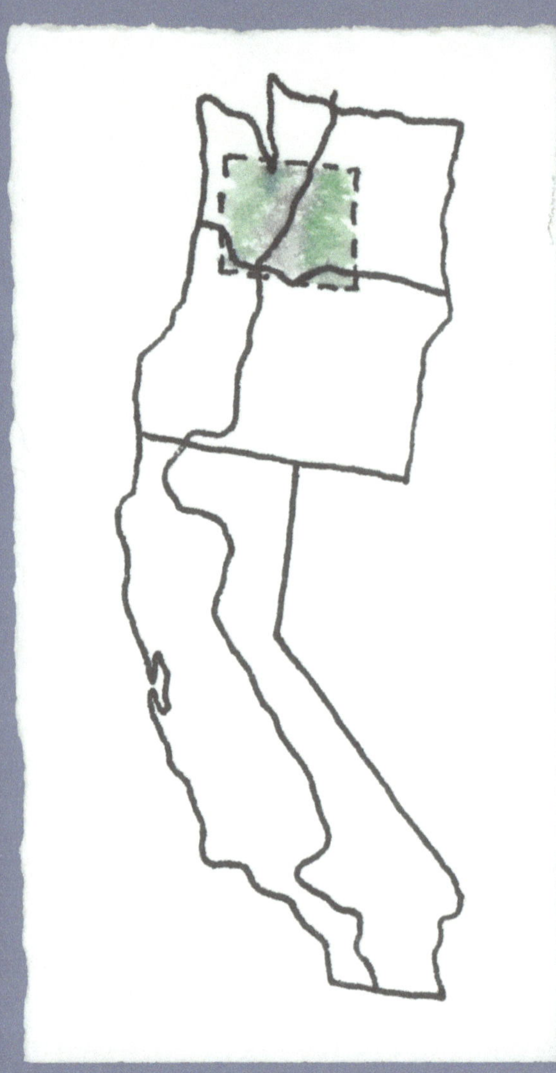

Northbound: Cascade Locks, OR to Stevens Pass, WA

July 28 to August 13, 2023

Trail days:	16
Hiking days:	16
Trail miles:	2155.7 - 2466.7
Average miles per hiking day:	18.66
Fewest miles per hiking day:	14.66
Most miles per hiking day:	26.65

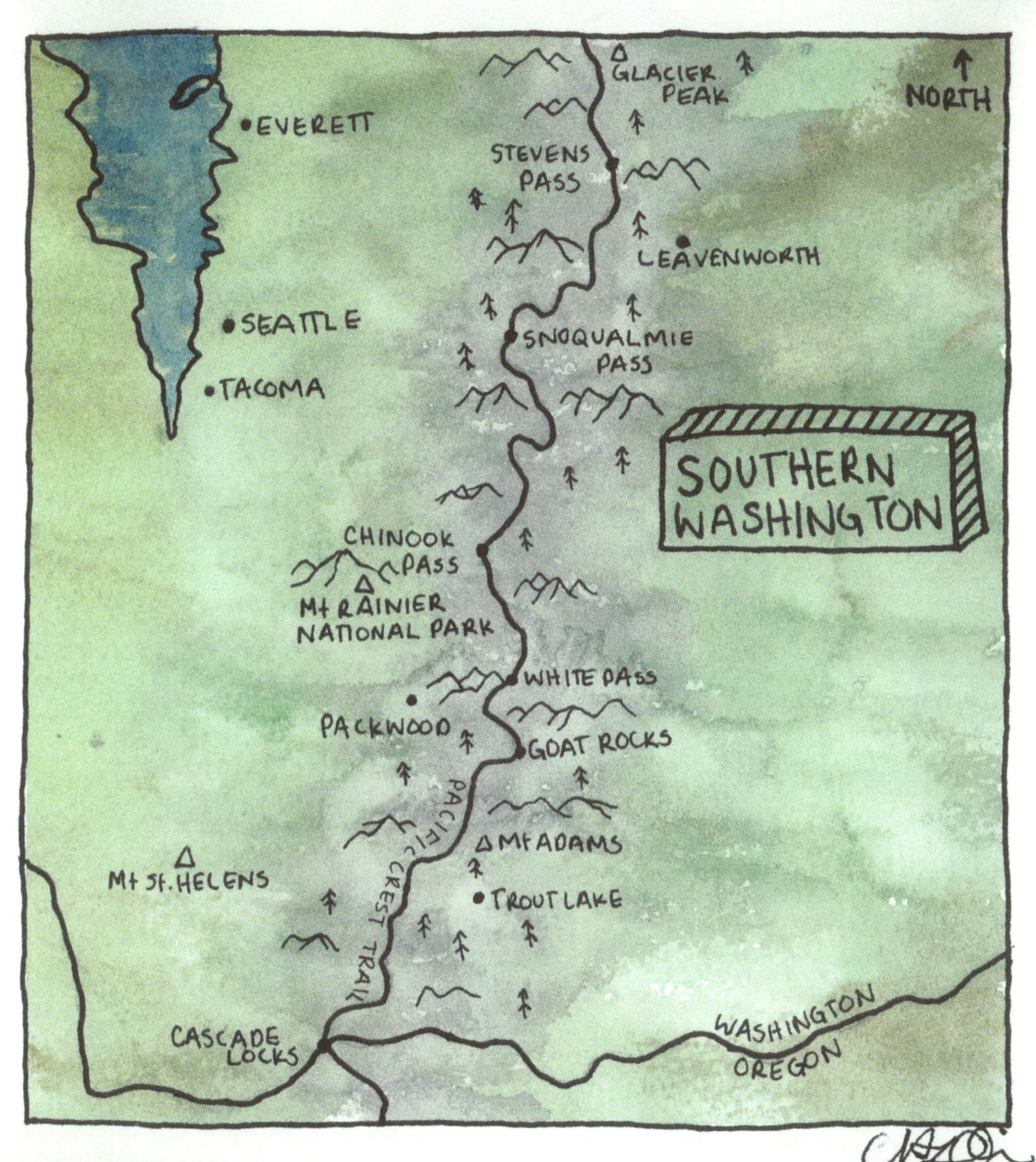

GLACIER PEAK
NORTH
EVERETT
STEVENS PASS
LEAVENWORTH
SEATTLE
SNOQUALMIE PASS
TACOMA
SOUTHERN WASHINGTON
CHINOOK PASS
Mt RAINIER NATIONAL PARK
WHITE PASS
PACKWOOD
GOAT ROCKS
PACIFIC CREST TRAIL
Mt ADAMS
Mt St. HELENS
TROUT LAKE
CASCADE LOCKS
WASHINGTON
OREGON

The Most Lush Forest on the PCT

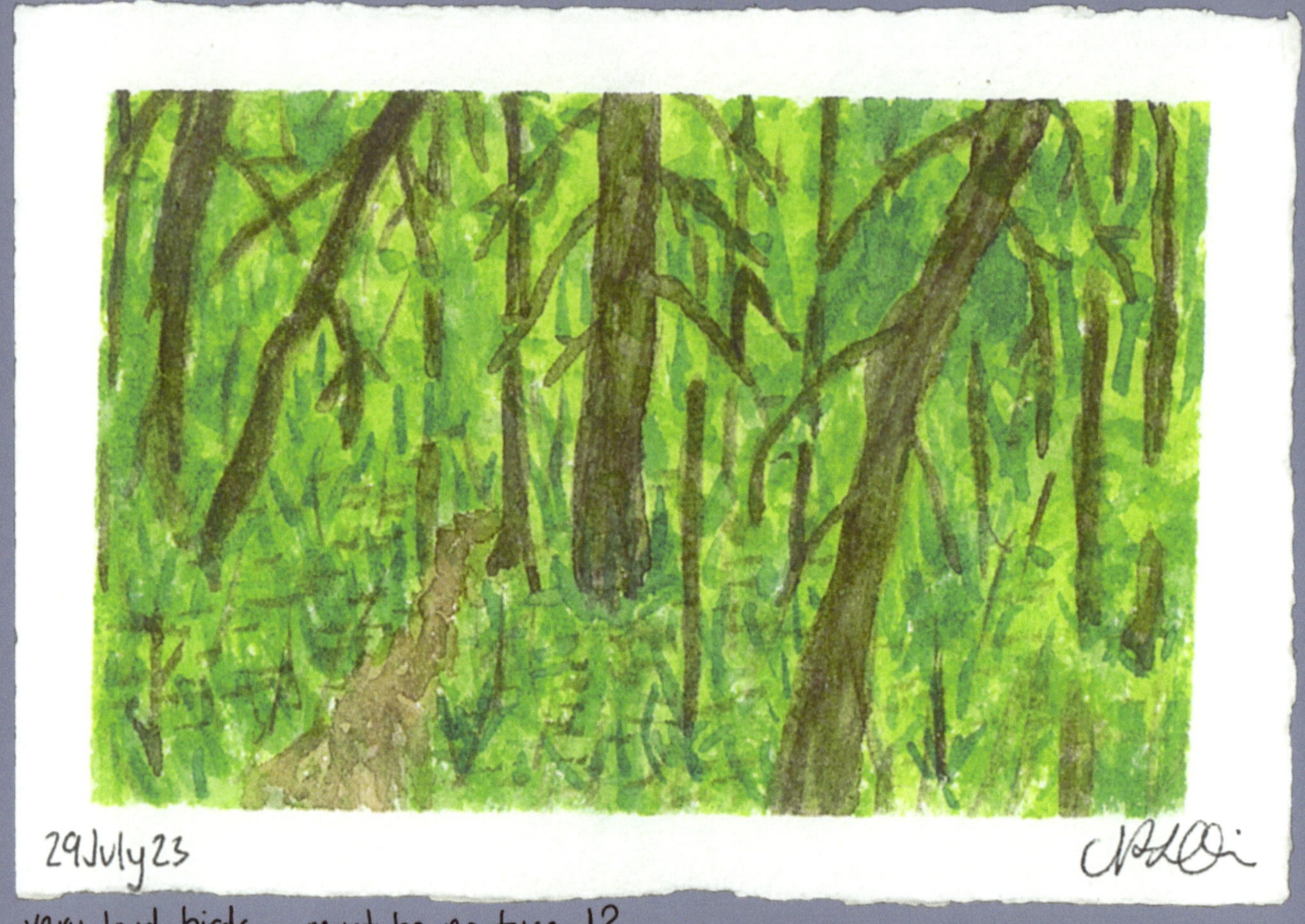

very loud birds. . . must be nocturnal?

Table Mountain to Rock Creek

Trail day:	104	Ascent:	+4747’
Hiking day:	87	Descent:	-3071’
Trail miles:	2155.7 - 2172.5	Minimum elevation:	843’
Hiking miles:	17.39	Maximum elevation:	3457’

A Dreamy View of Mt Hood and Mt Adams from Sedum Point

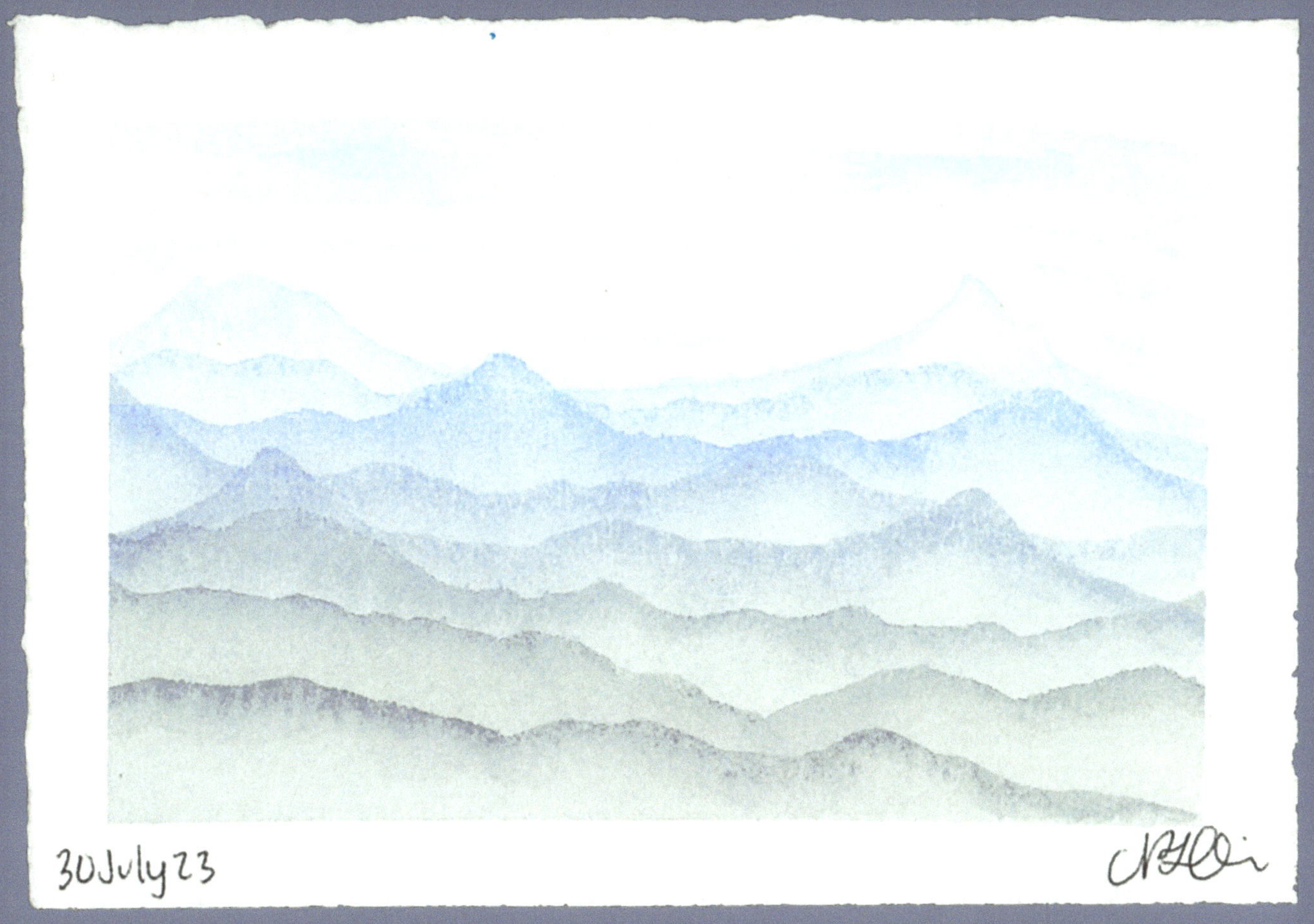

Rock Creek to Big Huckleberry Trailhead

Trail day:	105	Ascent:	+3629'
Hiking day:	88	Descent:	-3337'
Trail miles:	2172.5 - 2189.2	Minimum elevation:	326'
Hiking miles:	18.41	Maximum elevation:	984'

Mt Adams from Indian Heaven Wilderness

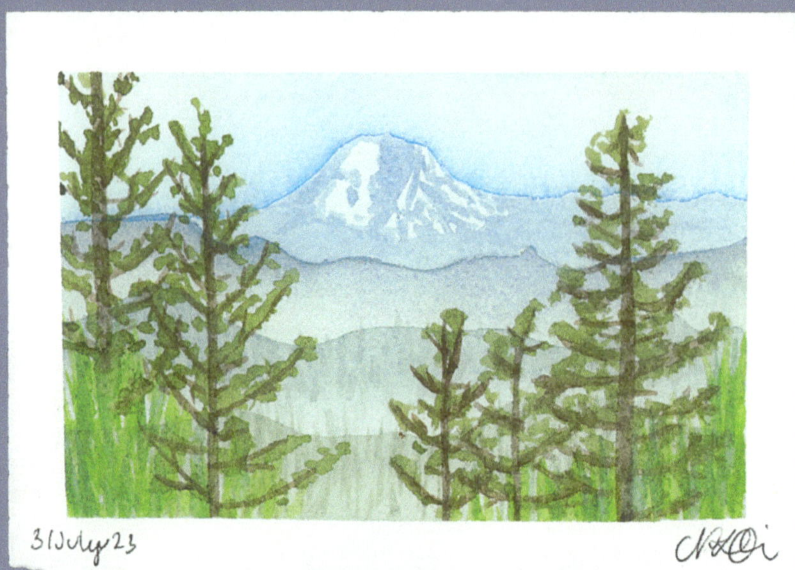

slug the same color as pickled jalapeno.

Big Huckleberry Trailhead to Blue Lake

Trail day:	106
Hiking day:	89
Trail miles:	2189.2 - 2208.0
Hiking miles:	18.34
Ascent:	+3852’
Descent:	-1959’
Minimum elevation:	2799’
Maximum elevation:	4984’

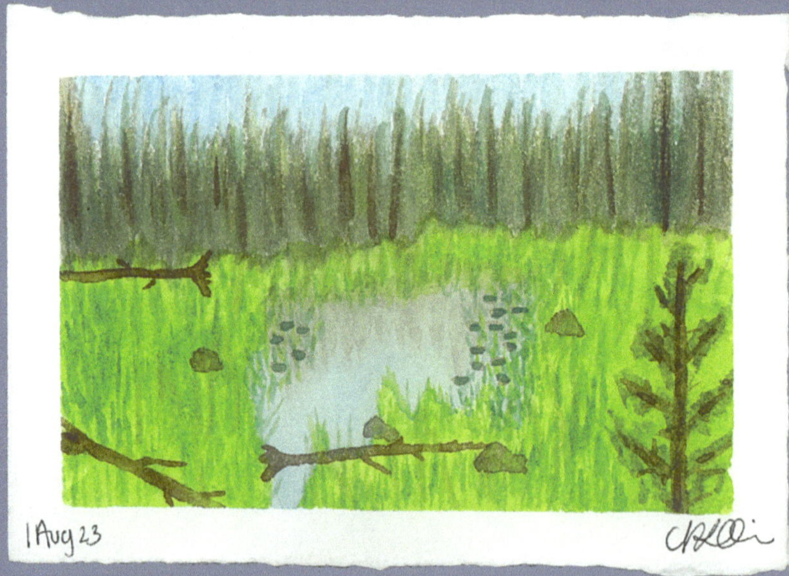

Blue Lake to Indian Heaven Wilderness

Trail day:	107
Hiking day:	90
Trail miles:	2208.0 - 2229.7
Hiking miles:	22.19
Ascent:	+2979’
Descent:	-3196’
Minimum elevation:	3367’
Maximum elevation:	5197’

A Marshy Meadow with Lily Pads in Indian Heaven Wilderness

Mt Adams with Lava Rocks, Burned Trees, Regrowth, and Meadows

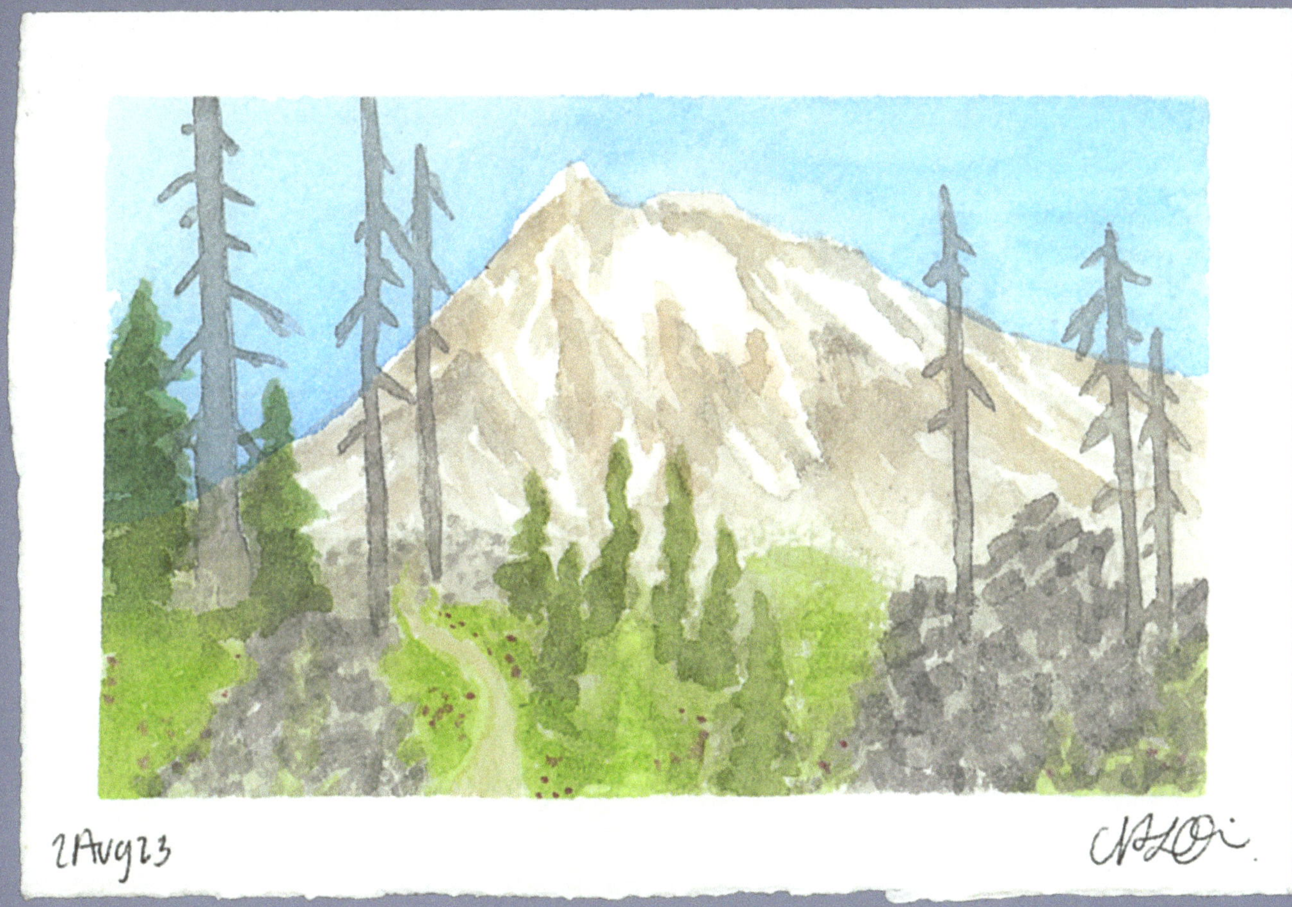

embrace the suck and call it a journey.

Indian Heaven Wilderness to Mt Adams Wilderness

Trail day:	108	Ascent:	+2904’
Hiking day:	91	Descent:	-1476’
Trail miles:	2229.7 - 2243.1	Minimum elevation:	3909’
Hiking miles:	14.66	Maximum elevation:	6144’

View of Mt Rainier from Mt Adams Wilderness

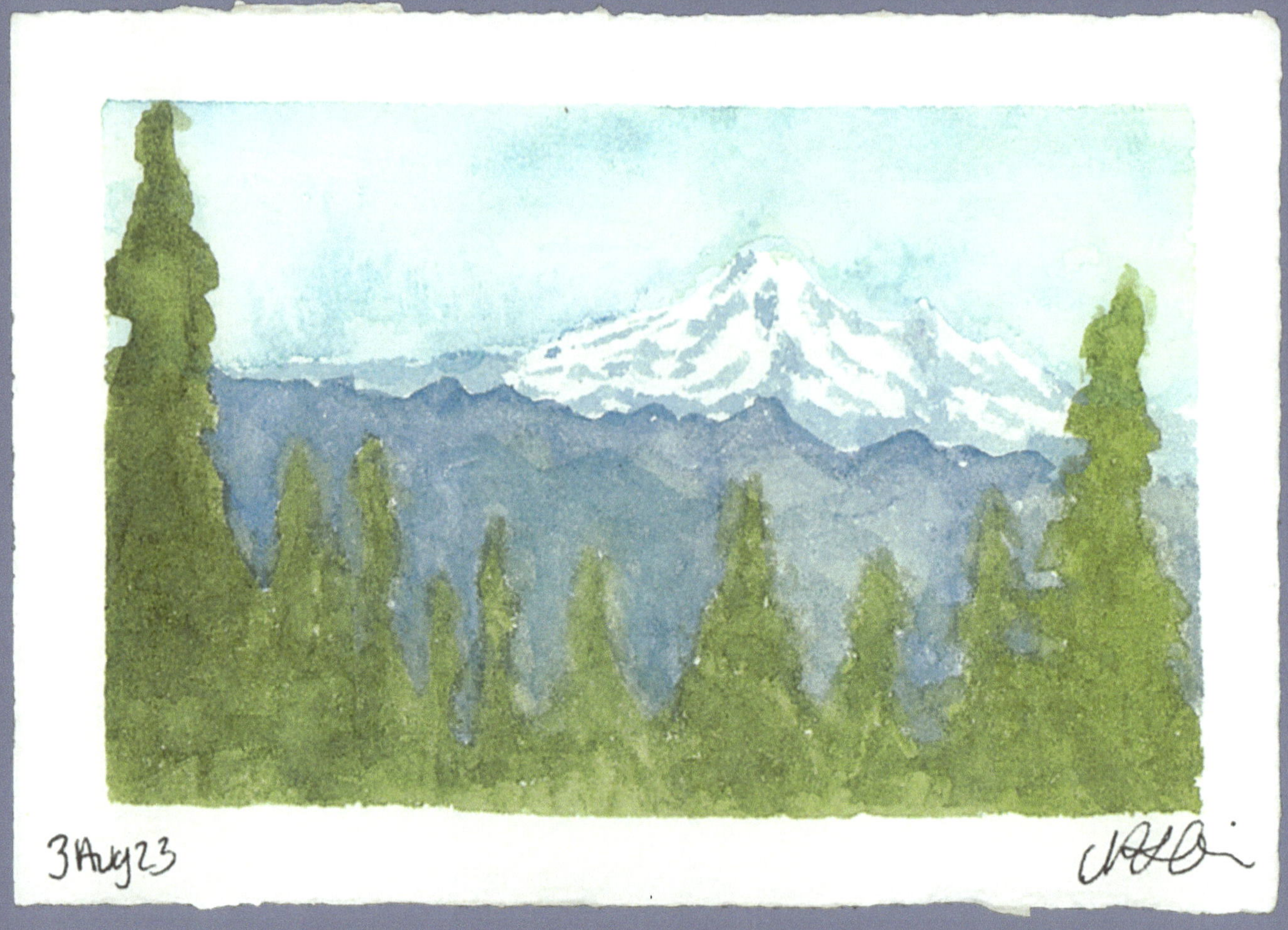

Mt Adams Wilderness to Walupt Lake

Trail day:	109	Ascent:	+2421’
Hiking day:	92	Descent:	-2589’
Trail miles:	2243.1 - 2262.1	Minimum elevation:	4481’
Hiking miles:	19.00	Maximum elevation:	5133’

Knife's Edge in Goat Rocks Wilderness

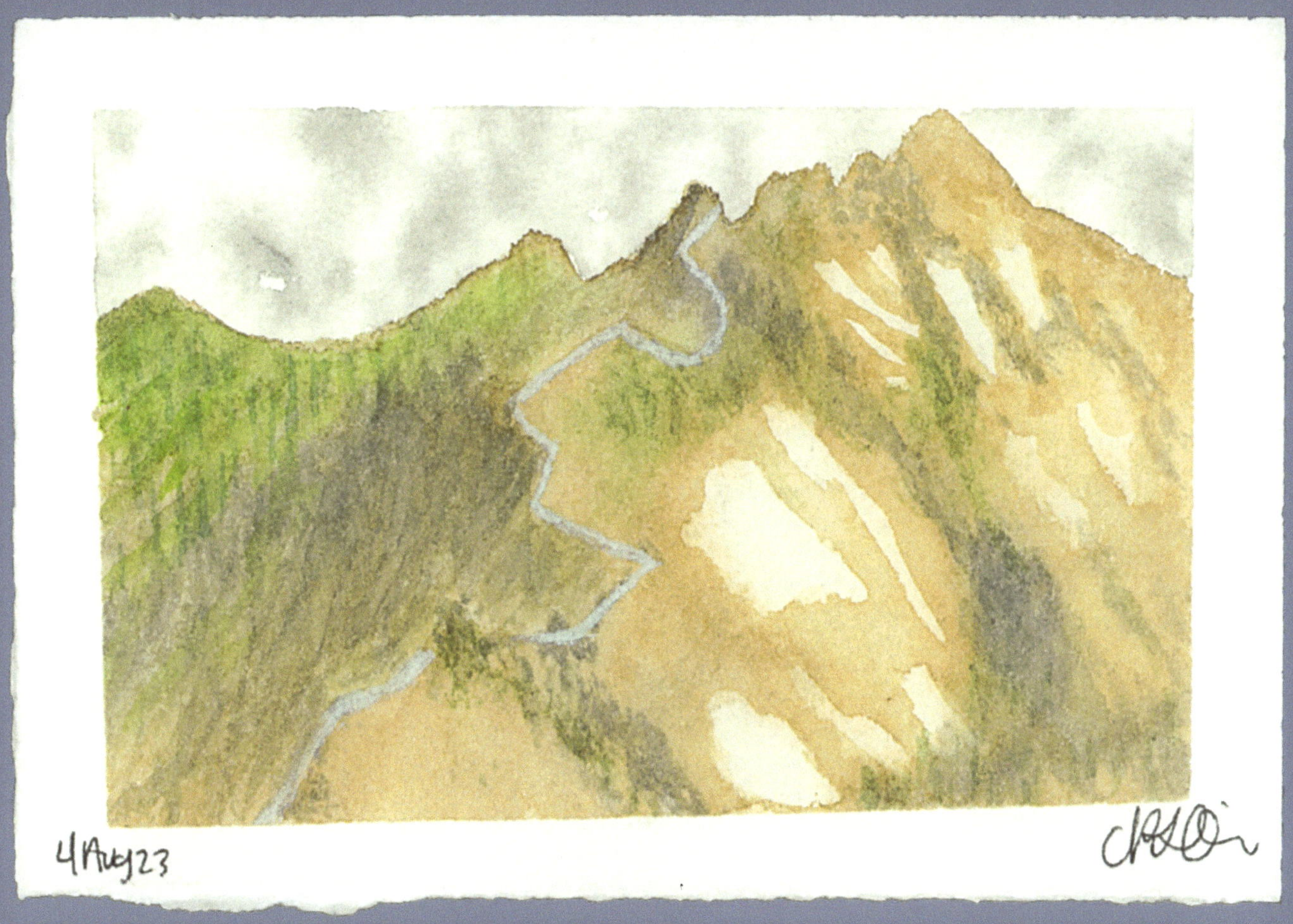

Walupt Lake to Goat Rocks Wilderness

Trail day:	110	Ascent:	+4514'
Hiking day:	93	Descent:	-4249'
Trail miles:	2262.1 - 2282.6	Minimum elevation:	4924'
Hiking miles:	23.45	Maximum elevation:	7586'

Leaving Goat Rocks near White's Pass Ski Area

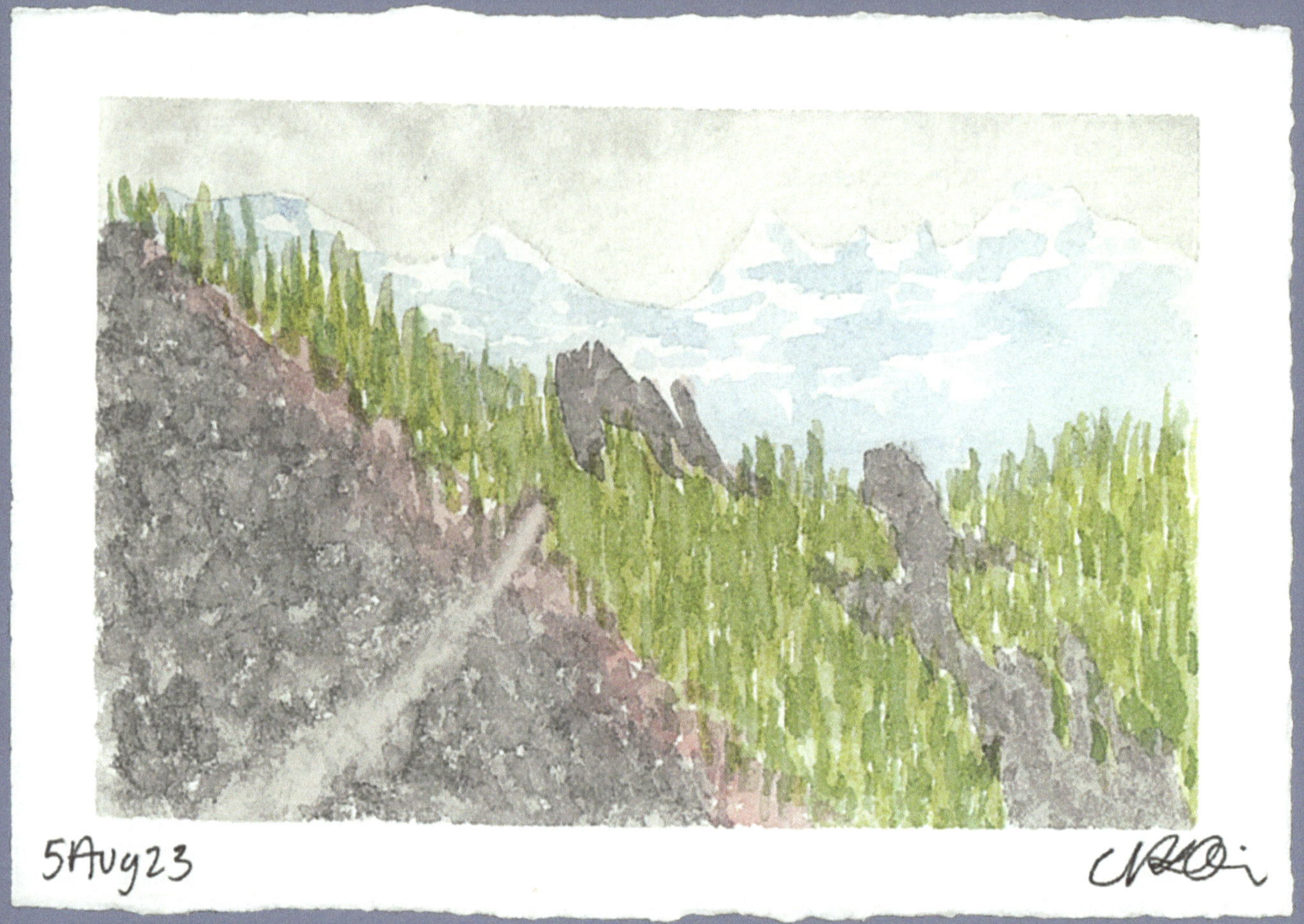

Goats Rock Wilderness to White's Pass

Trail day:	111	Ascent:	+2372'
Hiking day:	94	Descent:	-3967'
Trail miles:	2282.6 - 2297.6	Minimum elevation:	4398'
Hiking miles:	15.00	Maximum elevation:	6560'

A Boardwalk through a Meadow in William O. Douglas Wilderness

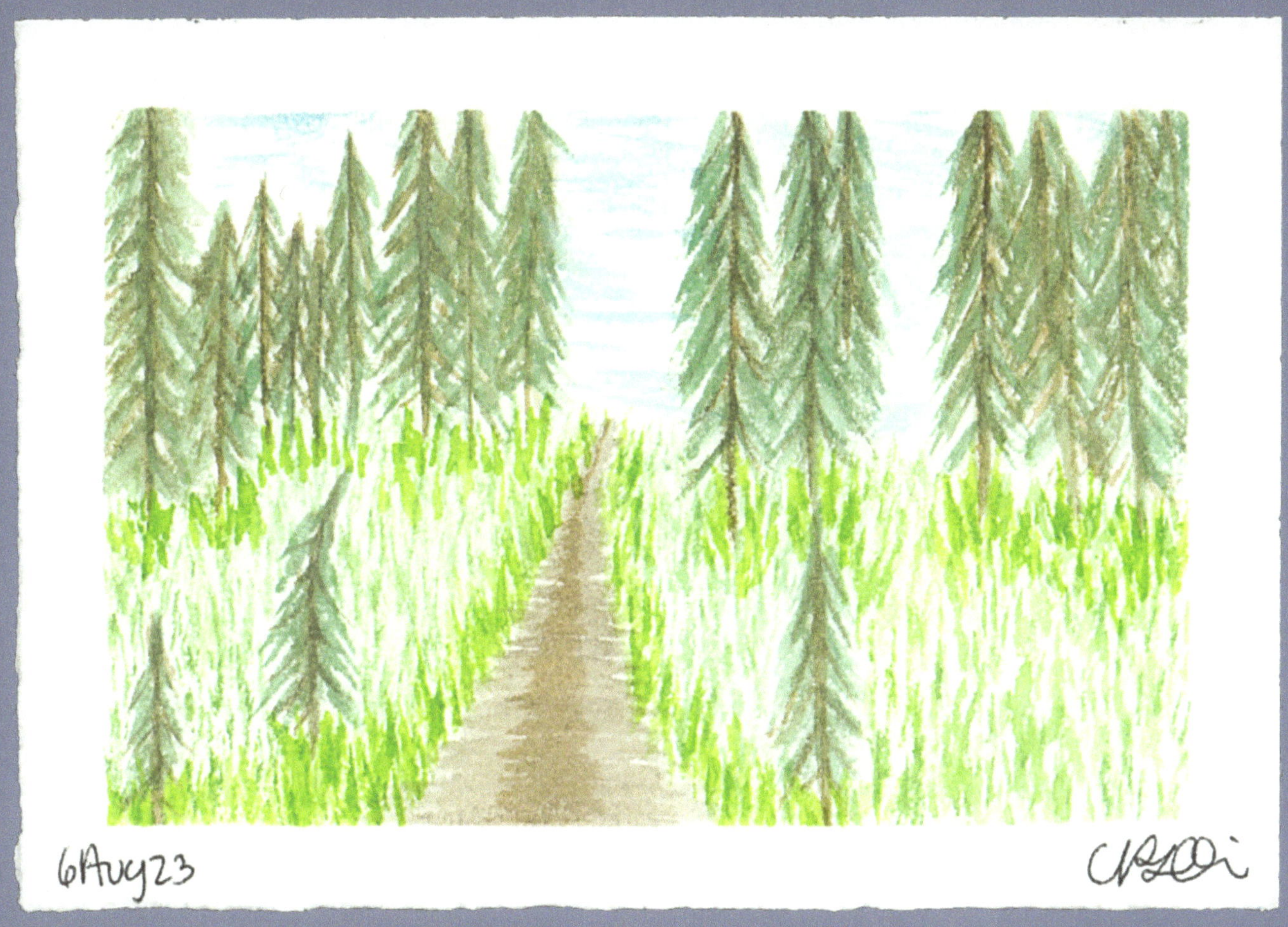

White's Pass to Bumping River

Trail day:	112	Ascent:	+1650'
Hiking day:	95	Descent:	-1926'
Trail miles:	2297.6 - 2311.3	Minimum elevation:	4150'
Hiking miles:	14.84	Maximum elevation:	5614'

Mt Rainier National Park Bridge over Highway 410 at Chinook Pass

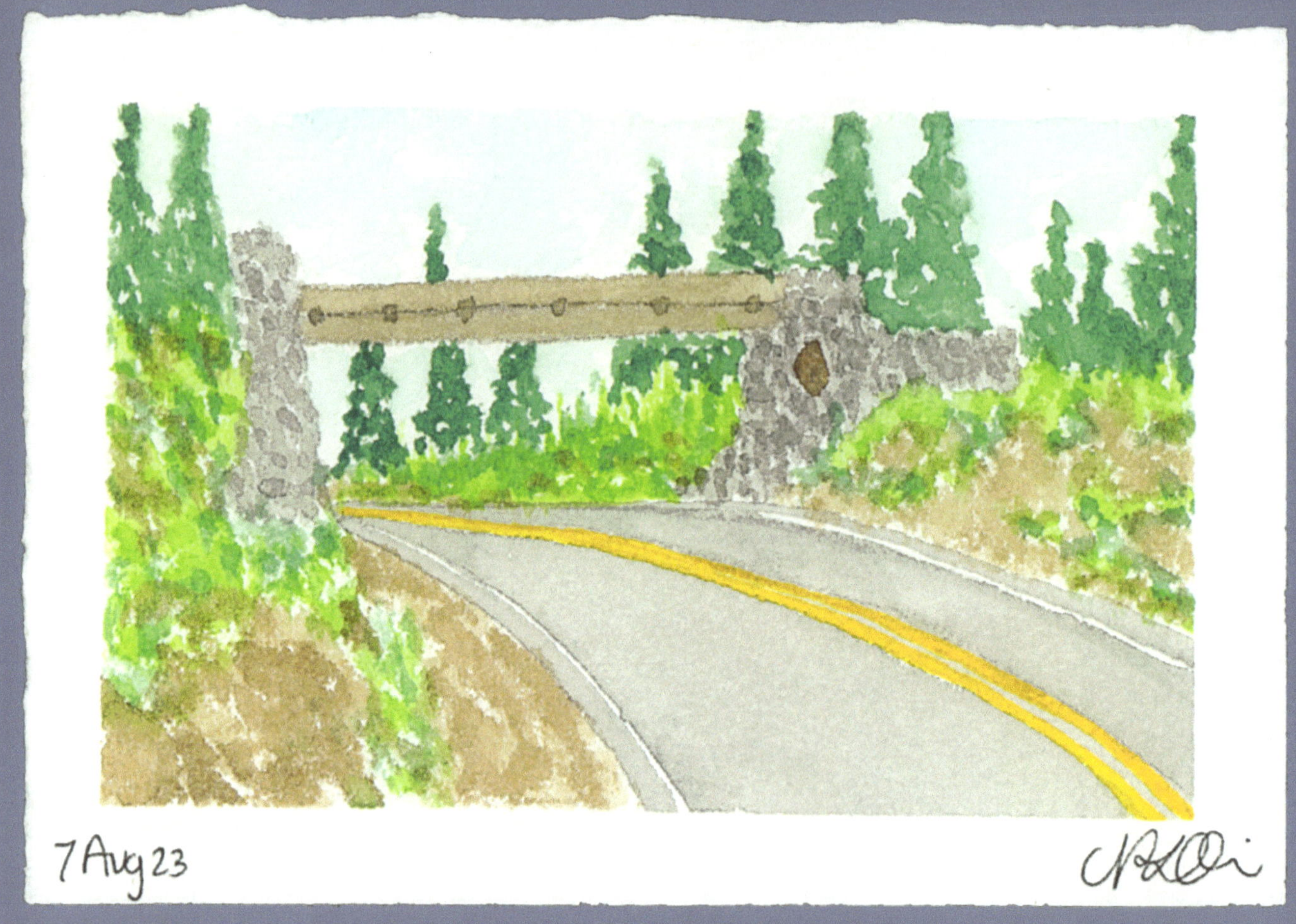

Bumping River to Sheep Lake at Chinook Pass

Trail day:	113	Ascent:	+3940’
Hiking day:	96	Descent:	-2336’
Trail miles:	2311.3 - 2328.4	Minimum elevation:	4150’
Hiking miles:	18.76	Maximum elevation:	5873’

Mt Rainier from Crystal Mountain Resort

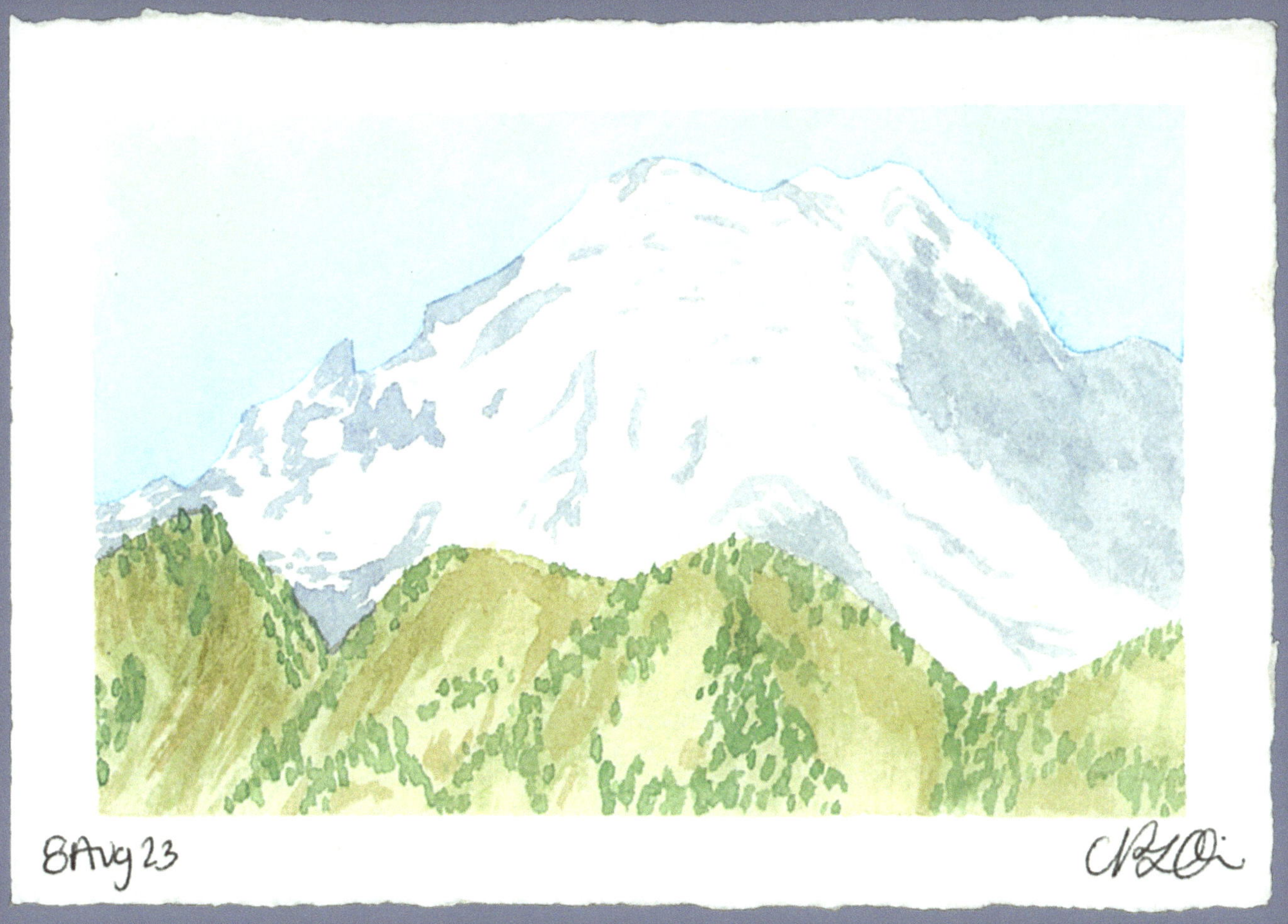

Sheep Lake to Norse Peak Wilderness

Trail day:	114	Ascent:	+3763'
Hiking day:	97	Descent:	-4436'
Trail miles:	2328.4 - 2354.4	Minimum elevation:	4797'
Hiking miles:	26.65	Maximum elevation:	6506'

A Field of Huckleberries

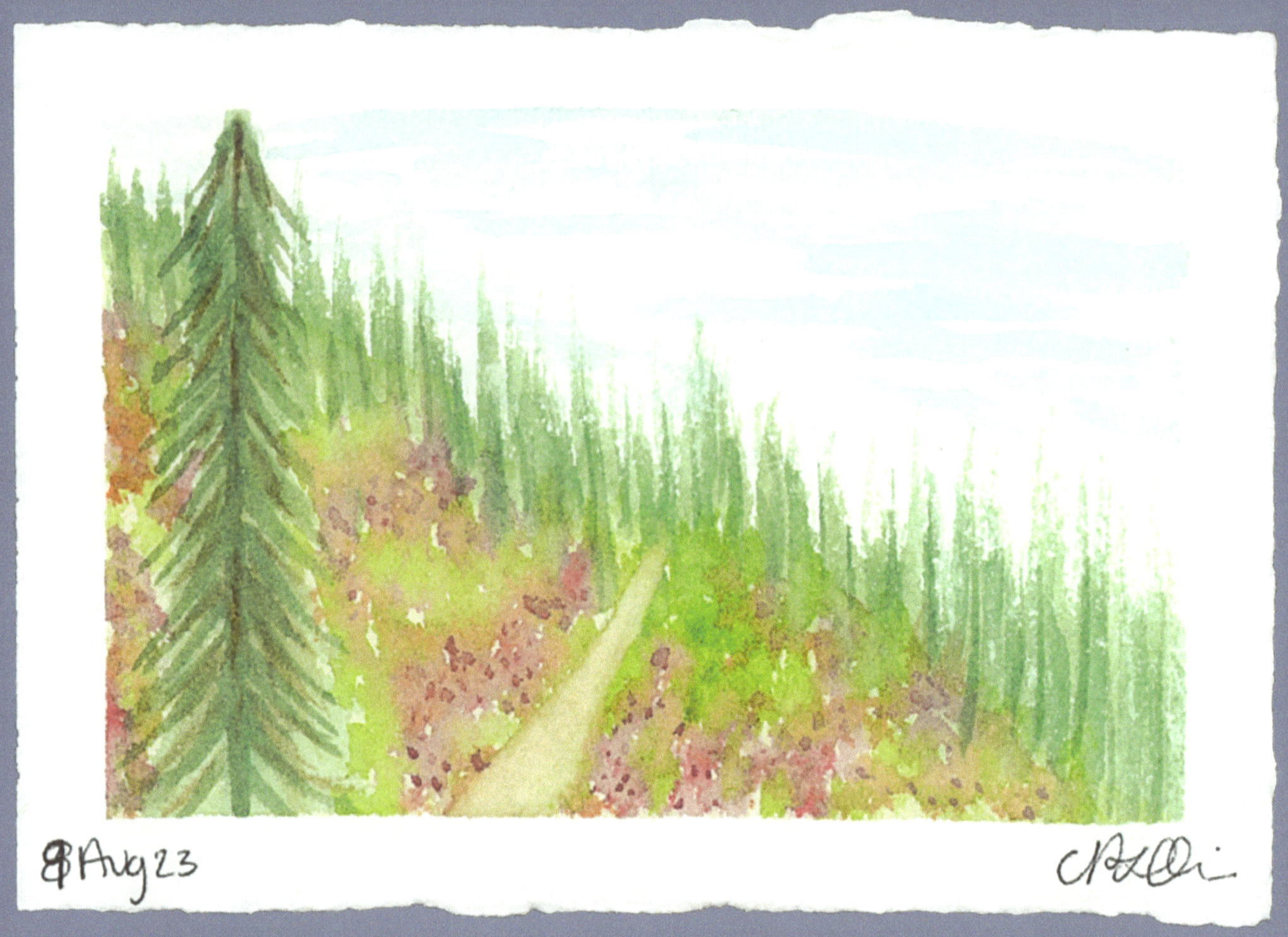

Norse Peak Wilderness to Mt Baker National Forest

Trail day:	115	Ascent:	+5000’
Hiking day:	98	Descent:	-6293’
Trail miles:	2354.4 - 2379.7	Minimum elevation:	3507’
Hiking miles:	25.83	Maximum elevation:	5651’

Washington Alpine Club at Snoqualmie Pass

Mt Baker National Forest to
Snoqualmie Pass

Trail day:	116
Hiking day:	99
Trail miles:	2379.7 - 2396.1
Hiking miles:	16.11
Ascent:	+2795’
Descent:	-3622’
Minimum elevation:	2904’
Maximum elevation:	4524’

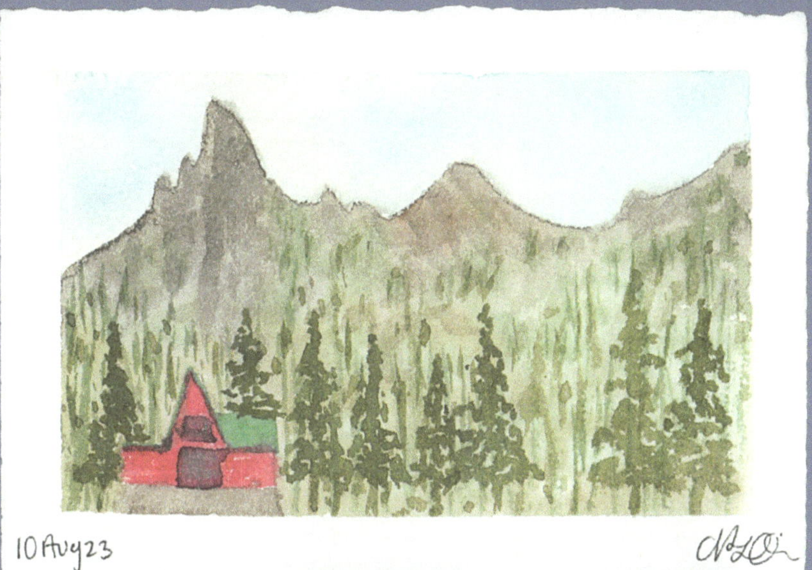

Snoqualmie Pass to Lemah Creek

Trail day:	117
Hiking day:	100
Trail miles:	2396.1 - 2417.3
Hiking miles:	23.50
Ascent:	+5446’
Descent:	-5135’
Minimum elevation:	2948’
Maximum elevation:	5963’

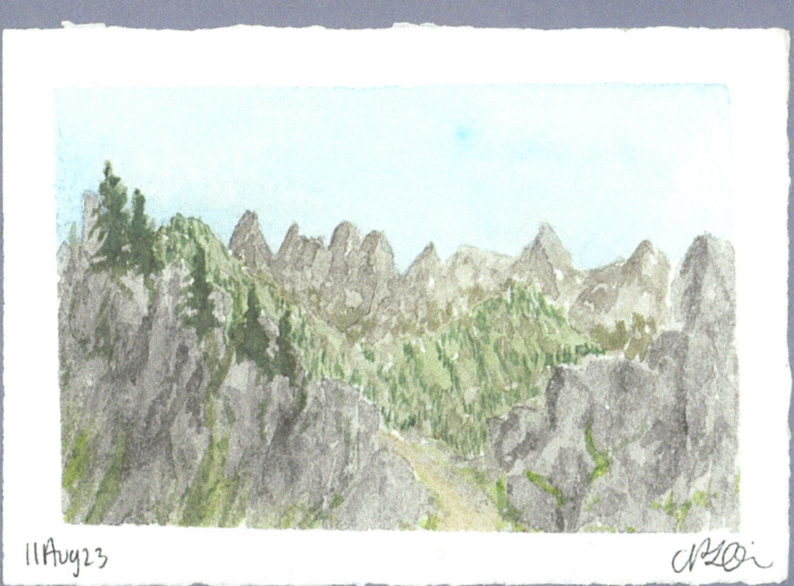

Kendall Katwalk in the Alpine Lakes Wilderness

Mt Daniel from the Descent toward Waptus Lake

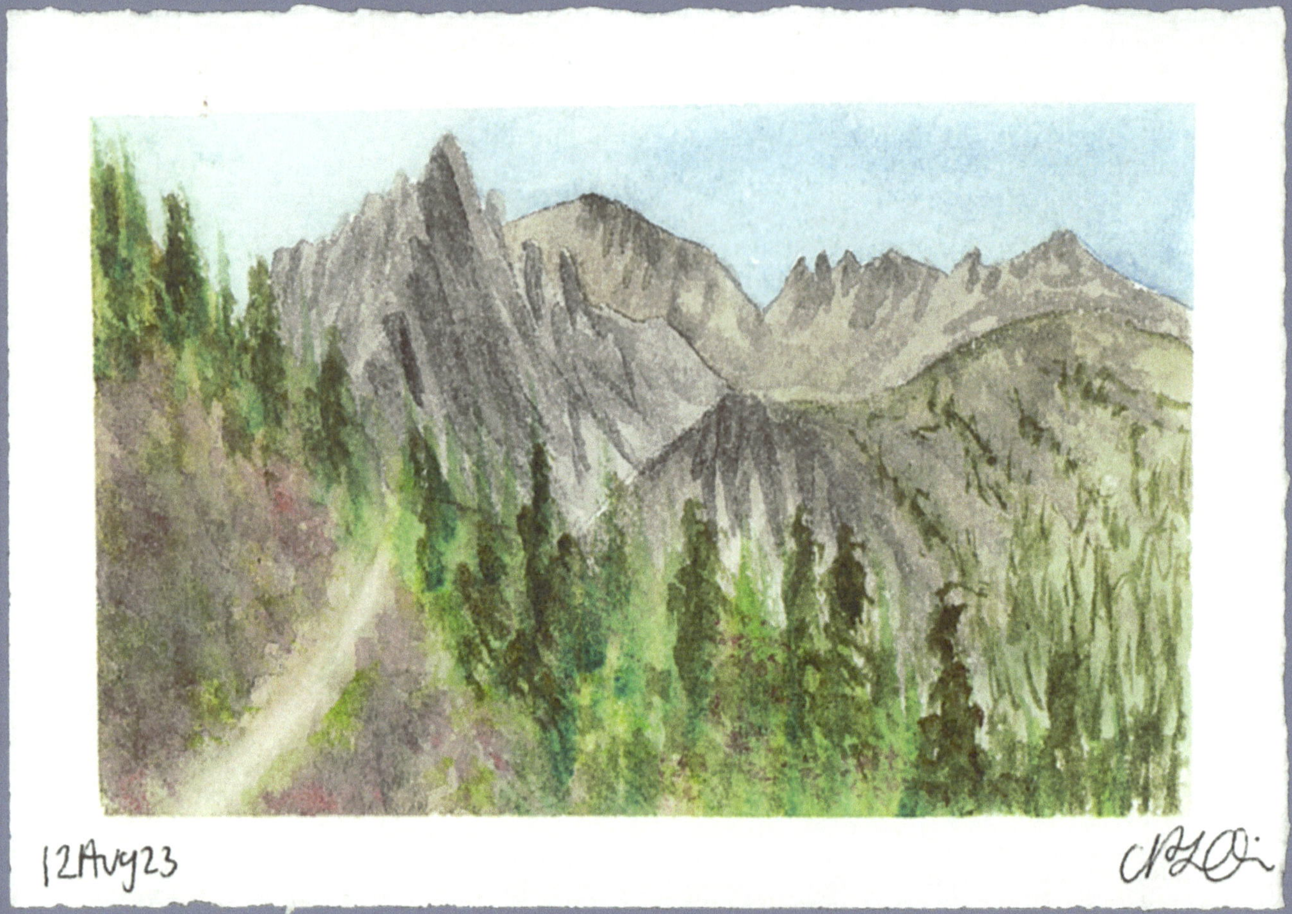

"burry ur poop"

Lemah Creek to Cathedral Rock

Trail day:	118	Ascent:	+5561’
Hiking day:	101	Descent:	-4301’
Trail miles:	2417.3 - 2442.6	Minimum elevation:	3043’
Hiking miles:	25.80	Maximum elevation:	5590’

Trap Lake in Wenatchee National Forest

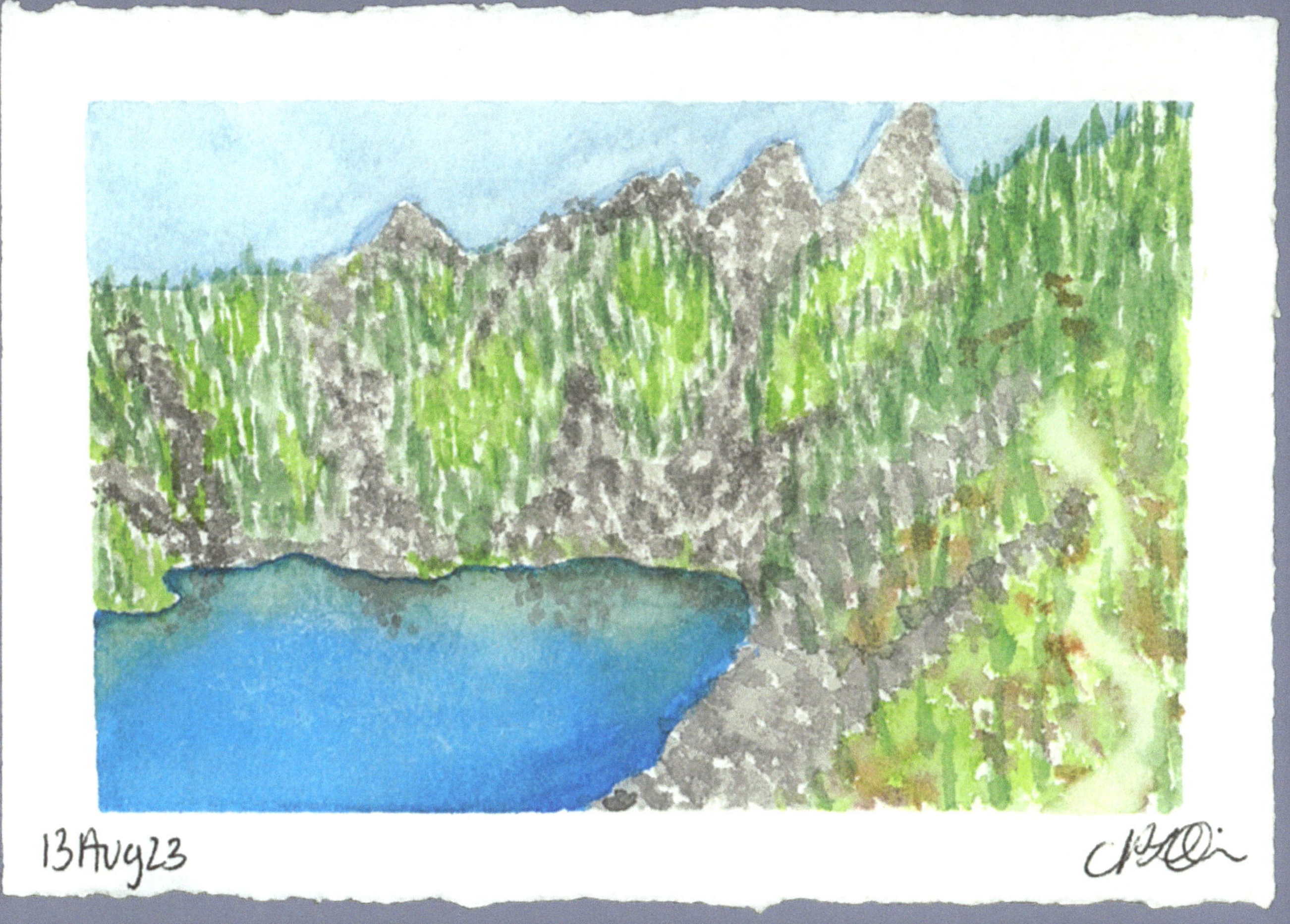

Cathedral Rock to Stevens Pass

Trail day:	119	Ascent:	+5444’
Hiking day:	102	Descent:	-5521’
Trail miles:	2442.6 - 2466.7	Minimum elevation:	3848’
Hiking miles:	25.20	Maximum elevation:	5921’

Central California

Sierra Nevada

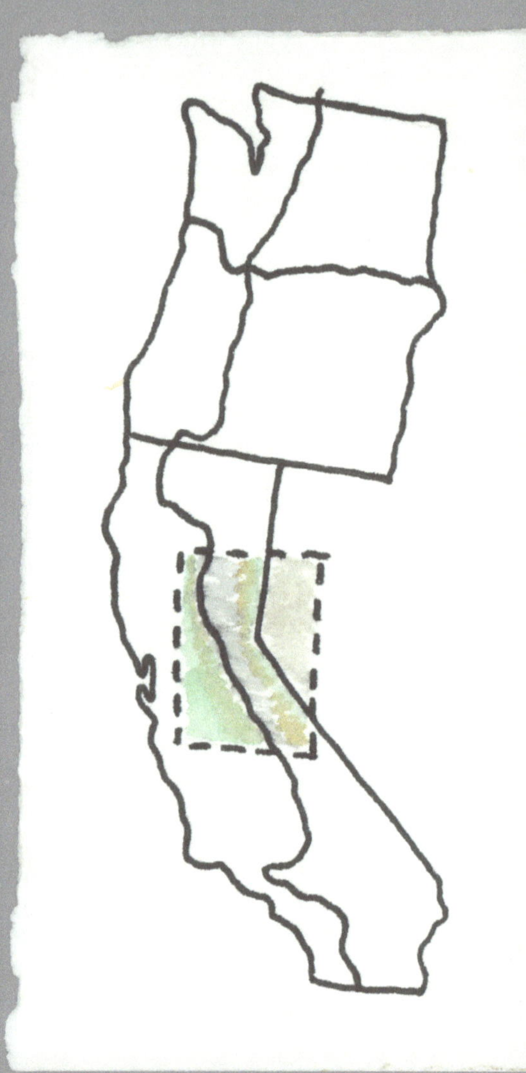

Southbound: Chester, CA to Kennedy Meadows South, CA

August 18 to September 17, 2023

Trail days:	31
Hiking days:	30
Trail miles:	1332.4 - 703.4
Average miles per hiking day:	20.96
Fewest miles per hiking day:	13.20
Most miles per hiking day:	29.04

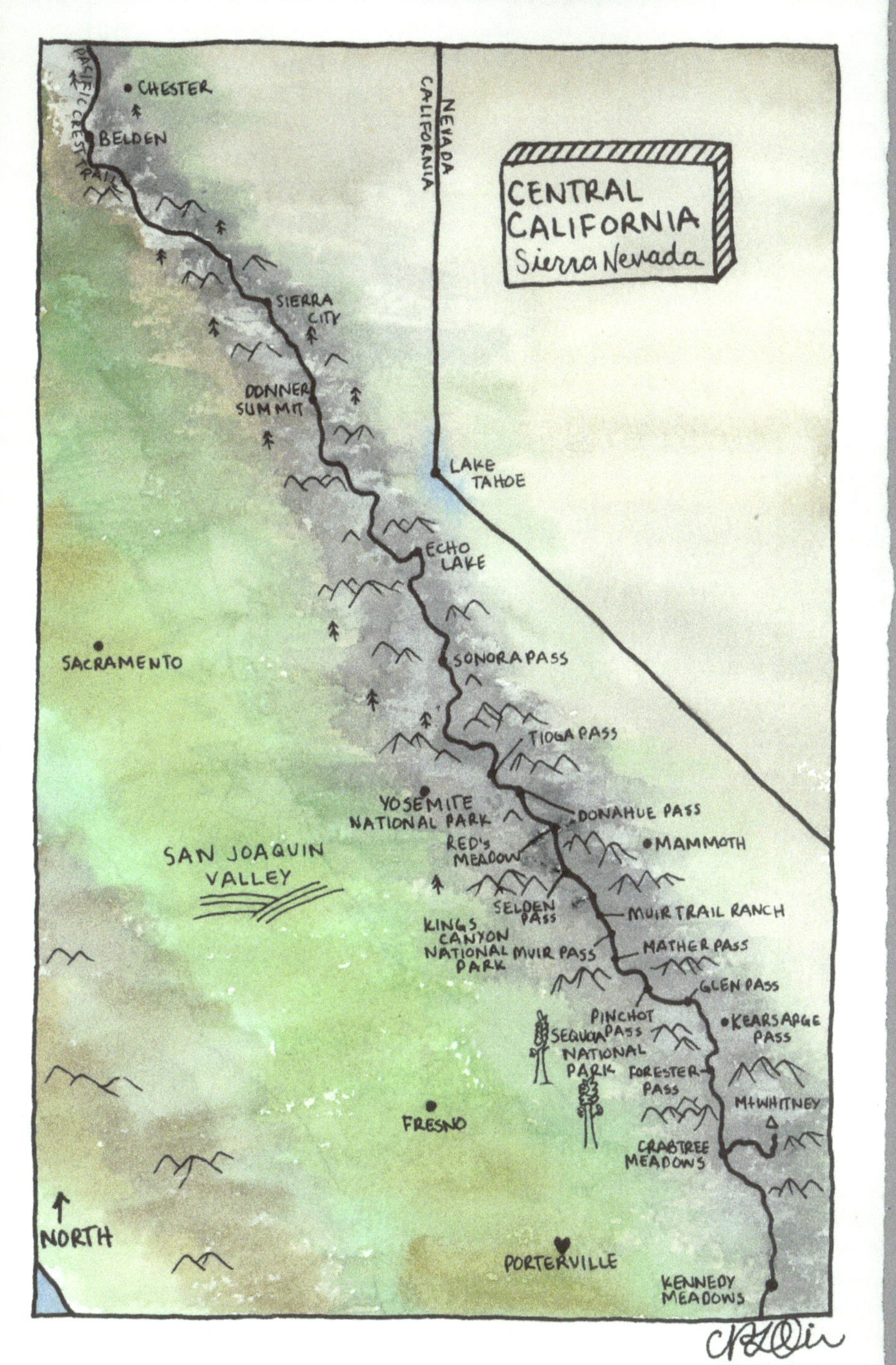
CENTRAL CALIFORNIA
Sierra Nevada
PACIFIC CREST TRAIL
CHESTER
BELDEN
NEVADA
CALIFORNIA
SIERRA CITY
DONNER SUMMIT
LAKE TAHOE
ECHO LAKE
SACRAMENTO
SONORA PASS
TIOGA PASS
YOSEMITE NATIONAL PARK
DONAHUE PASS
RED'S MEADOW
MAMMOTH
SAN JOAQUIN VALLEY
SELDEN PASS
MUIR TRAIL RANCH
KINGS CANYON NATIONAL PARK
MUIR PASS
MATHER PASS
GLEN PASS
PINCHOT PASS
KEARSARGE PASS
SEQUOIA NATIONAL PARK
FORESTER PASS
MT WHITNEY
FRESNO
CRABTREE MEADOWS
NORTH
PORTERVILLE
KENNEDY MEADOWS

Dixie Burn Area in Lassen National Forest

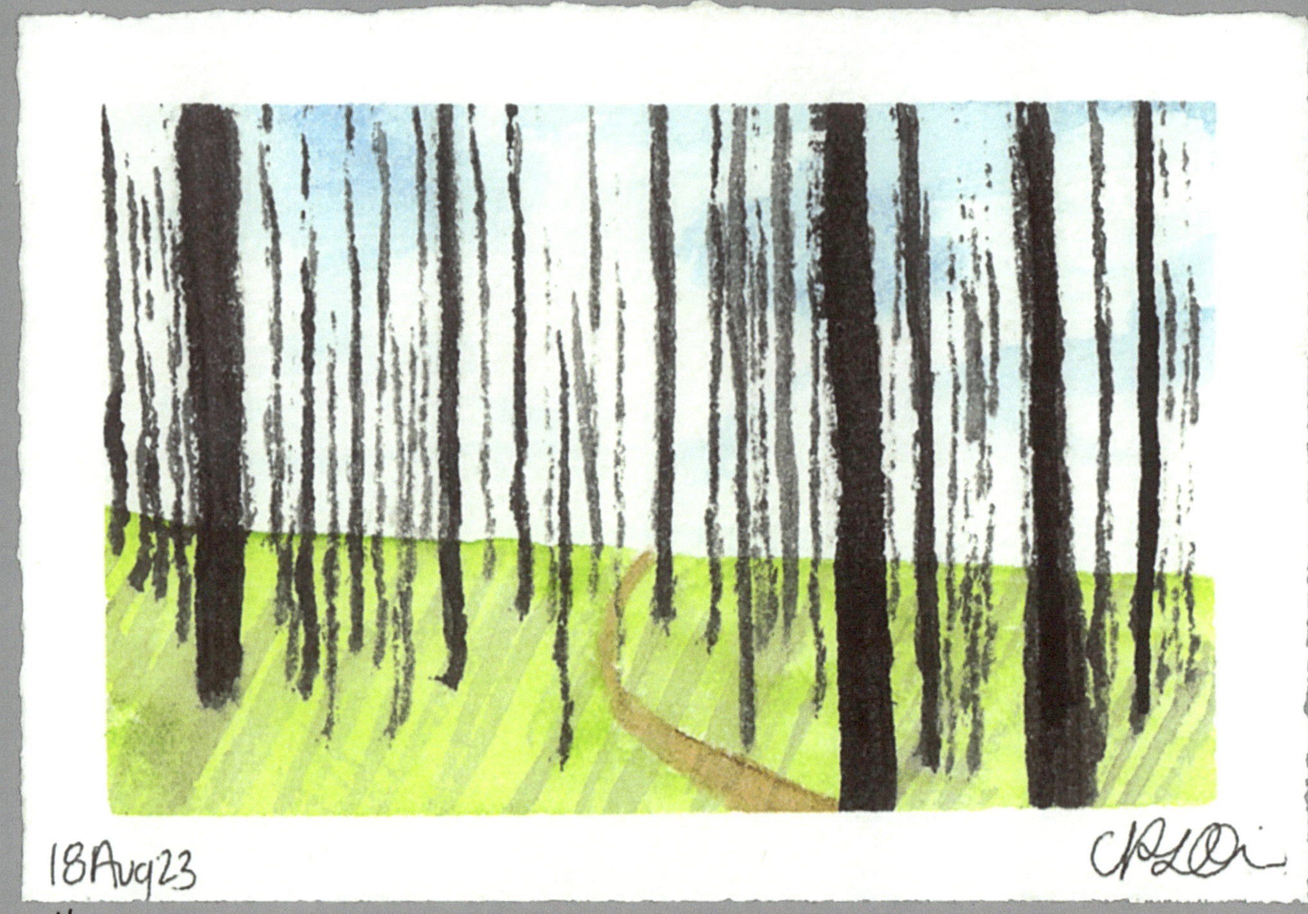

all it takes is all you have.

Chester to Robbers Spring

Trail day:	124	Ascent:	+3376'
Hiking day:	103	Descent:	-2244'
Trail miles:	1332.4 - 1314.3	Minimum elevation:	4873'
Hiking miles:	16.67	Maximum elevation:	7621'

Belden Town Bridge

Robbers Spring to Belden

Trail day:	125
Hiking day:	104
Trail miles:	1314.3 - 1287.9
Hiking miles:	29.72
Ascent:	+3557’
Descent:	-7517’
Minimum elevation:	2260’
Maximum elevation:	7179’

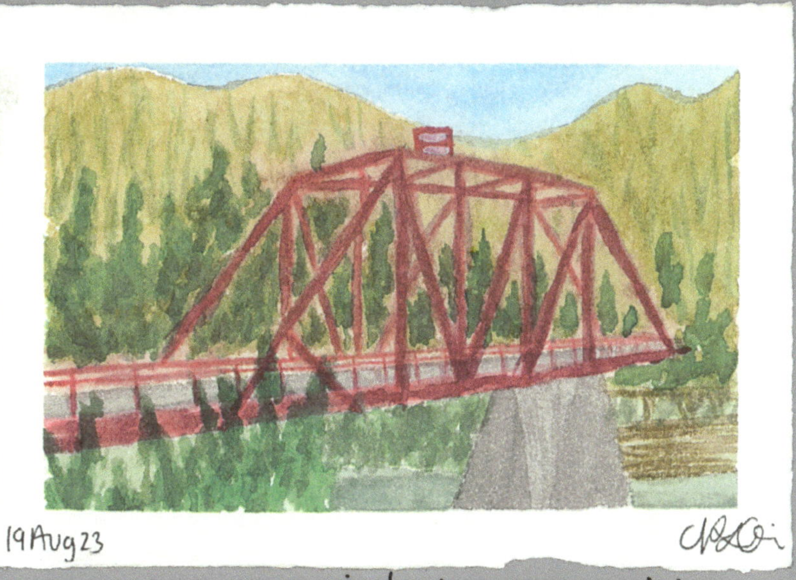

just doing the best I can...

Belden to Big Creek Road in Buck’s Lake Wilderness

Trail day:	126
Hiking day:	105
Trail miles:	1287.9 - 1264.6
Hiking miles:	24.46
Ascent:	+6263’
Descent:	-2962’
Minimum elevation:	2207’
Maximum elevation:	7026’

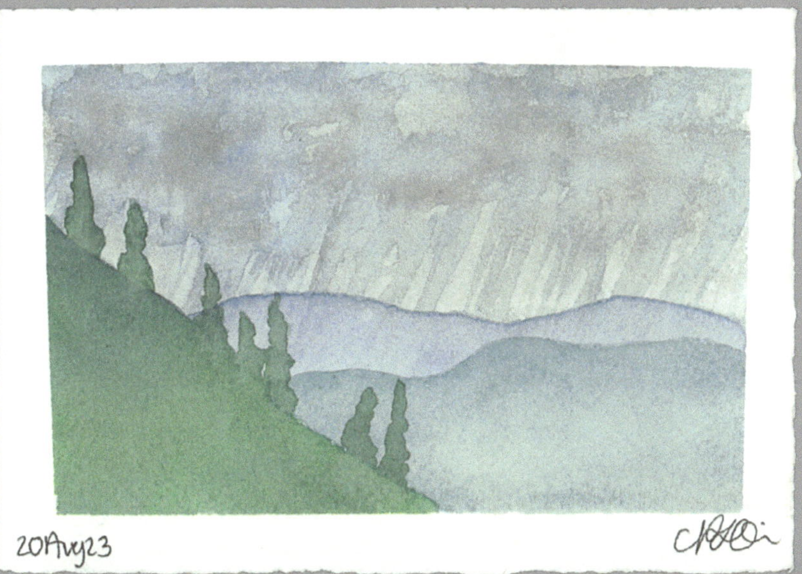

Tropical Storm Hilary Incoming to Quincy

Bridge over North Fork of the Feather Wild and Scenic River

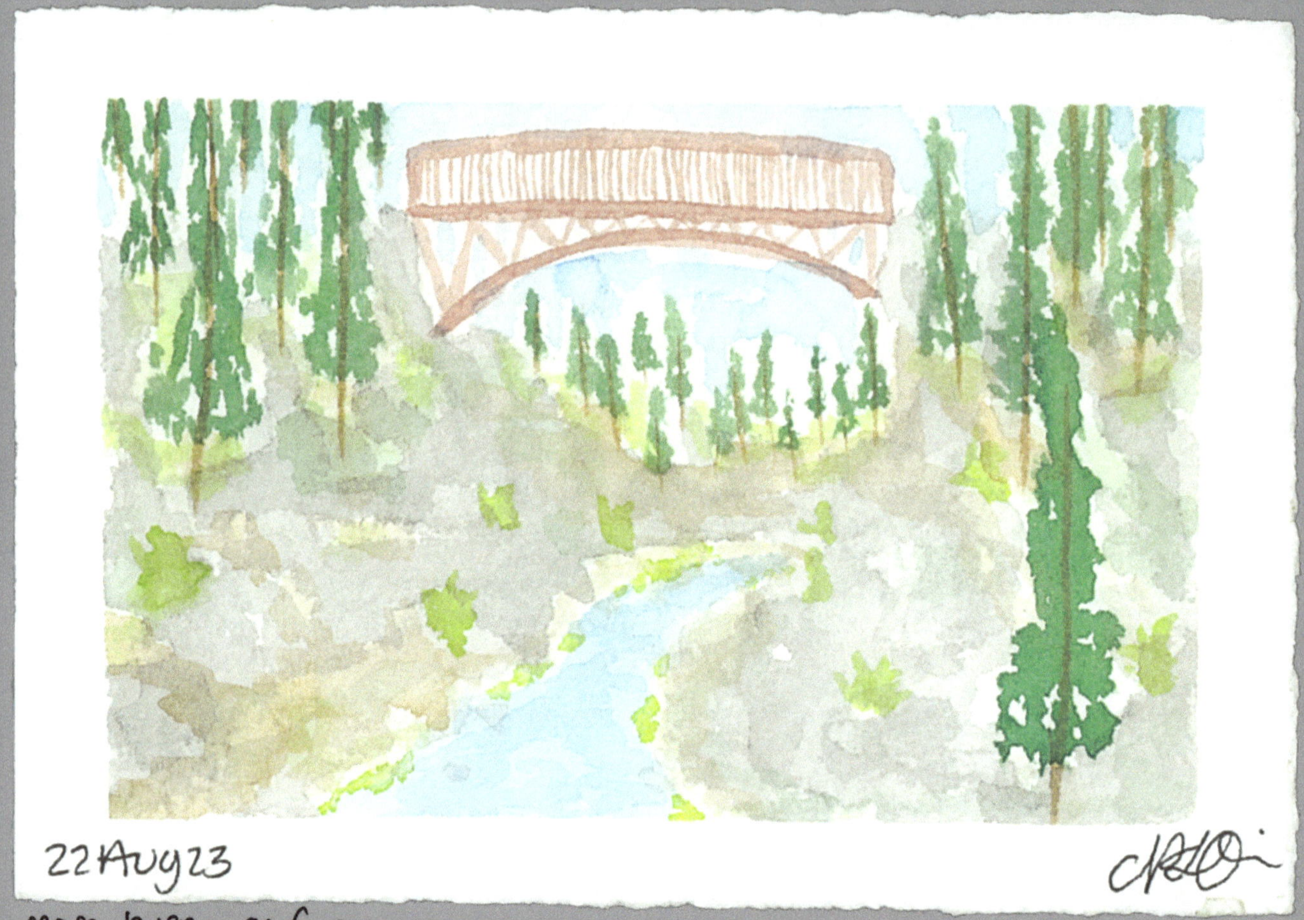

more burn... as far as can see

Big Creek Road to Alder Spring

Trail day:	128	Ascent:	+5267’
Hiking day:	106	Descent:	-4693’
Trail miles:	1264.6 - 1238.0	Minimum elevation:	2990’
Hiking miles:	26.63	Maximum elevation:	6085’

Sierra Butte from Old Packer Alternate

Alder Spring to Old Packer Alternate

Trail day:	129
Hiking day:	107
Trail miles:	1238.0 - 1209.5
Hiking miles:	28.76
Ascent:	+5397'
Descent:	-4052'
Minimum elevation:	5892'
Maximum elevation:	7490'

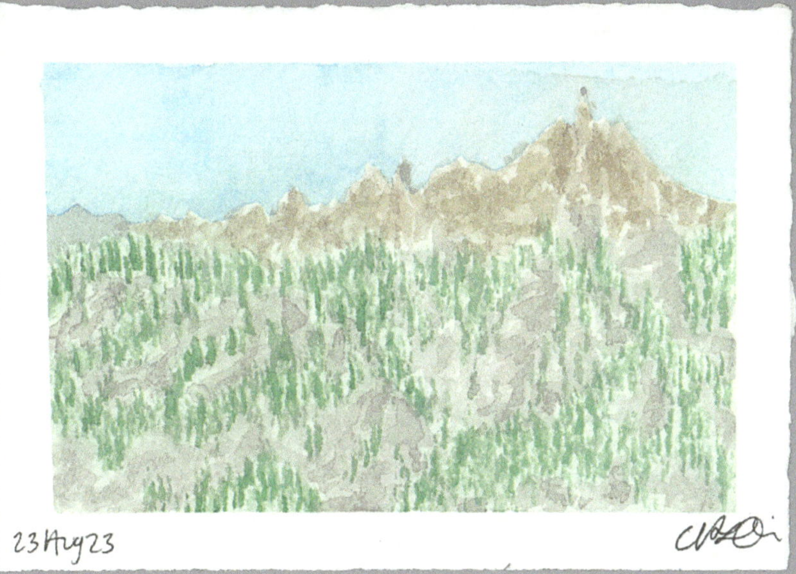

starving. need more snacks.

Old Packer Alternate to
Jackson Meadows Reservoir

Trail day:	130
Hiking day:	108
Trail miles:	1209.5 - 1181.1
Hiking miles:	28.58
Ascent:	+5670'
Descent:	-5862'
Minimum elevation:	4598'
Maximum elevation:	8546'

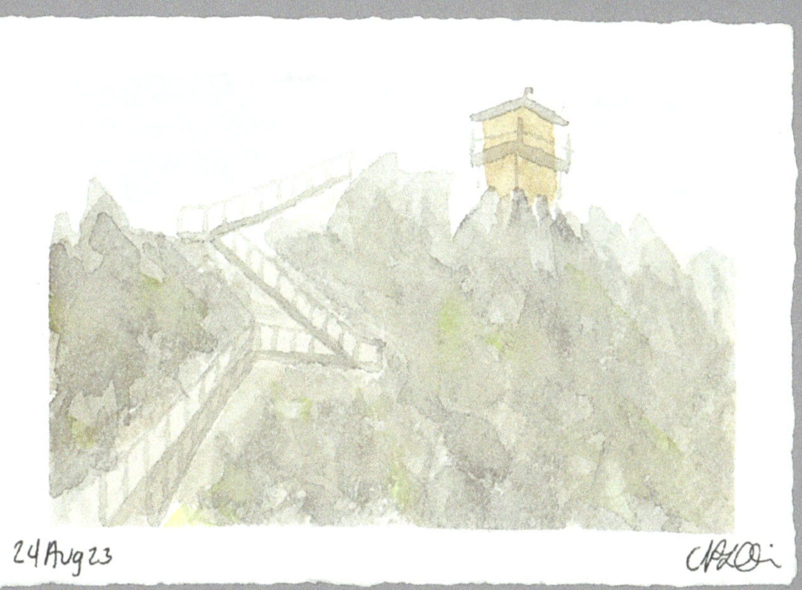

Fire Lookout at the Top of Sierra Butte

PCT Descending beneath Castle Peak toward Donner Pass

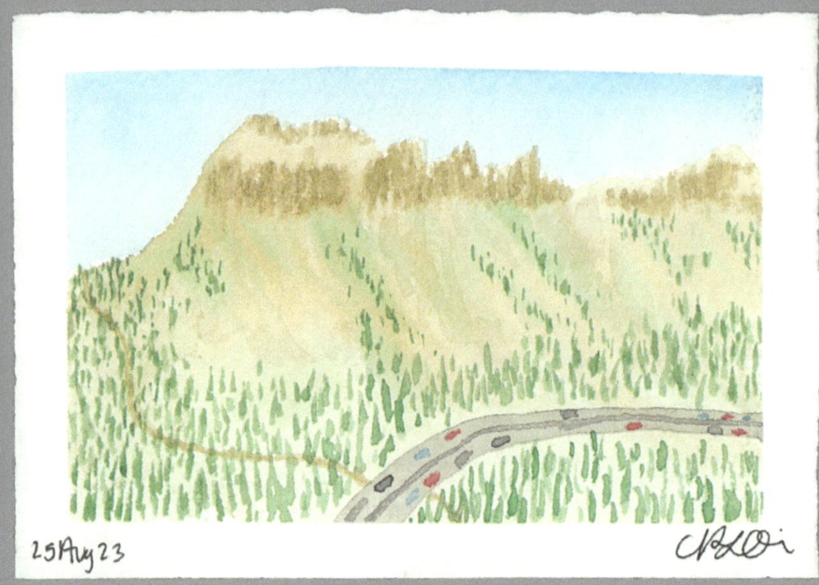

Jackson Meadows Reservoir to Donner Pass

Trail day:	131
Hiking day:	109
Trail miles:	1181.4 - 1158.6
Hiking miles:	23.02
Ascent:	+3929'
Descent:	-3842'
Minimum elevation:	7149'
Maximum elevation:	8390'

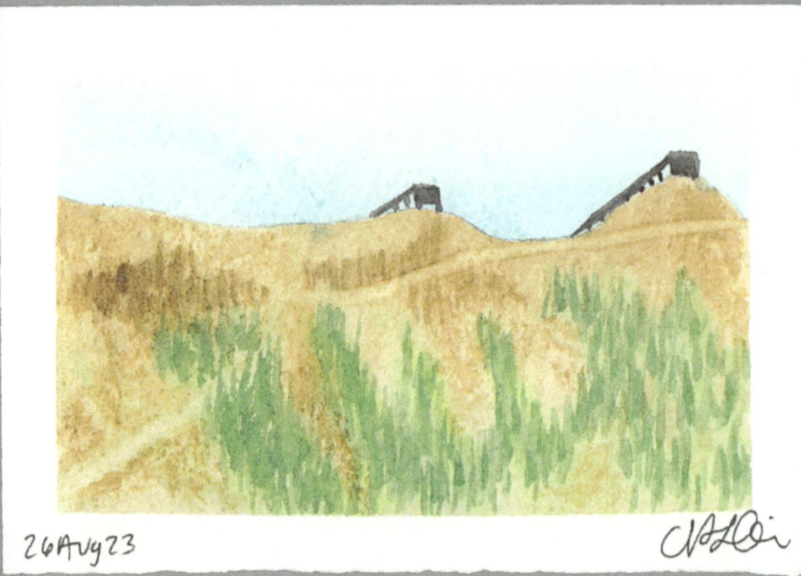

Donner Pass to Five Lakes in Granite Chief Wilderness

Trail day:	132
Hiking day:	110
Trail miles:	1158.6 - 1137.0
Hiking miles:	22.09
Ascent:	+4341'
Descent:	-4163'
Minimum elevation:	7016'
Maximum elevation:	8722'

Tahoe Palisades Chairlifts on Granite Chief

Lake Tahoe from Lake Fontanillis at Sunset

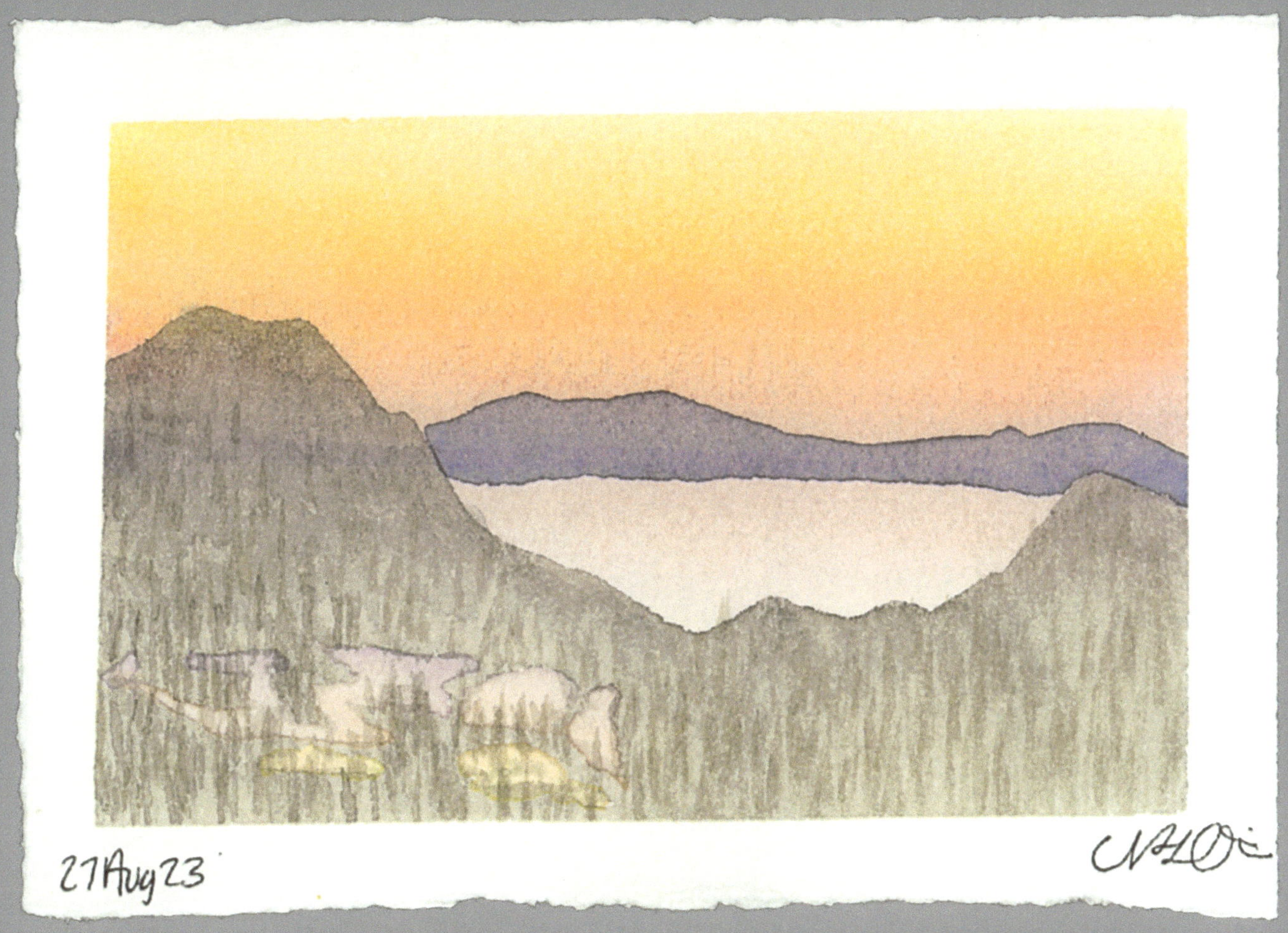

Five Lakes to Lake Fontanillis in Desolation Wilderness

Trail day:	133	Ascent:	+4606’
Hiking day:	111	Descent:	-3632’
Trail miles:	1137.0 - 1109.6	Minimum elevation:	6988’
Hiking miles:	28.17	Maximum elevation:	8413’

Lake Aloha

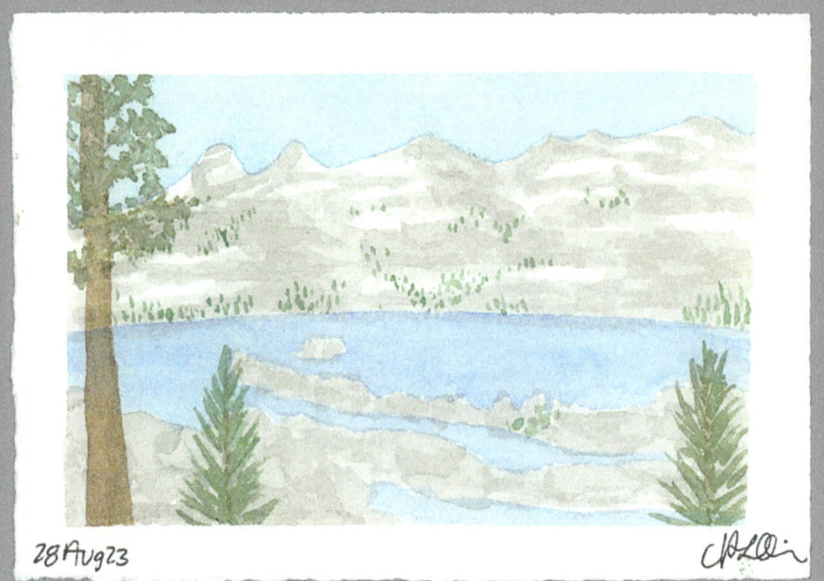

Lake Fontanillis to Echo Lake

Trail day:	134
Hiking day:	112
Trail miles:	1109.7 - 1093.4
Hiking miles:	16.99
Ascent:	+2343’
Descent:	-3169’
Minimum elevation:	7447’
Maximum elevation:	9368’

hike on!

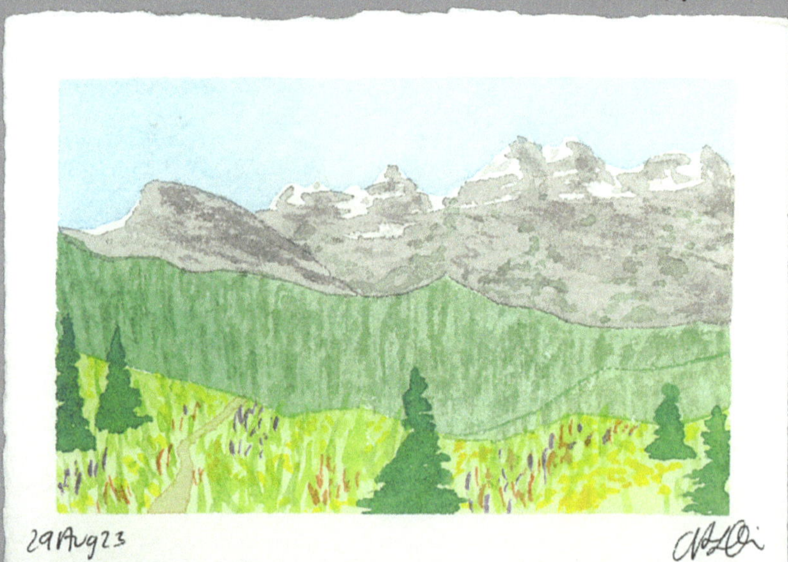

Echo Lake to the Nipple in Mokelumne Wilderness

Trail day:	135
Hiking day:	113
Trail miles:	1093.4 - 1068.1
Hiking miles:	26.27
Ascent:	+5361’
Descent:	-4304’
Minimum elevation:	7278’
Maximum elevation:	9085’

Carson Pass

Jagged Lava Peaks near Ebbetts Pass

The Nipple to Wolf Creek in Carson-Iceberg Wilderness

Trail day:	136
Hiking day:	114
Trail miles:	1068.1 - 1040.1
Hiking miles:	29.04
Ascent:	+5062’
Descent:	-5177’
Minimum elevation:	7785’
Maximum elevation:	9320’

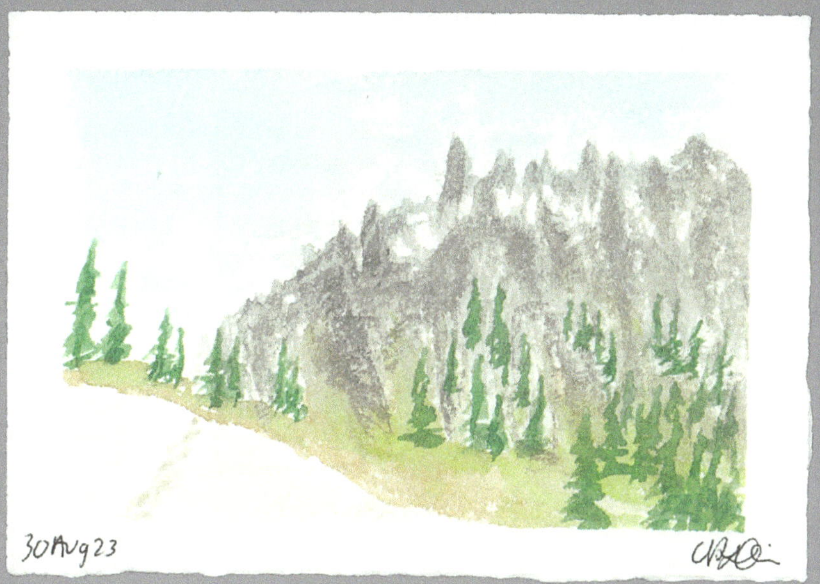

shower, laundry, resupply, new shoes, ice cream.

Wolf Creek to Sonora Pass

Trail day:	137
Hiking day:	115
Trail miles:	1040.4 - 1018.1
Hiking miles:	22.43
Ascent:	+5404’
Descent:	-4213’
Minimum elevation:	8154’
Maximum elevation:	10500’

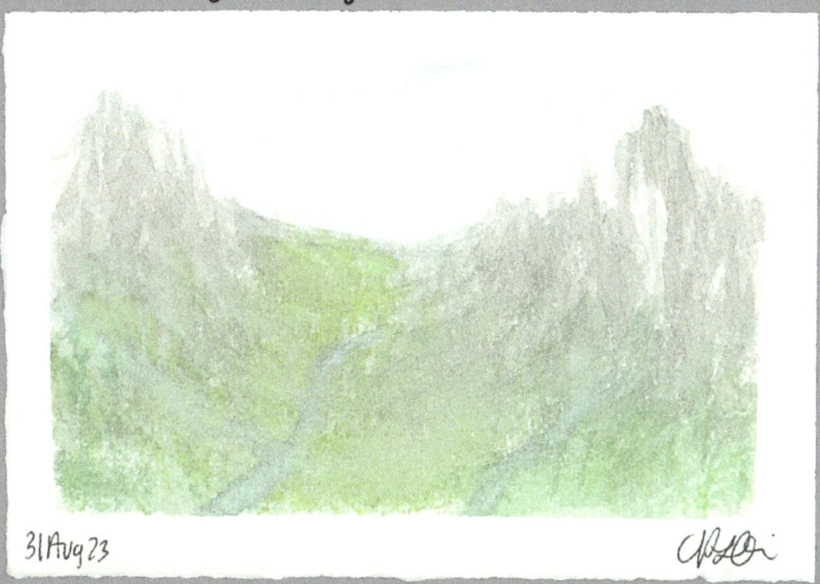

East Fork of the Carson River Leading toward Sonora Peak

Lichen-Covered Window into the Snowy, Stormy Emigrant Wilderness

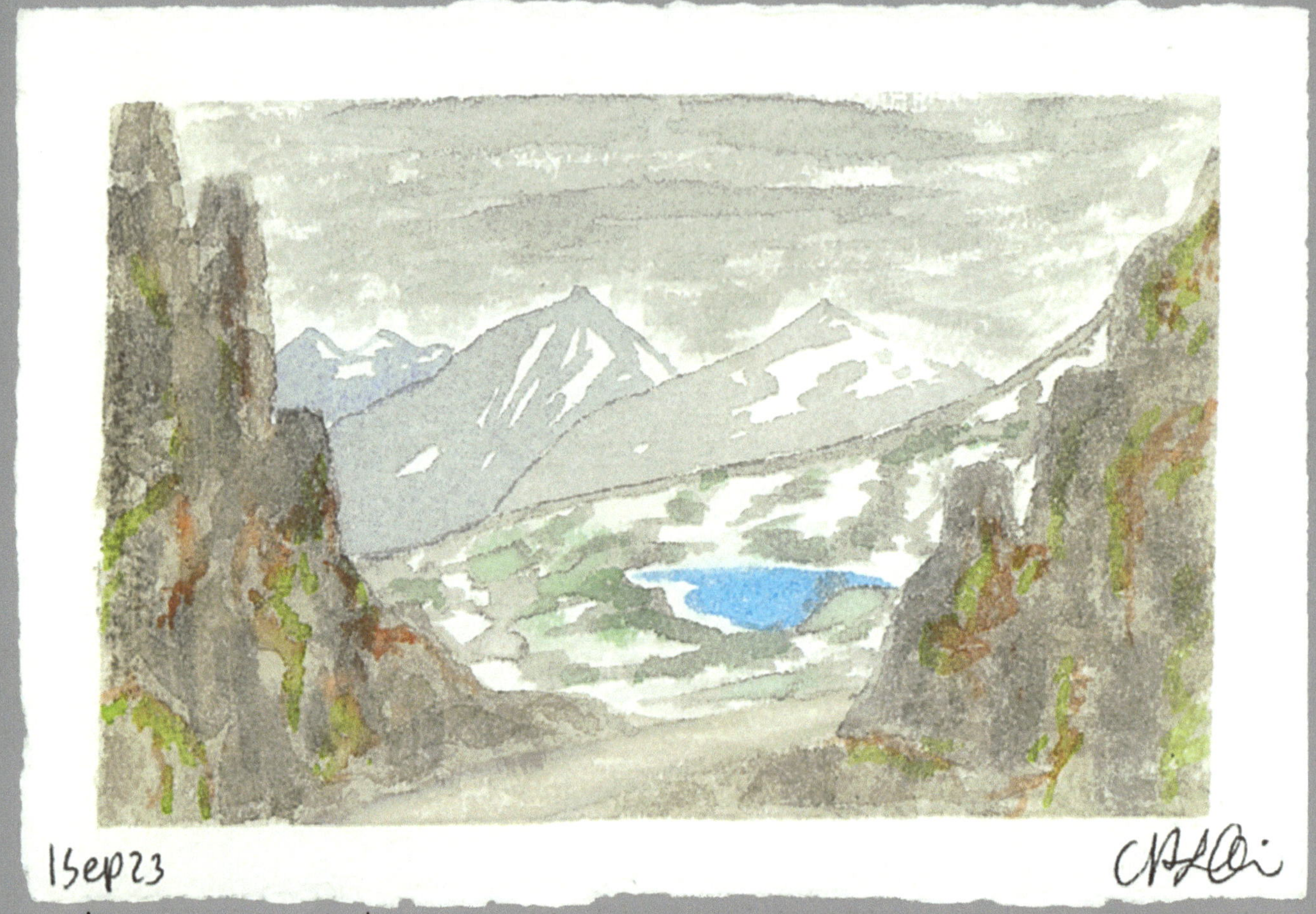

wind won't kill me but gravity will.

Sonora Pass to Dorothy Lake

Trail day:	138	Ascent:	+6572’
Hiking day:	116	Descent:	-6791’
Trail miles:	1018.1 - 997.6	Minimum elevation:	8551’
Hiking miles:	22.12	Maximum elevation:	11001’

Benson Lake, the Sierra Riviera

Dorothy Lake to Benson Lake

Trail day:	139
Hiking day:	117
Trail miles:	997.6 - 973.5
Hiking miles:	25.33
Ascent:	+4058’
Descent:	-5883’
Minimum elevation:	7614’
Maximum elevation:	9433’

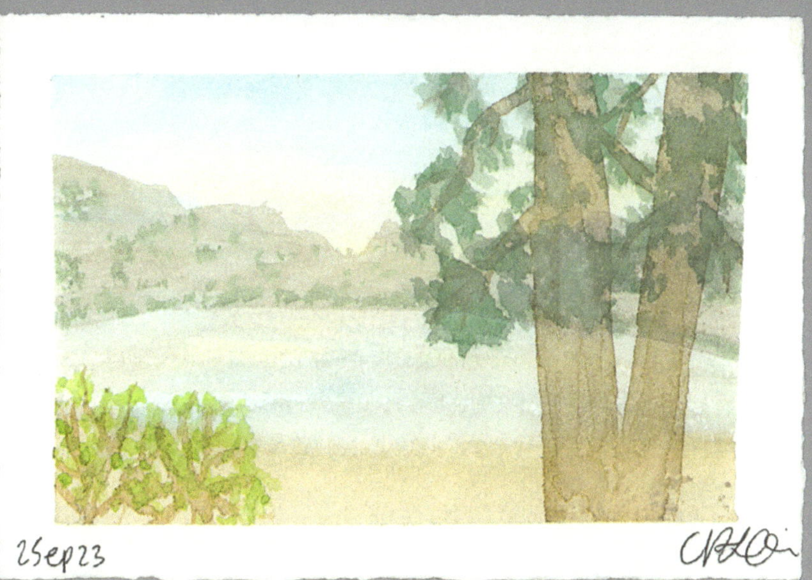

very wet... very cold.

Benson Lake to Glen Aulin High Sierra Camp

Trail day:	140
Hiking day:	118
Trail miles:	973.5 - 949.5
Hiking miles:	27.67
Ascent:	+5623’
Descent:	-5348’
Minimum elevation:	7605’
Maximum elevation:	10114’

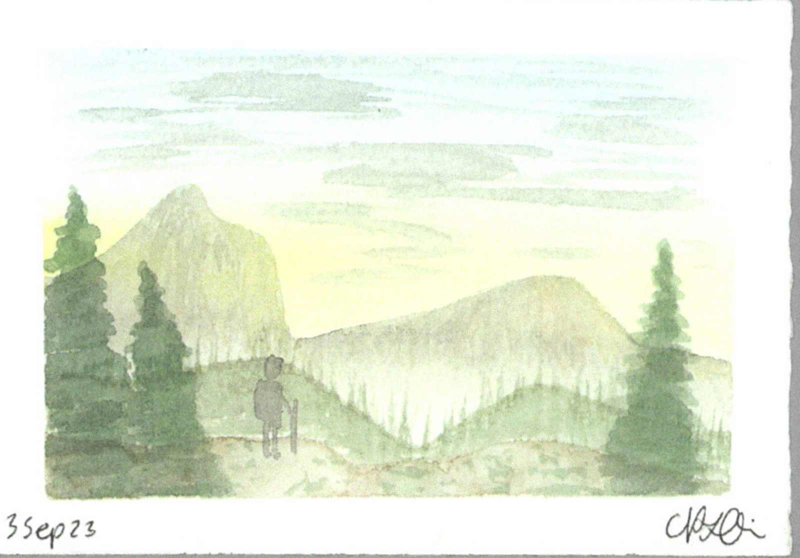

Benson Pass Looking North after a Storm Passed

Reflections on a Large Pond on the South Side of Donahue Pass

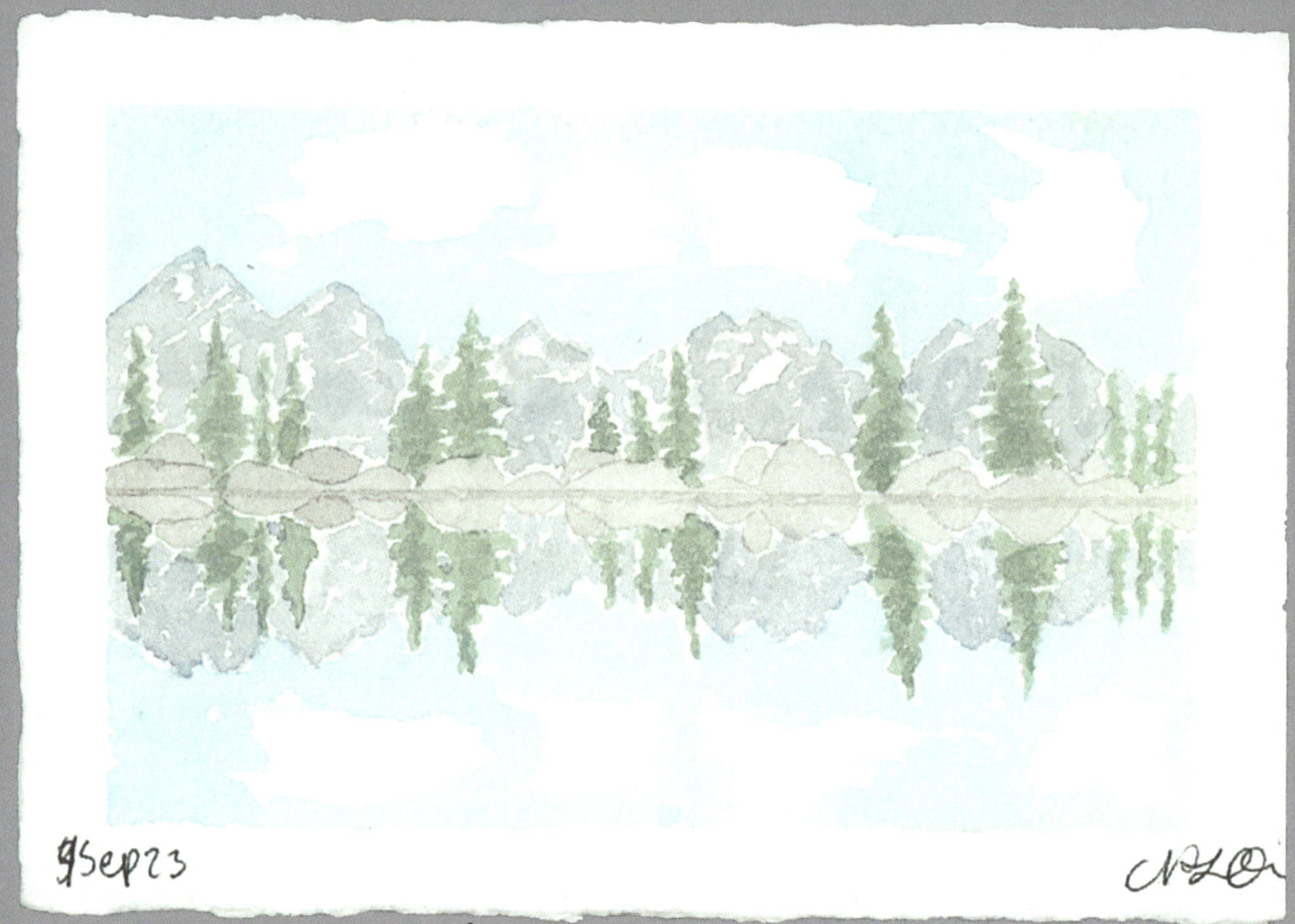

soooooo awesome to see friends after very shitty day yesterday

Glen Aulin High Sierra Camp to Donahue Pass

Trail day:	141	Ascent:	+3963’
Hiking day:	119	Descent:	-1722’
Trail miles:	949.5 - 928.5	Minimum elevation:	7888’
Hiking miles:	23.90	Maximum elevation:	11065’

Mt Ritter from Thousand Island Lake

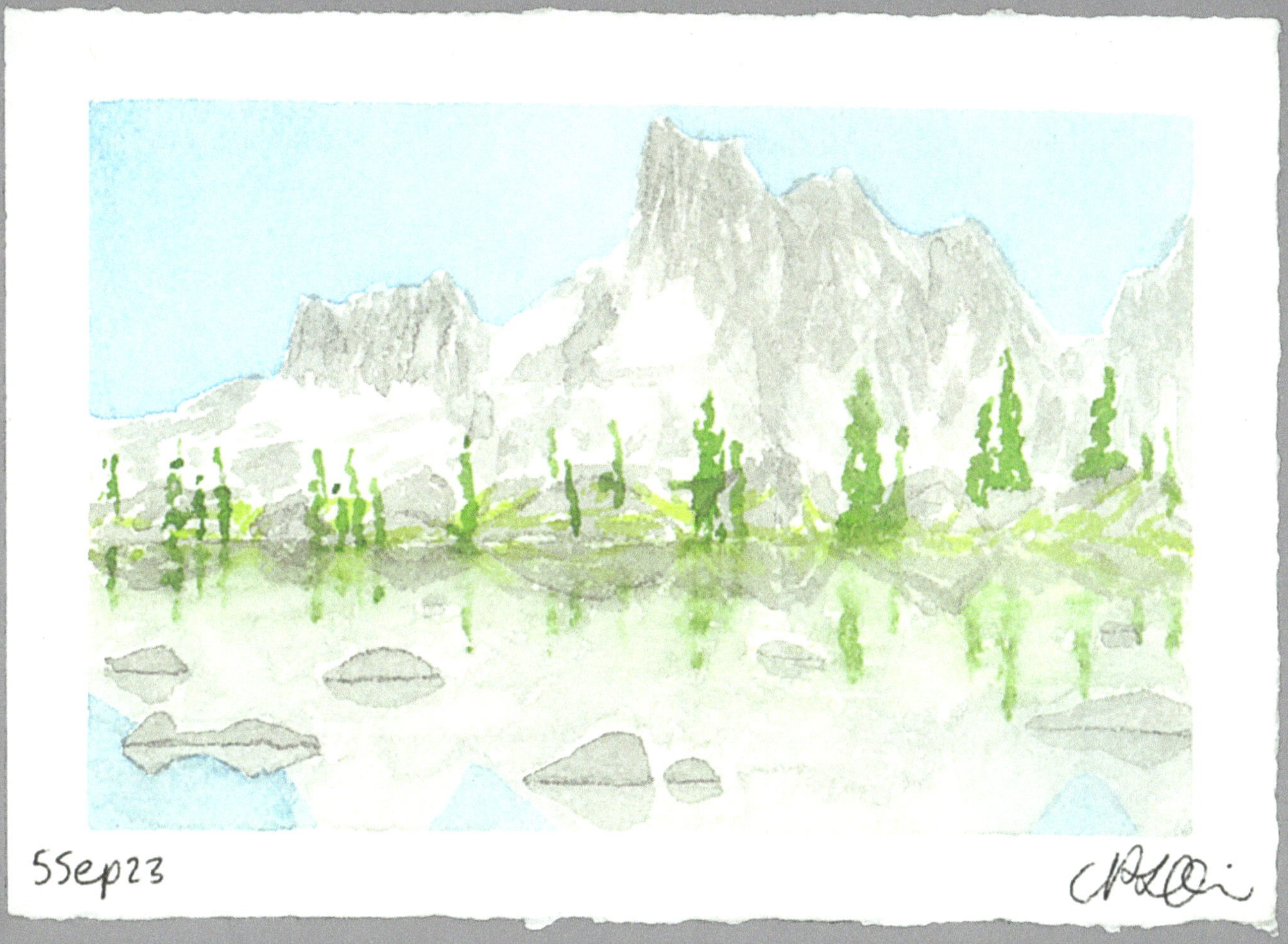

Donahue Pass to Red's Meadow

Trail day:	142	Ascent:	+3015'
Hiking day:	120	Descent:	-5443'
Trail miles:	928.5 - 907.5	Minimum elevation:	7596'
Hiking miles:	22.18	Maximum elevation:	10217'

Squaw Lake on Silver Pass at Sundown

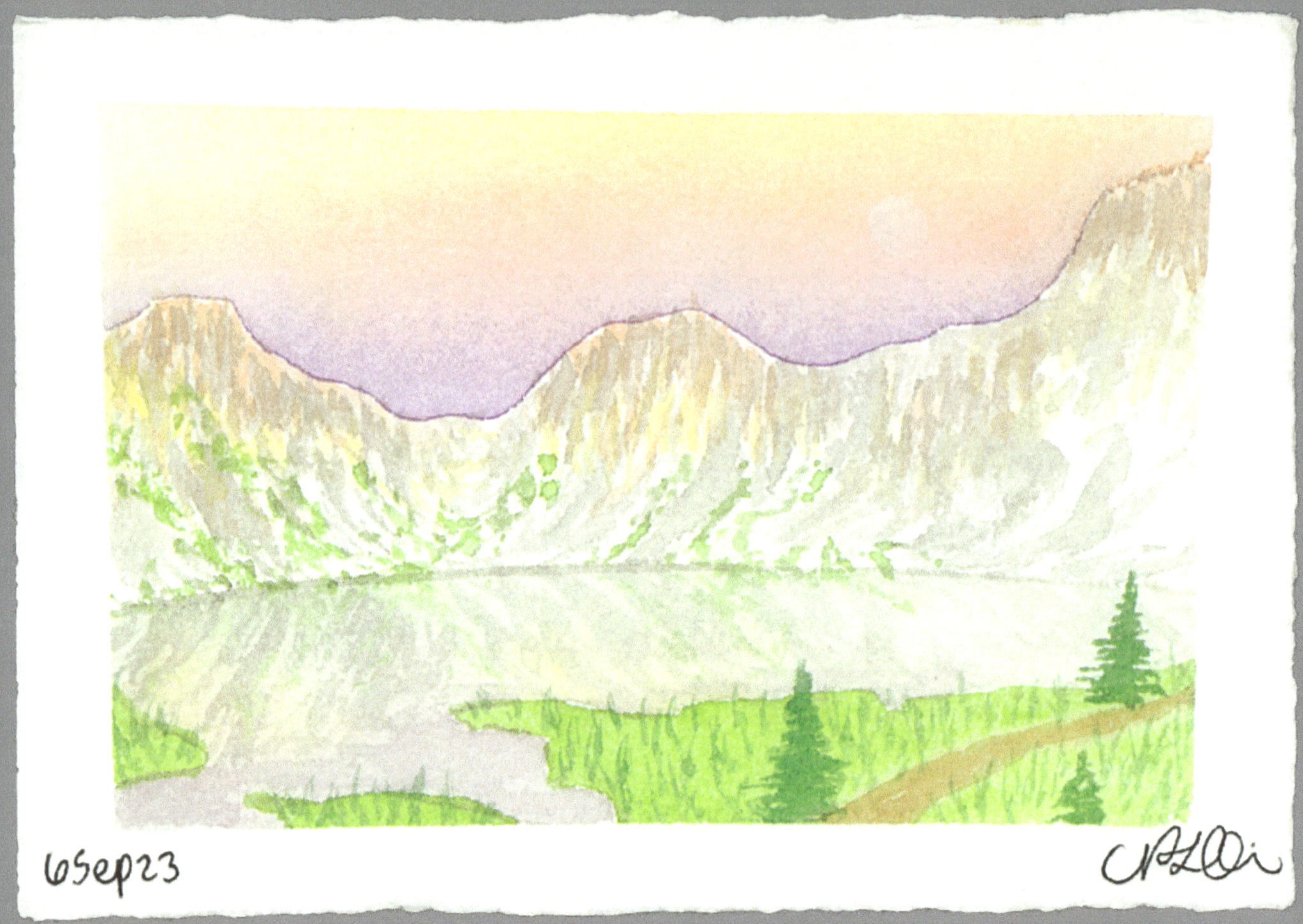

Alpine glow ♡

Red's Meadow to Silver Pass

Trail day:	143	Ascent:	+5279'
Hiking day:	121	Descent:	-2740'
Trail miles:	907.5 - 887.7	Minimum elevation:	7732'
Hiking miles:	21.79	Maximum elevation:	10539'

Marie Lakes from Selden Pass

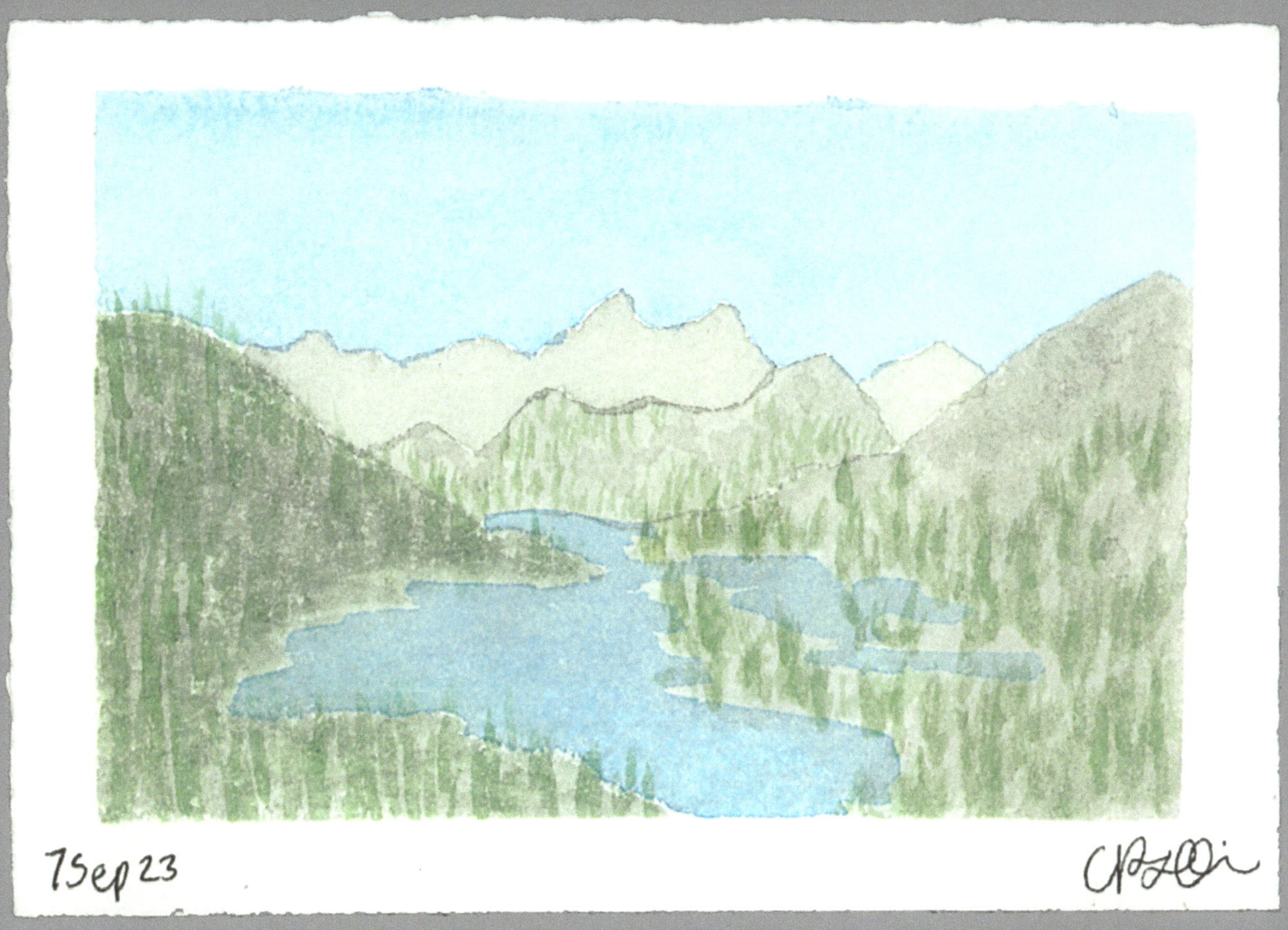

Silver Pass to Heart Lake

Trail day:	144	Ascent:	+5043'
Hiking day:	122	Descent:	-4751'
Trail miles:	887.7 - 865.9	Minimum elevation:	7855'
Hiking miles:	24.05	Maximum elevation:	10908'

Muir Pass from Evolution Creek

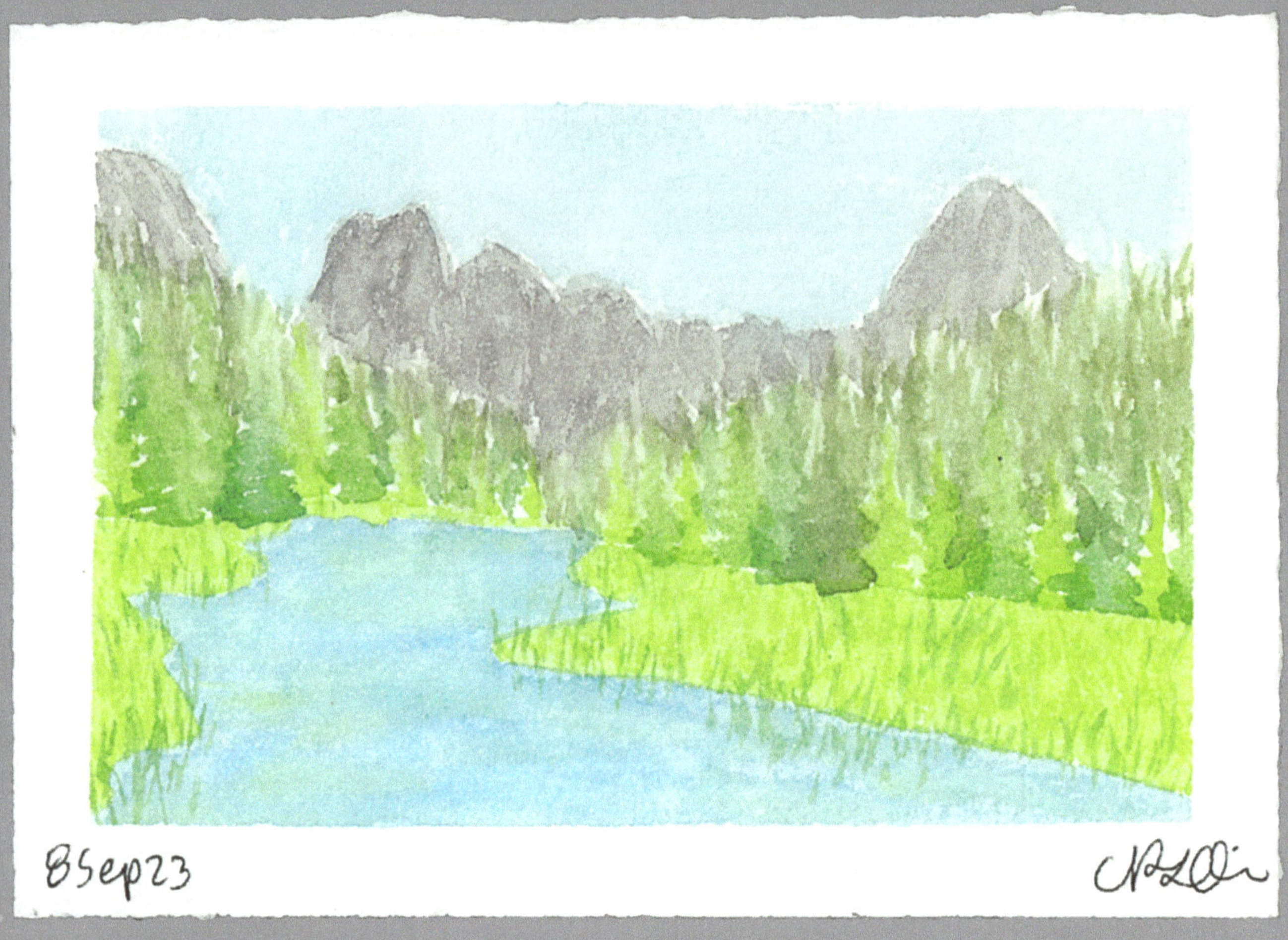

Heart Lake to Wanda Lake

Trail day:	145	Ascent:	+4921’
Hiking day:	123	Descent:	-3993’
Trail miles:	865.9 - 841.7	Minimum elevation:	7696’
Hiking miles:	27.40	Maximum elevation:	11466’

Palisade Lakes and Peaks from Mather Pass

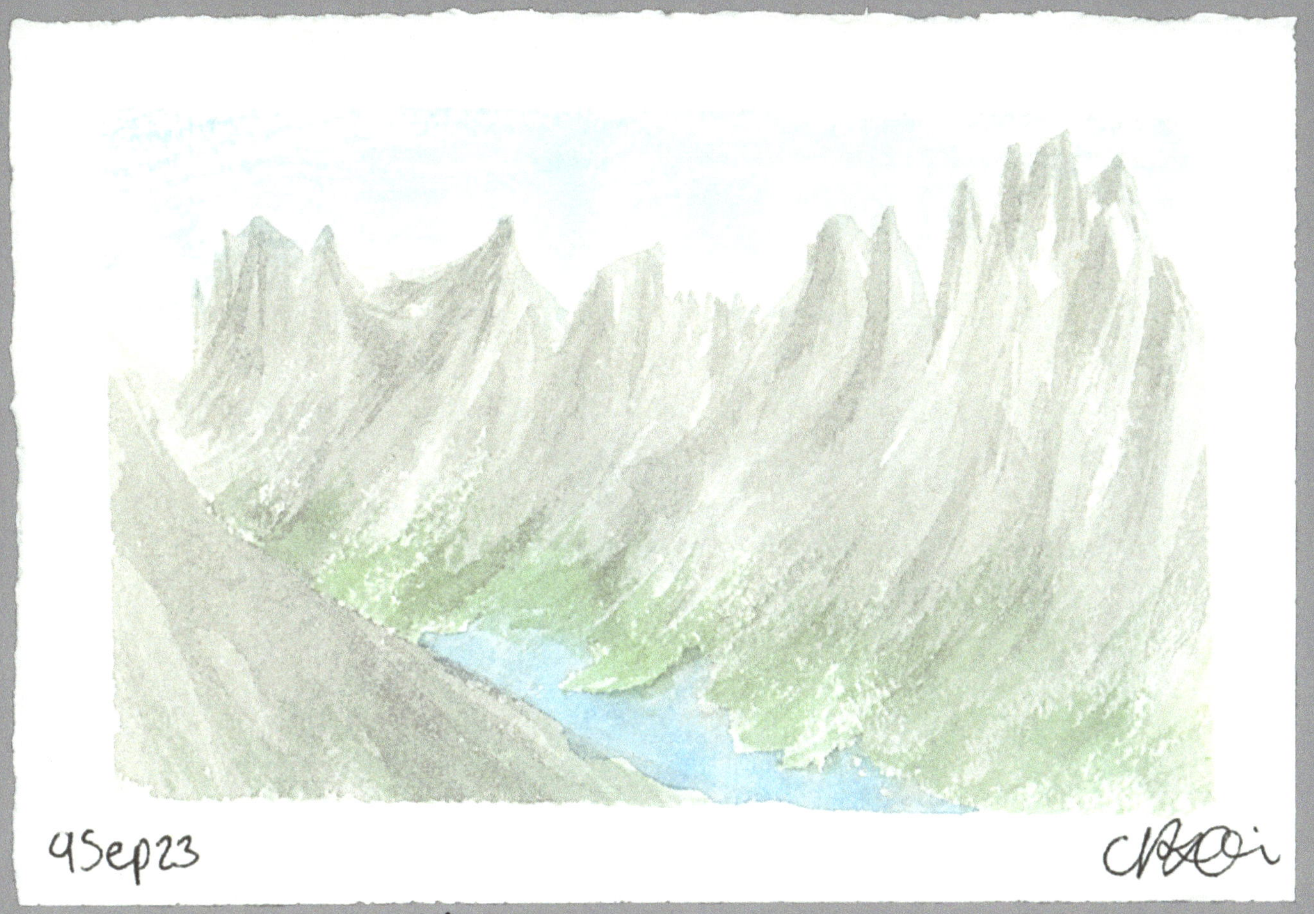

hiked alone. in dark. up Muir Pass. in storm. across snowfields.

Wanda Lake to Mather Pass

Trail day:	146	Ascent:	+5203’
Hiking day:	124	Descent:	-5177’
Trail miles:	841.7 - 816.6	Minimum elevation:	8021’
Hiking miles:	27.53	Maximum elevation:	12070’

Woods Creek Suspension Bridge

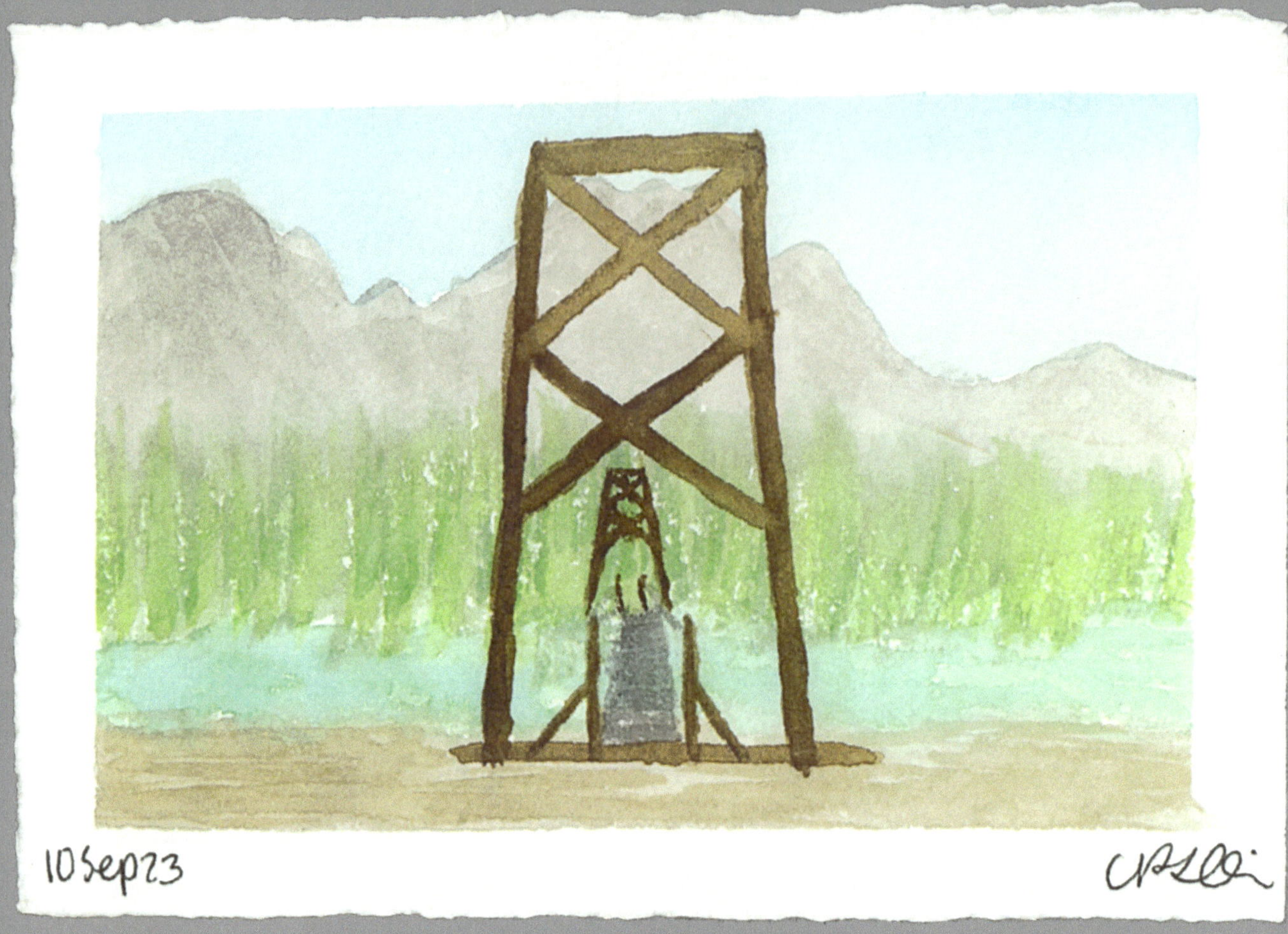

Mather Pass to Rae Lakes

Trail day:	147	Ascent:	+4639’
Hiking day:	125	Descent:	-5558’
Trail miles:	816.6 - 795.5	Minimum elevation:	8530’
Hiking miles:	24.35	Maximum elevation:	12071’

Glen Pass from Rae Lakes

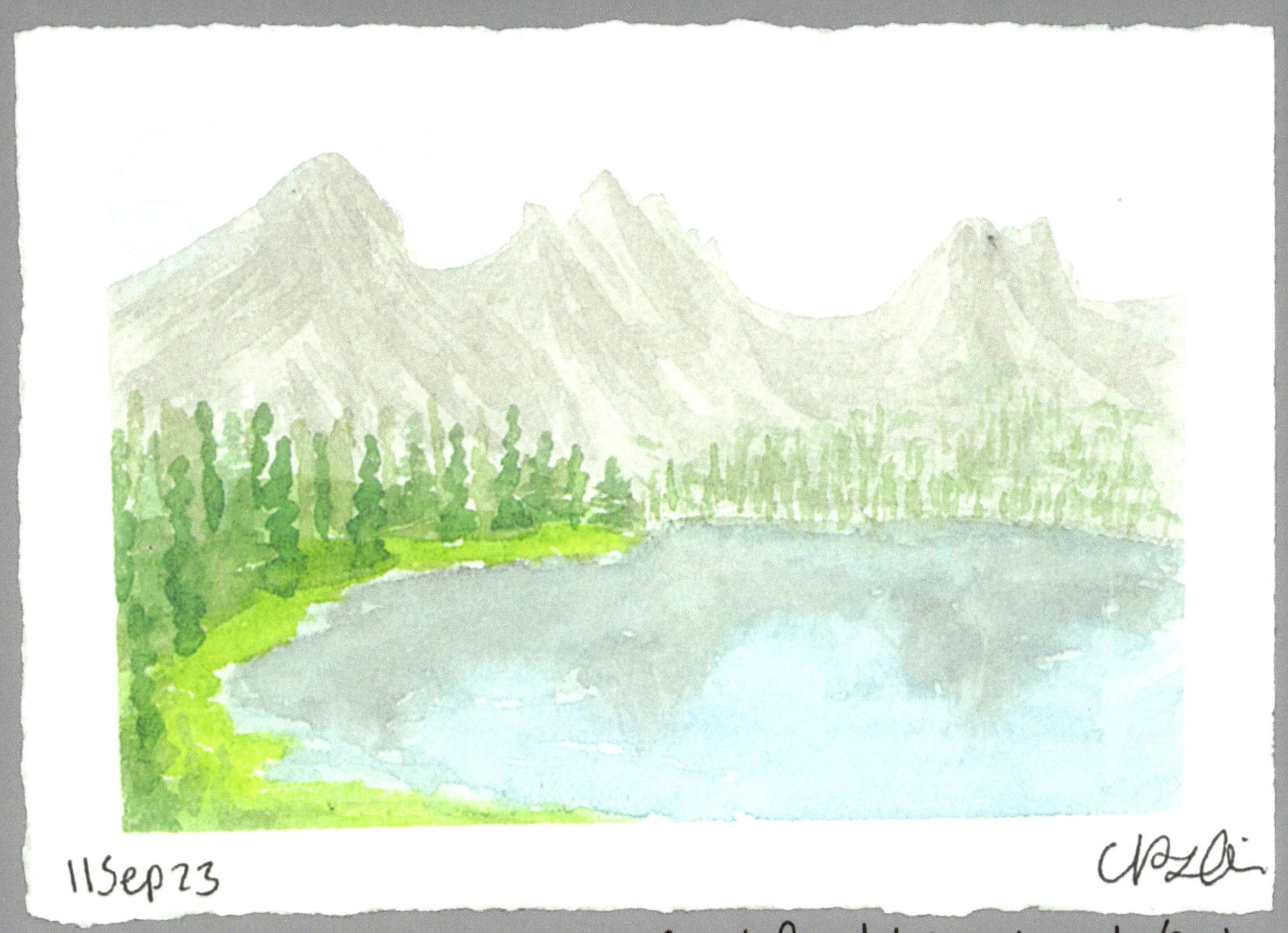

resupply from dad. plans changed w/Bogdan.

Rae Lakes to North of Forester Pass

Trail day:	148	Ascent:	+3553’
Hiking day:	126	Descent:	-2854’
Trail miles:	795.5 - 783.7	Minimum elevation:	9546’
Hiking miles:	13.20	Maximum elevation:	11945’

Mt Whitney from Big Horn Plateau

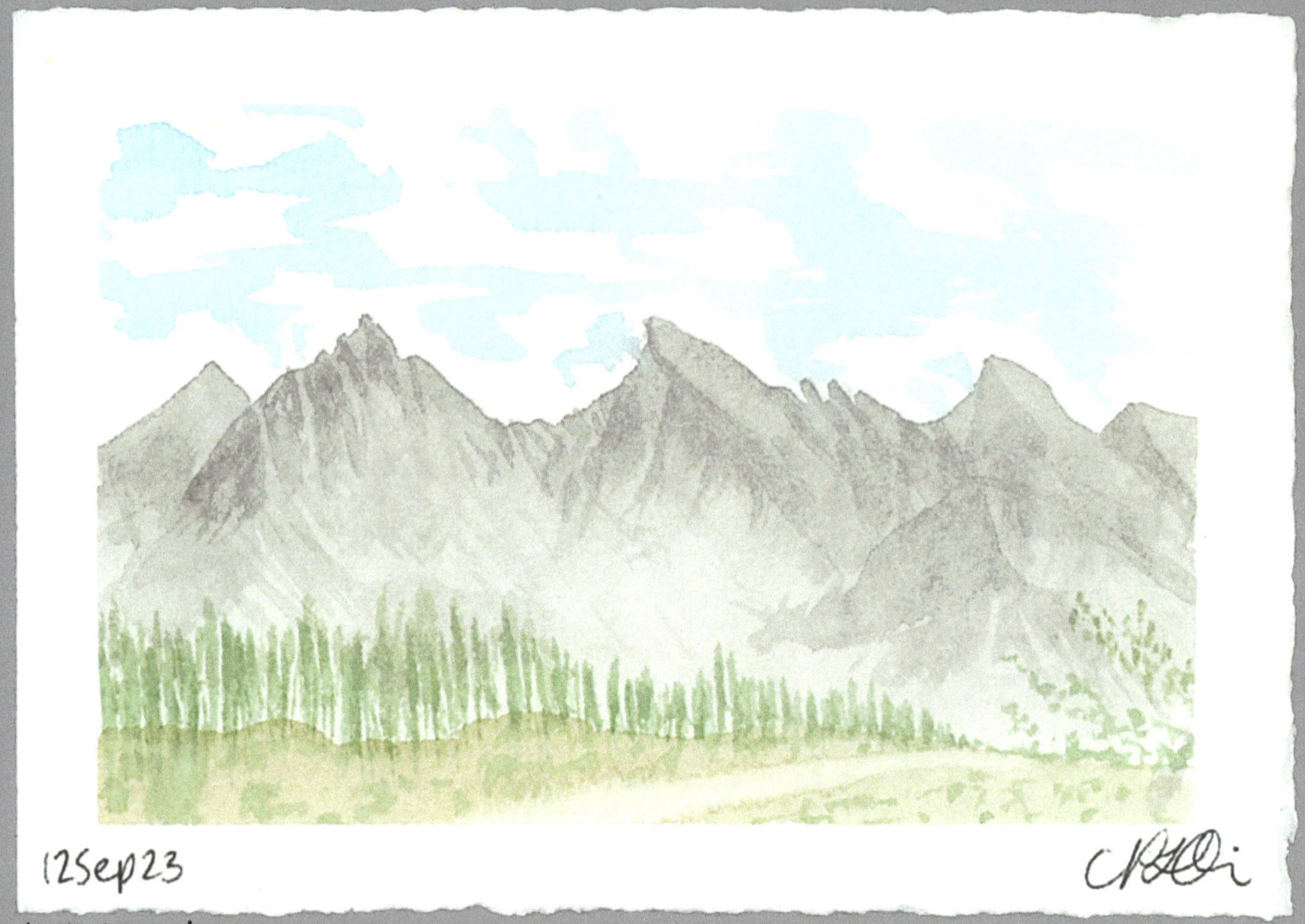

birthday at home amung the granite peaks.

Forester Pass to Crabtree Meadows

Trail day:	149	Ascent:	+3576’
Hiking day:	127	Descent:	-4098’
Trail miles:	783.7 - 768.1	Minimum elevation:	10396’
Hiking miles:	18.69	Maximum elevation:	13200’

Shelter on Mt Whitney Summit

Mt Whitney Trail

Trail day:	150
Hiking day:	128
Trail miles:	Side trail
Hiking miles:	16.77
Ascent:	+4334’
Descent:	-4334’
Minimum elevation:	10707’
Maximum elevation:	14505’

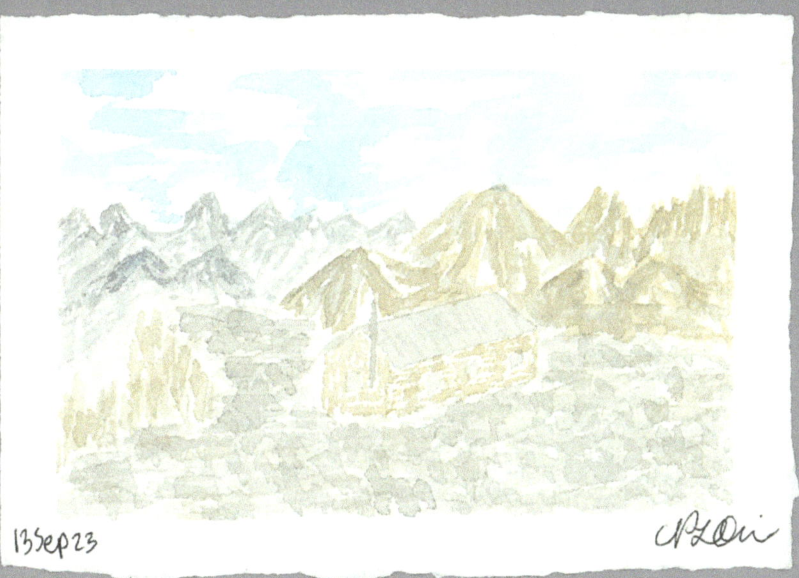

trail is river. river is trail.

Crabtree Meadows to Chicken Spring Lake

Trail day:	151
Hiking day:	129
Trail miles:	768.1 - 752.1
Hiking miles:	17.69
Ascent:	+3520’
Descent:	-2946’
Minimum elevation:	9554’
Maximum elevation:	11516’

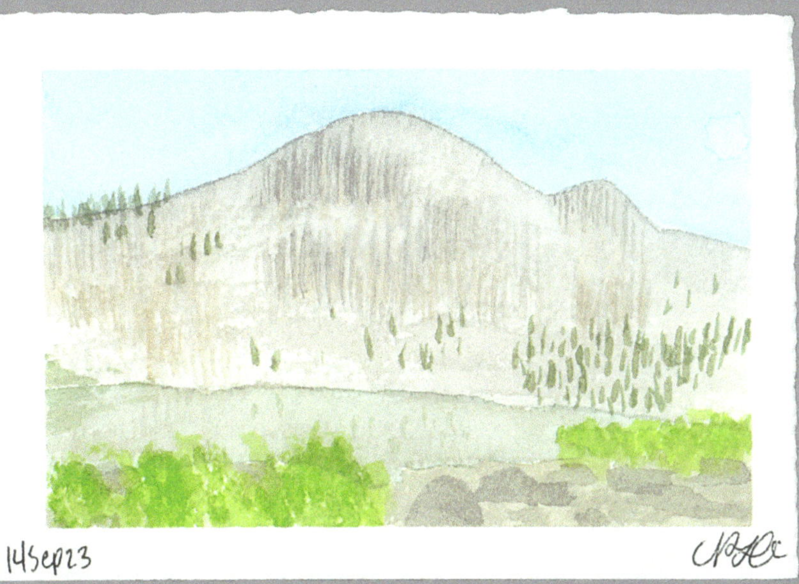

Chicken Spring Lake

Rock Formations on a Ridge Overlooking Owens Valley

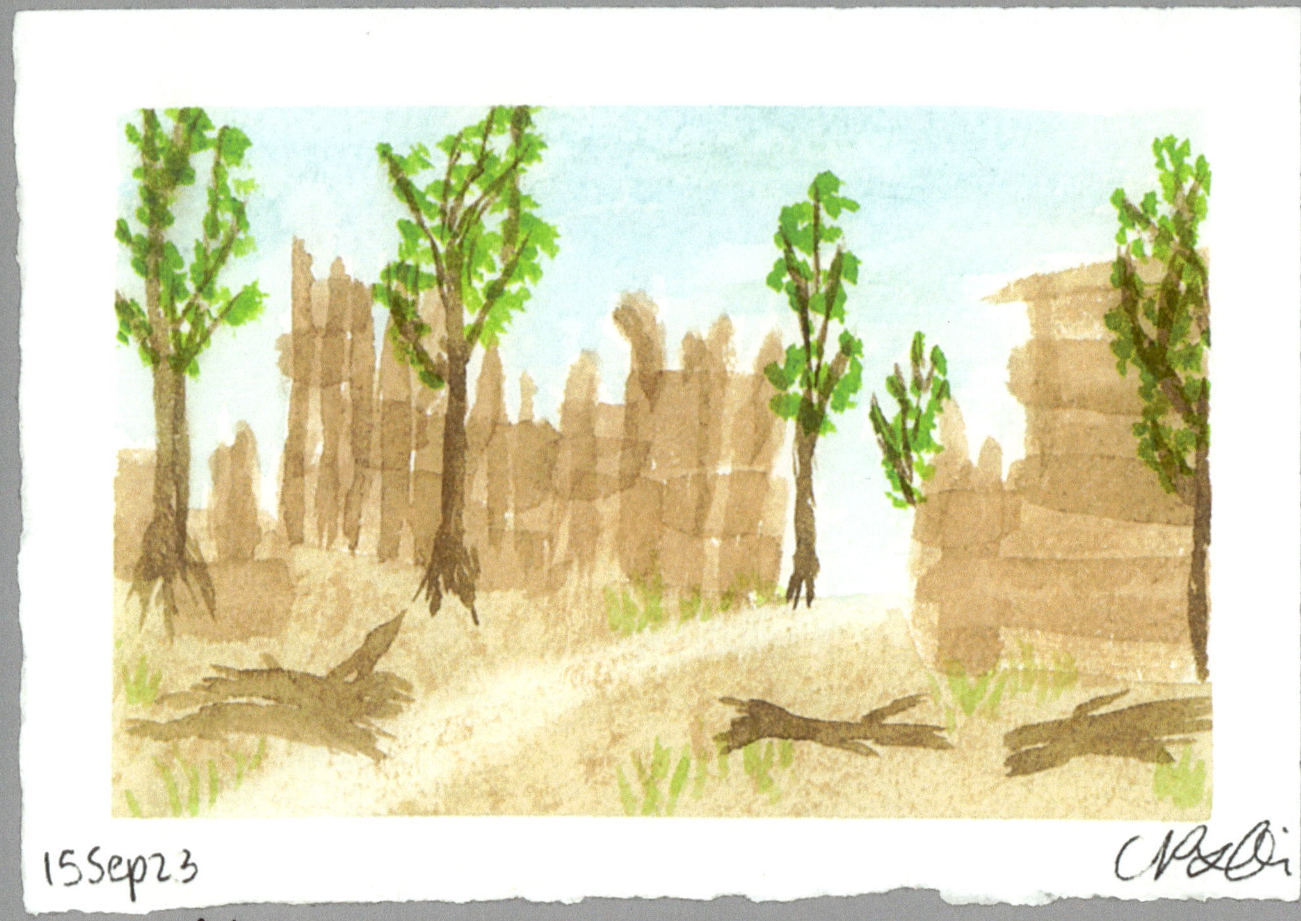

dont really feel like painting tonight.

Chicken Spring Lake to Golden Trout Wilderness

Trail day:	152	Ascent:	+1906’
Hiking day:	130	Descent:	-3009’
Trail miles:	752.1 - 735.0	Minimum elevation:	9604’
Hiking miles:	17.58	Maximum elevation:	11274’

Leaving the High Sierra

Golden Trout Wilderness to Monache Meadows

Trail day:	153
Hiking day:	131
Trail miles:	735.0 - 717.7
Hiking miles:	19.83
Ascent:	+1929'
Descent:	-4239'
Minimum elevation:	7844'
Maximum elevation:	10572'

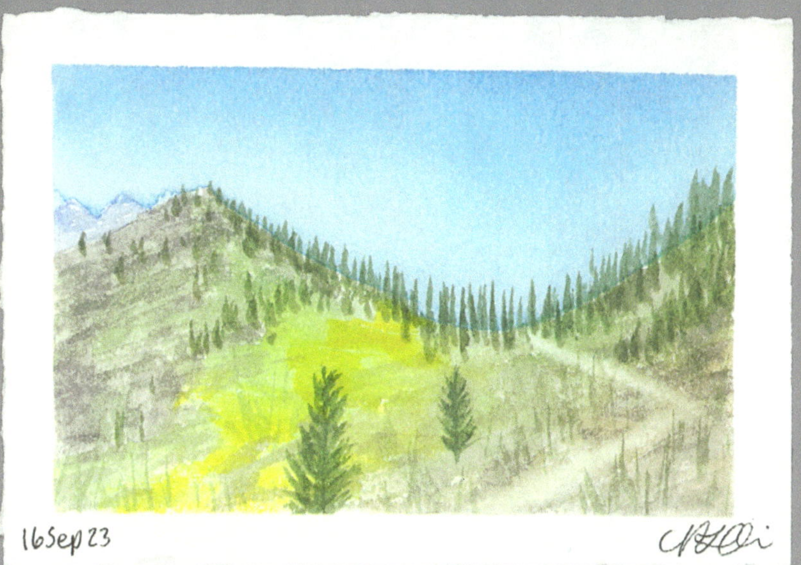

Monache Meadows to Kennedy Meadows South

Trail day:	154
Hiking day:	132
Trail miles:	717.7 - 703.4
Hiking miles:	14.77
Ascent:	+1207'
Descent:	-2992'
Minimum elevation:	6014'
Maximum elevation:	8388'

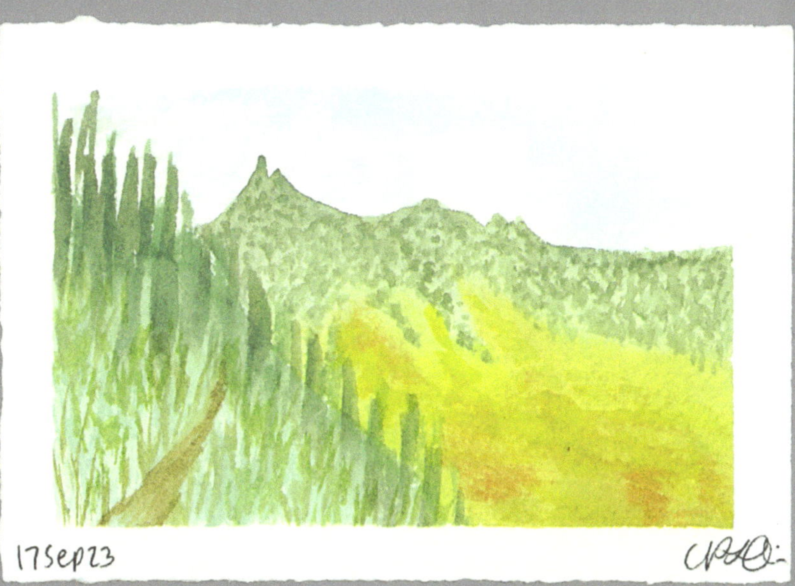

Monache Meadows

Northern Washington

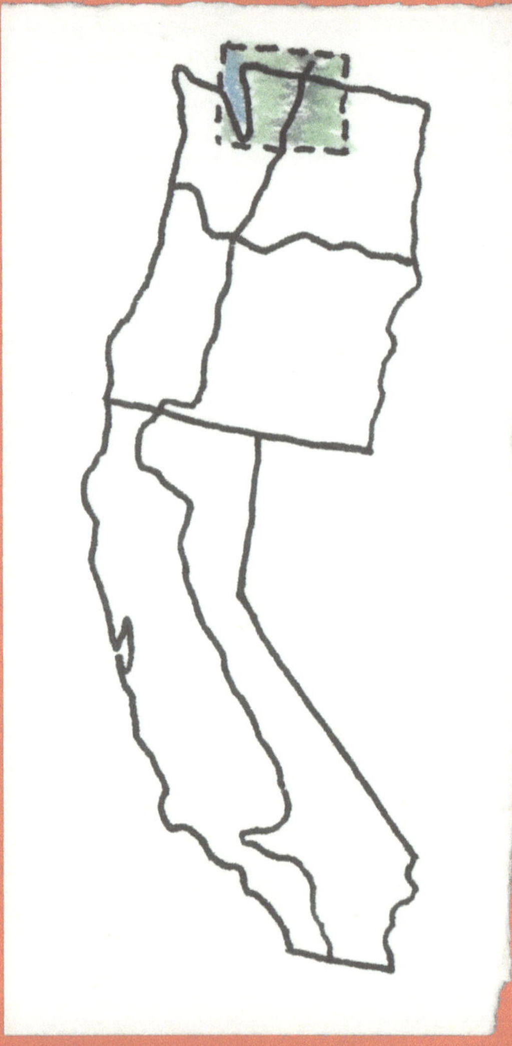

Northbound: Stevens Pass, WA to
Northern Terminus, then Manning Park, BC

September 20 to 30, 2023

Trail days:	11
Hiking days:	10
Trail miles:	2466.9 - 2655.1
Average miles per hiking day:	18.88
Fewest miles per hiking day:	5.01
Most miles per hiking day:	25.18

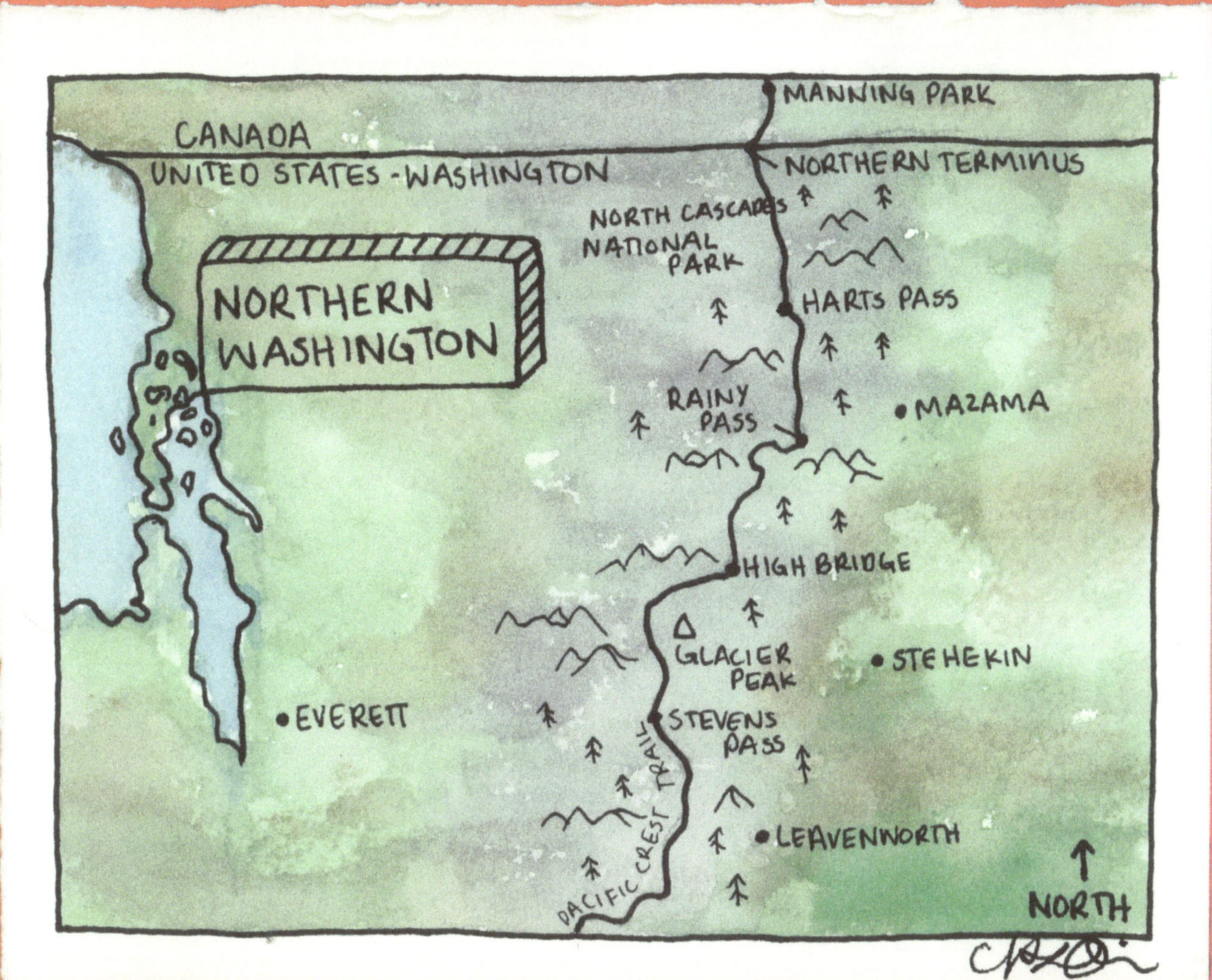
MANNING PARK
CANADA
UNITED STATES - WASHINGTON
NORTHERN TERMINUS
NORTH CASCADES NATIONAL PARK
NORTHERN WASHINGTON
HARTS PASS
RAINY PASS
MAZAMA
HIGH BRIDGE
GLACIER PEAK
STEHEKIN
EVERETT
STEVENS PASS
PACIFIC CREST TRAIL
LEAVENWORTH
NORTH

Lake Valhalla on a Misty Morning

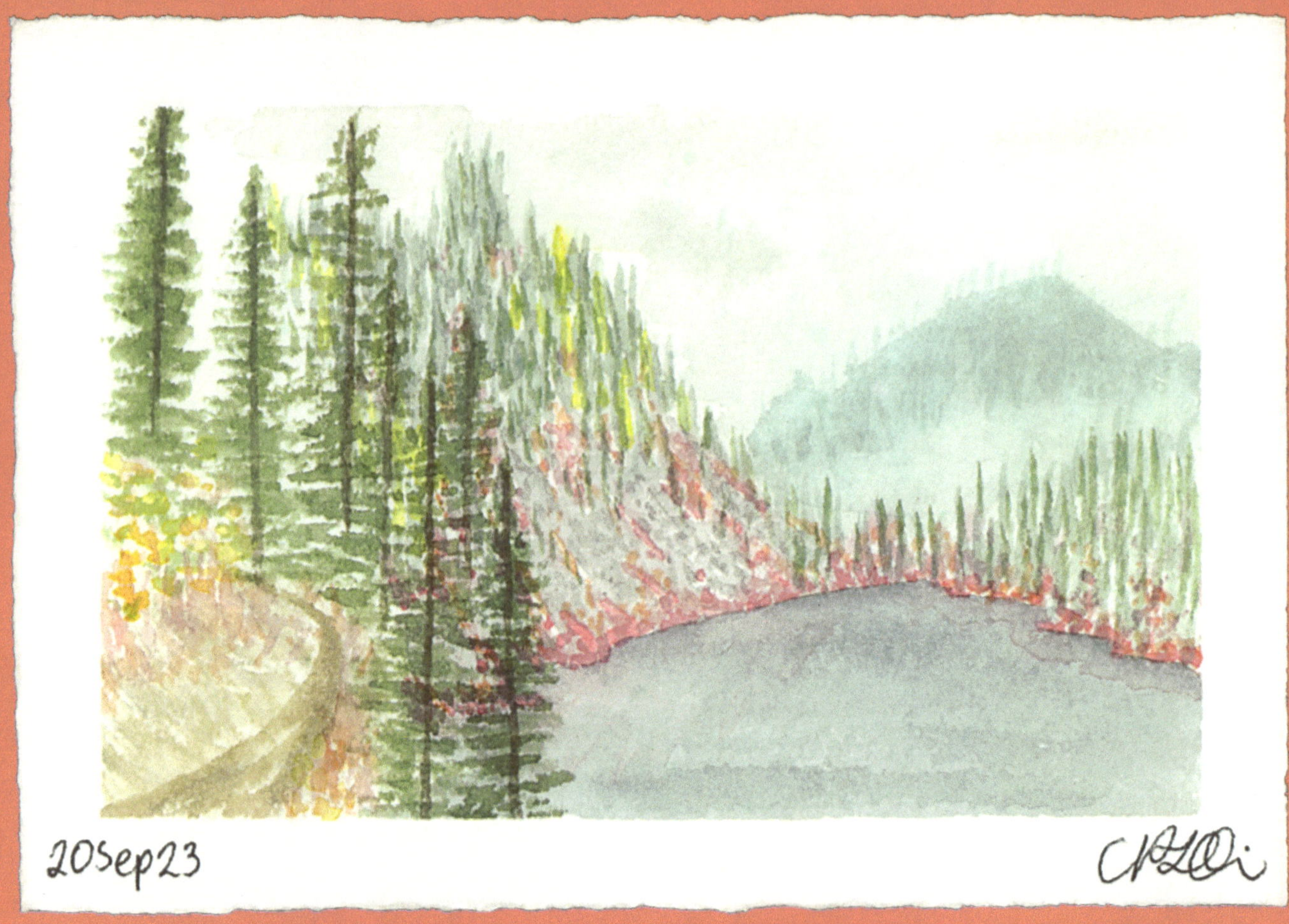

Stevens Pass to Pear Lake

Trail day:	157	Ascent:	+4324'
Hiking day:	133	Descent:	-3556'
Trail miles:	2466.9 - 2485.2	Minimum elevation:	3803'
Hiking miles:	19.34	Maximum elevation:	5572'

Glacier Peak Wilderness

Pear Lake to Red Pass

Trail day:	158
Hiking day:	134
Trail miles:	2485.2 - 2506.5
Hiking miles:	22.99
Ascent:	+5059’
Descent:	-3448’
Minimum elevation:	4213’
Maximum elevation:	6484’

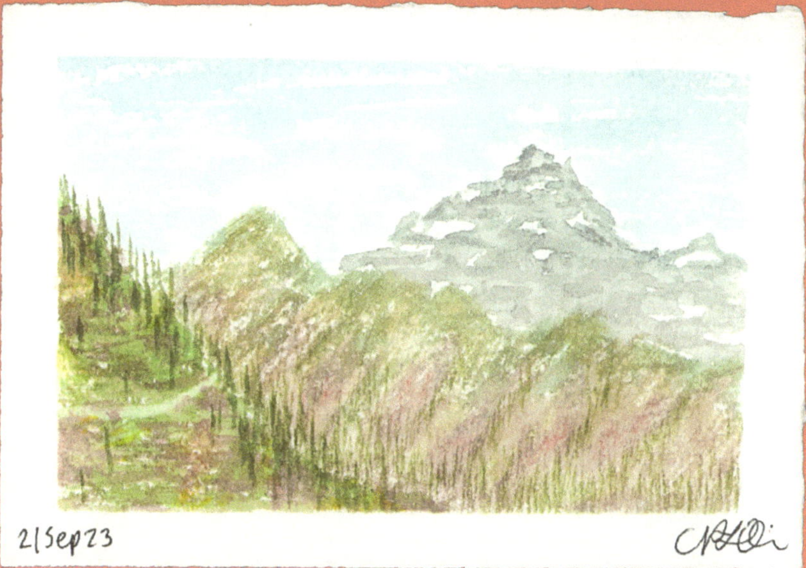

walked thru closure. did not catch fire. not criminal.

big fall. ascent from Milky Creek. Face plant. Humbled.

Red Pass to Glacier Peak Wilderness

Trail day:	159
Hiking day:	135
Trail miles:	2506.5 - 2531.5
Hiking miles:	25.18
Ascent:	+6109’
Descent:	-7024’
Minimum elevation:	3310’
Maximum elevation:	6488’

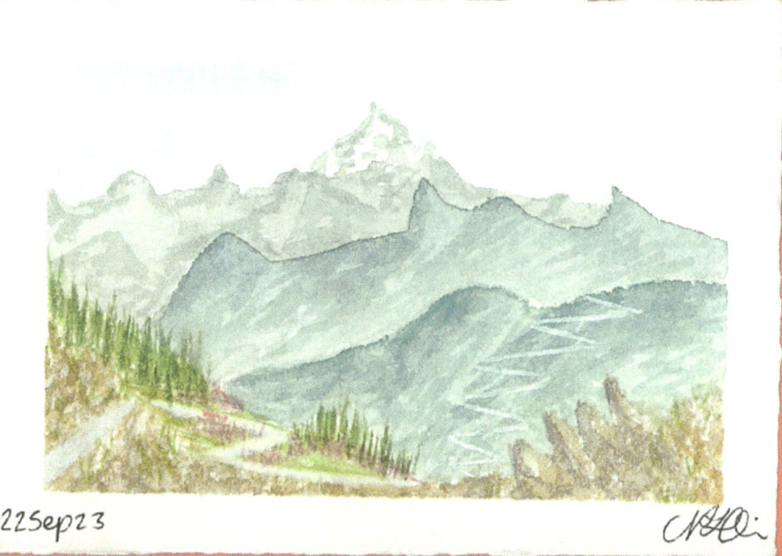

Endless Switchbacks in Glacier Peak Wilderness

Fall Colors in the Northern Cascades

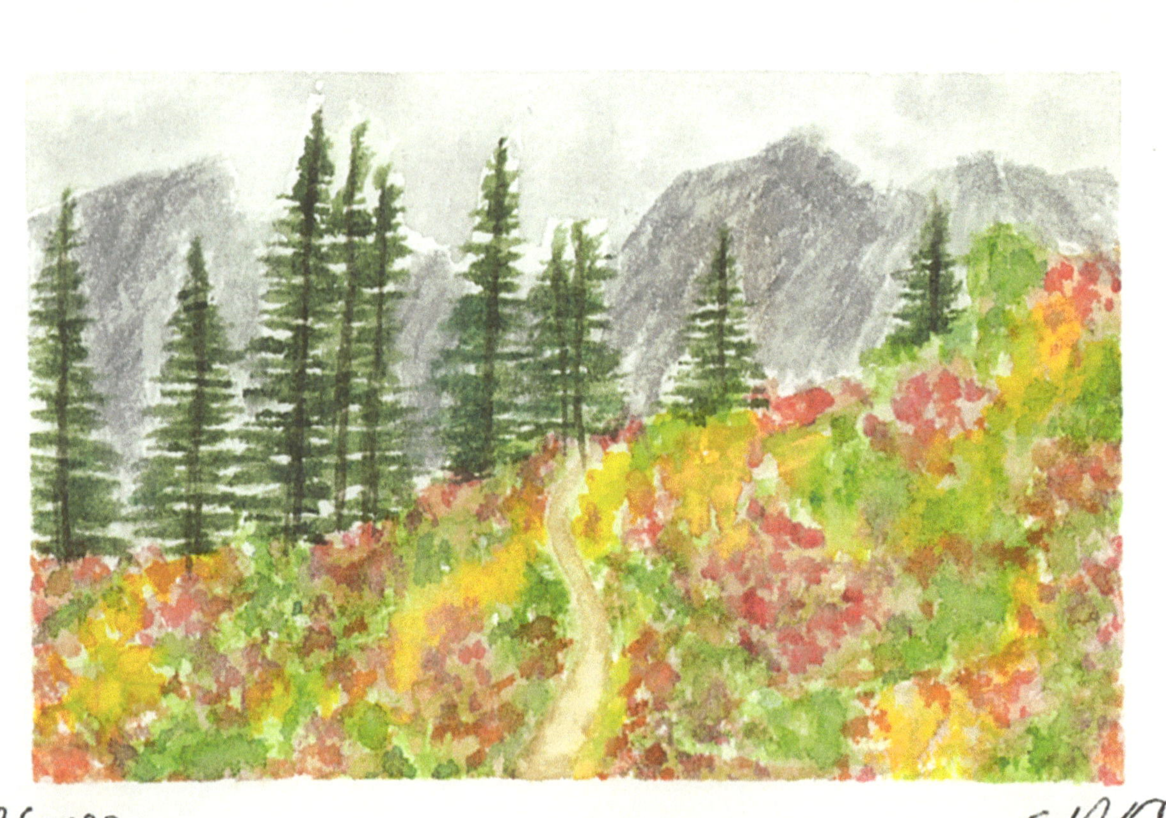

23Sep23

GIANT blowdowns. I am a tree climber now.

Glacier Peak Wilderness to Suiattle Pass

Trail day:	160	Ascent:	+4820’
Hiking day:	136	Descent:	-4567’
Trail miles:	2531.5 - 2555.1	Minimum elevation:	2426’
Hiking miles:	24.05	Maximum elevation:	5982’

Dome Creek Fire Smoke on a Rainy Day in the Agnes Creek Valley

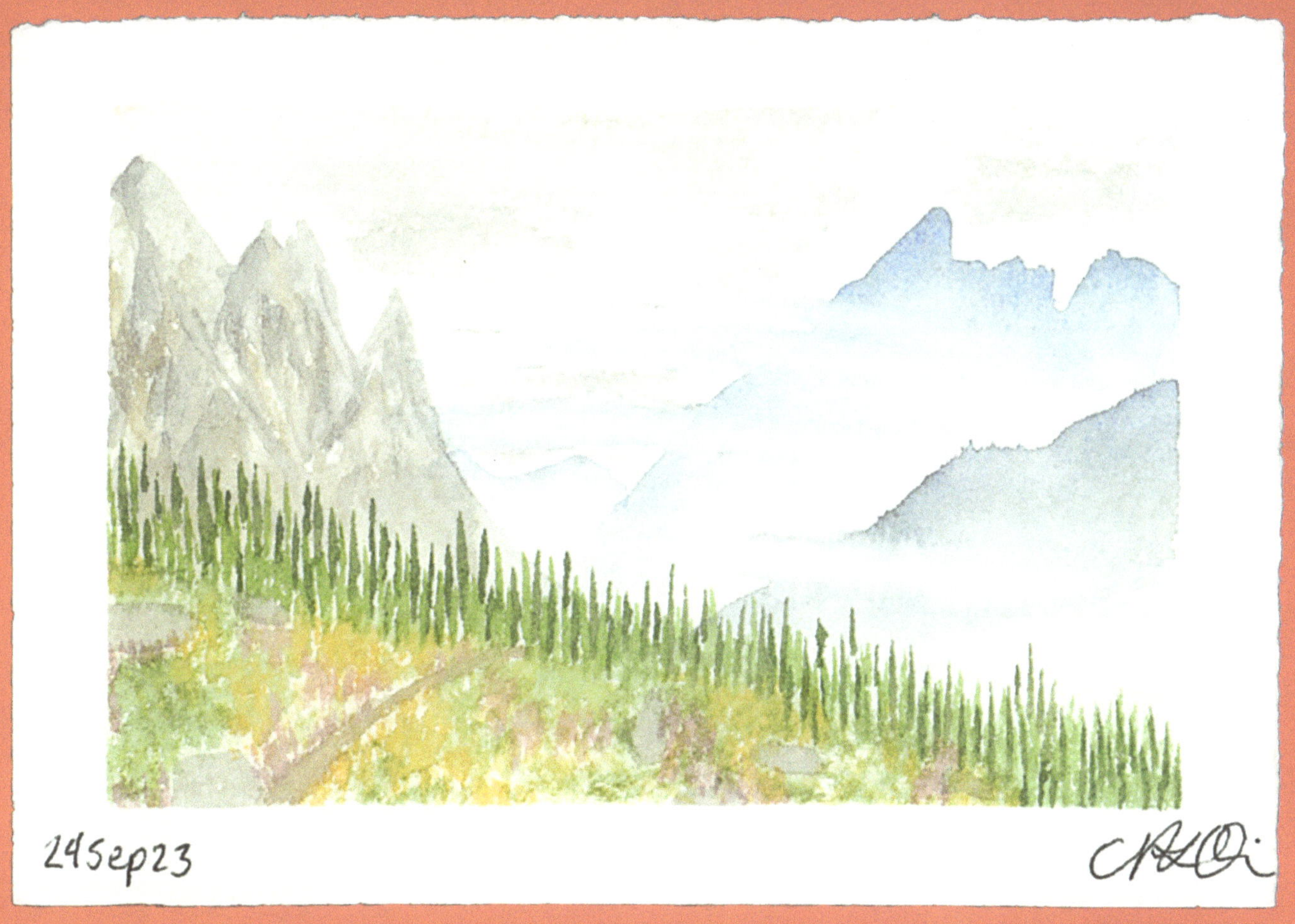

Suiattle Pass to High Bridge

Trail day:	161	Ascent:	+1637’
Hiking day:	137	Descent:	-5853’
Trail miles:	2555.1 - 2574.6	Minimum elevation:	1587’
Hiking miles:	18.65	Maximum elevation:	5830’

Lake Chelan from Stehekin

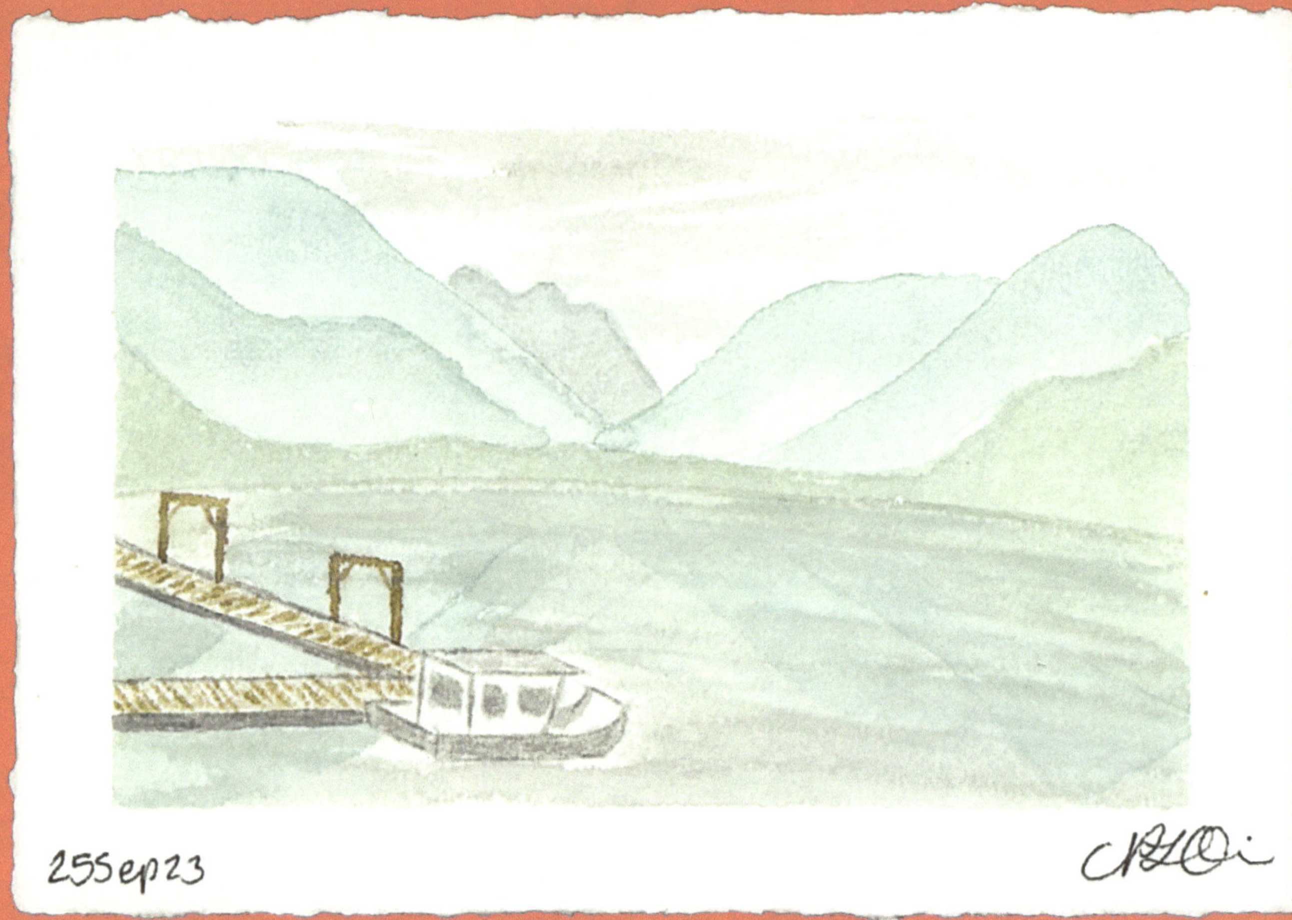

pools of water. warm + dry in sleeping bag.

High Bridge to Fireweed Camp

Trail day:	162	Ascent:	+3592’
Hiking day:	138	Descent:	-1544’
Trail miles:	2574.6 - 2588.9	Minimum elevation:	1581’
Hiking miles:	15.30	Maximum elevation:	3644’

A Rainy Day Leading to Rainy Pass

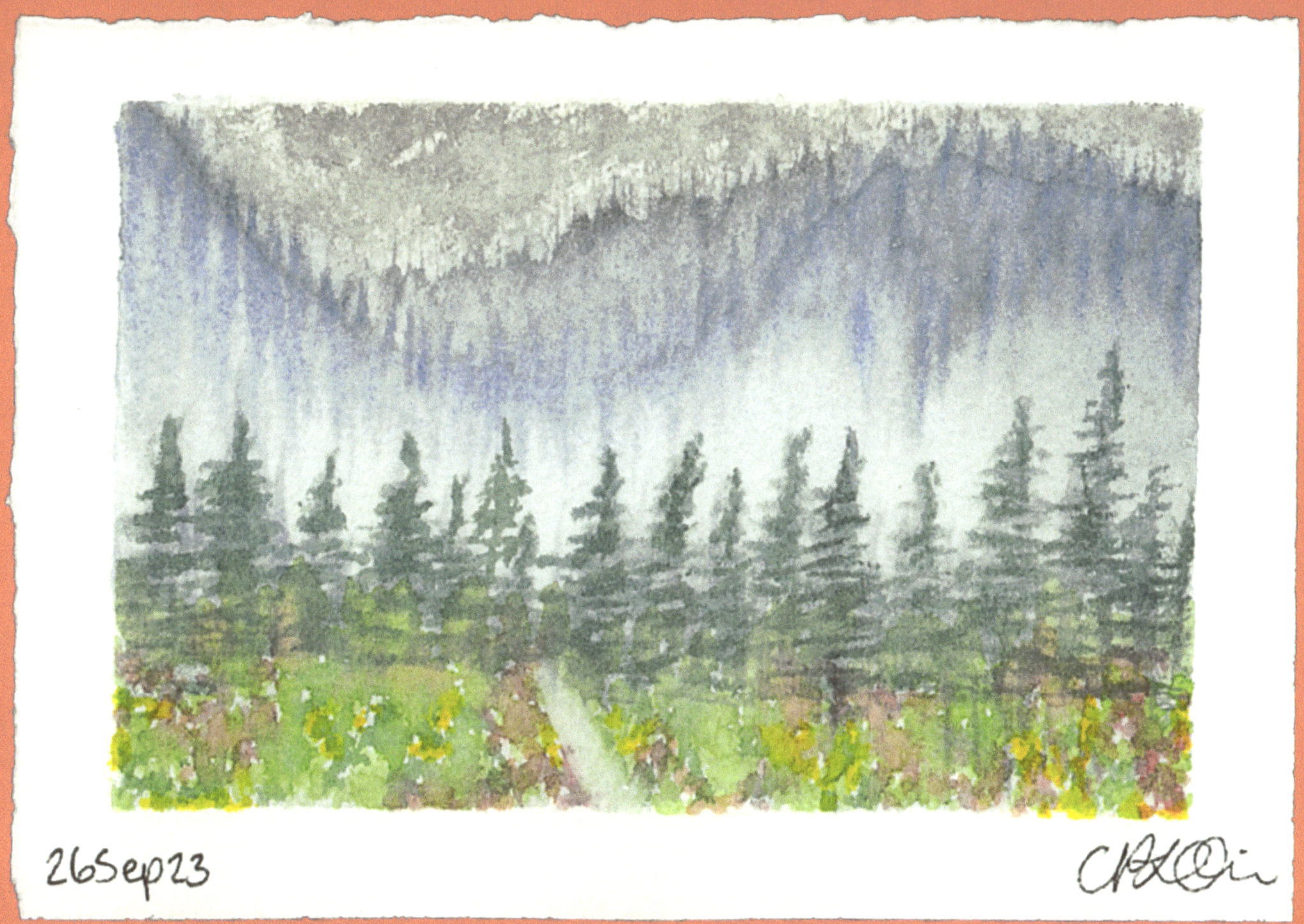

Fireweed Camp to Rainy Pass

Trail day:	163	Ascent:	+1404’
Hiking day:	139	Descent:	-159’
Trail miles:	2588.9 - 2593.8	Minimum elevation:	3623’
Hiking miles:	5.01	Maximum elevation:	4885’

A Switchback into Yellow Larch Trees

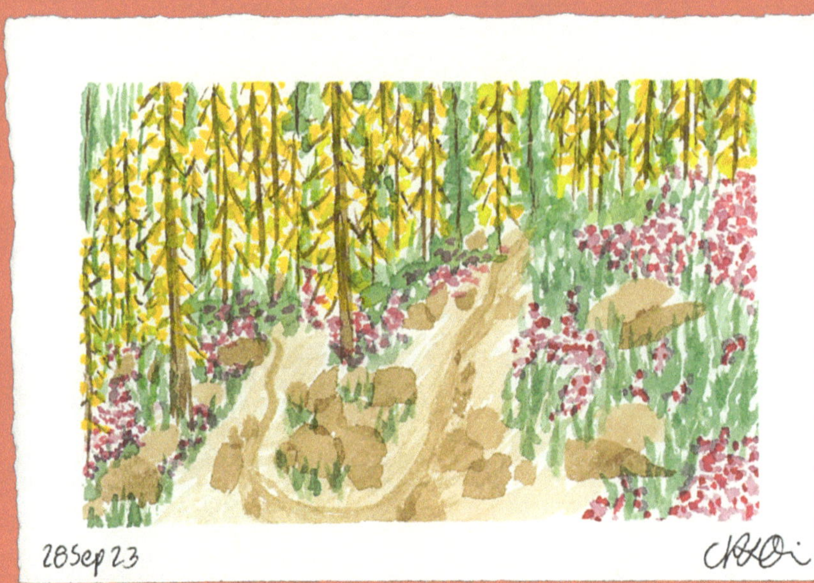

Rainy Pass to Grasshopper Pass

Trail day:	165
Hiking day:	140
Trail miles:	2593.8 - 2617.9
Hiking miles:	24.17
Ascent:	+5412'
Descent:	-3600'
Minimum elevation:	4270'
Maximum elevation:	6900'

Just keep getting out of the tent.

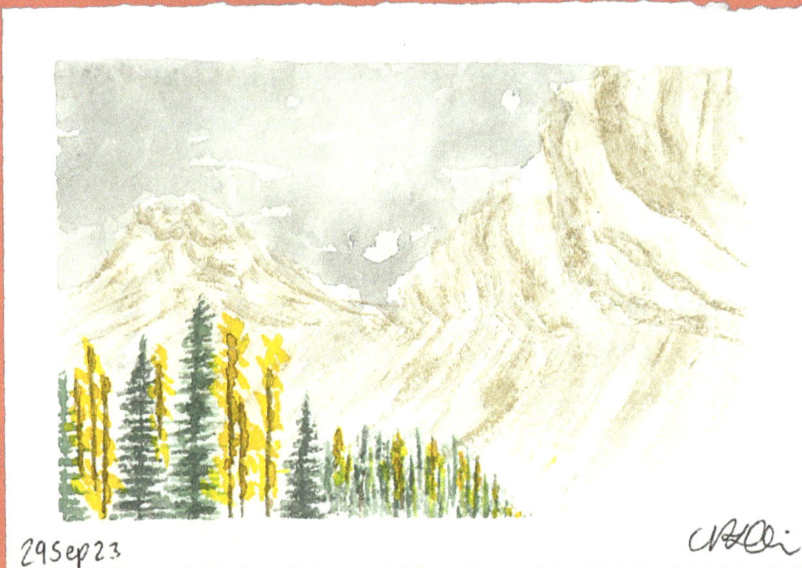

Grasshopper Pass to Rock Pass

Trail day:	166
Hiking day:	141
Trail miles:	2617.9 - 2640.6
Hiking miles:	23.96
Ascent:	+3683'
Descent:	-4204'
Minimum elevation:	5124'
Maximum elevation:	6995'

A Dusting of Snow near Rock Pass

The Northern Terminus

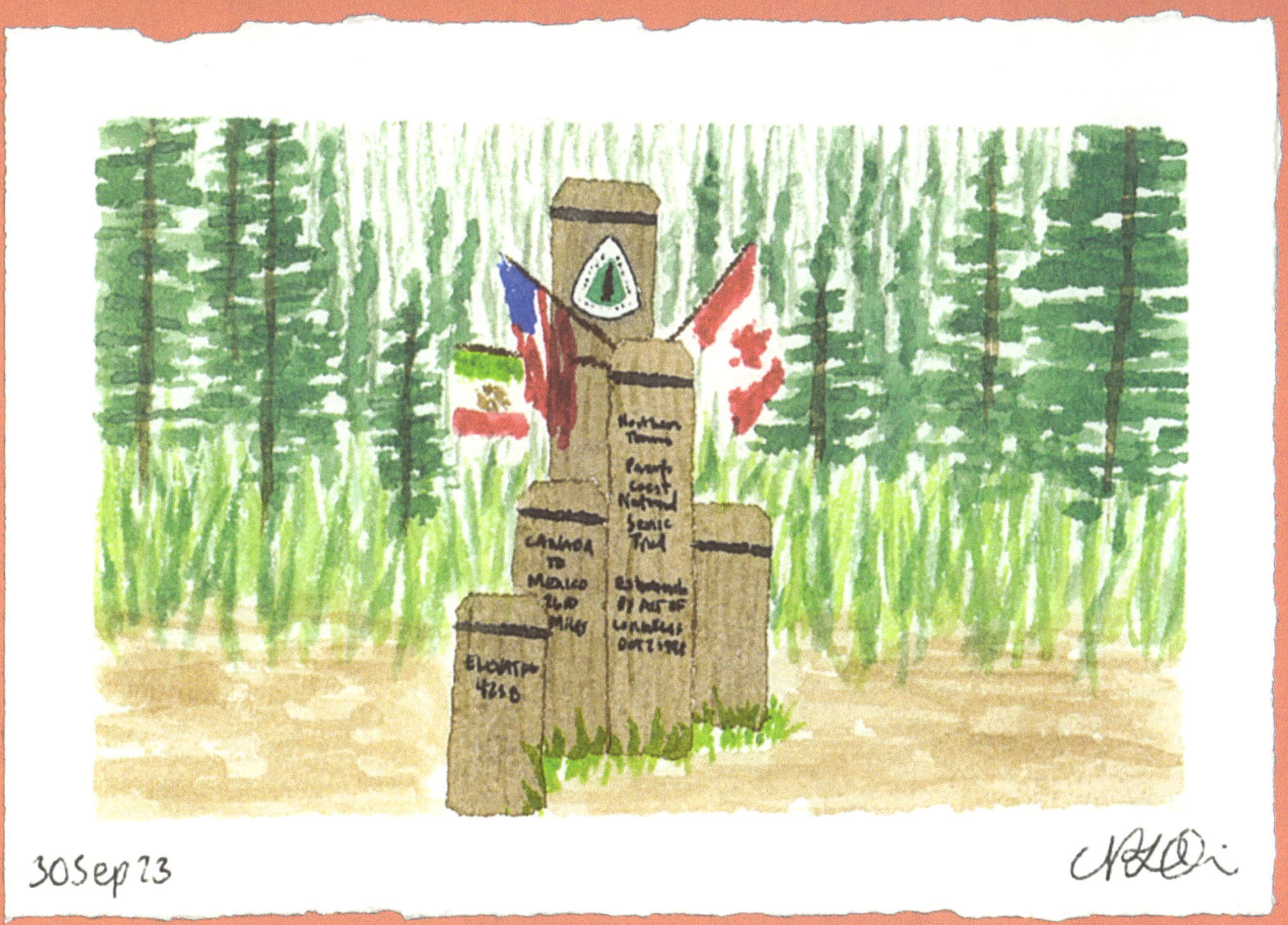

Rock Pass to Northern Terminus and then to Manning Park, BC

Trail day:	167	Ascent:	+2408’
Hiking day:	142	Descent:	-4669’
Trail miles:	2640.6 - 2655.1	Minimum elevation:	3795’
Hiking miles:	24.50	Maximum elevation:	7086’

Reflecting Back on the Southern Terminus

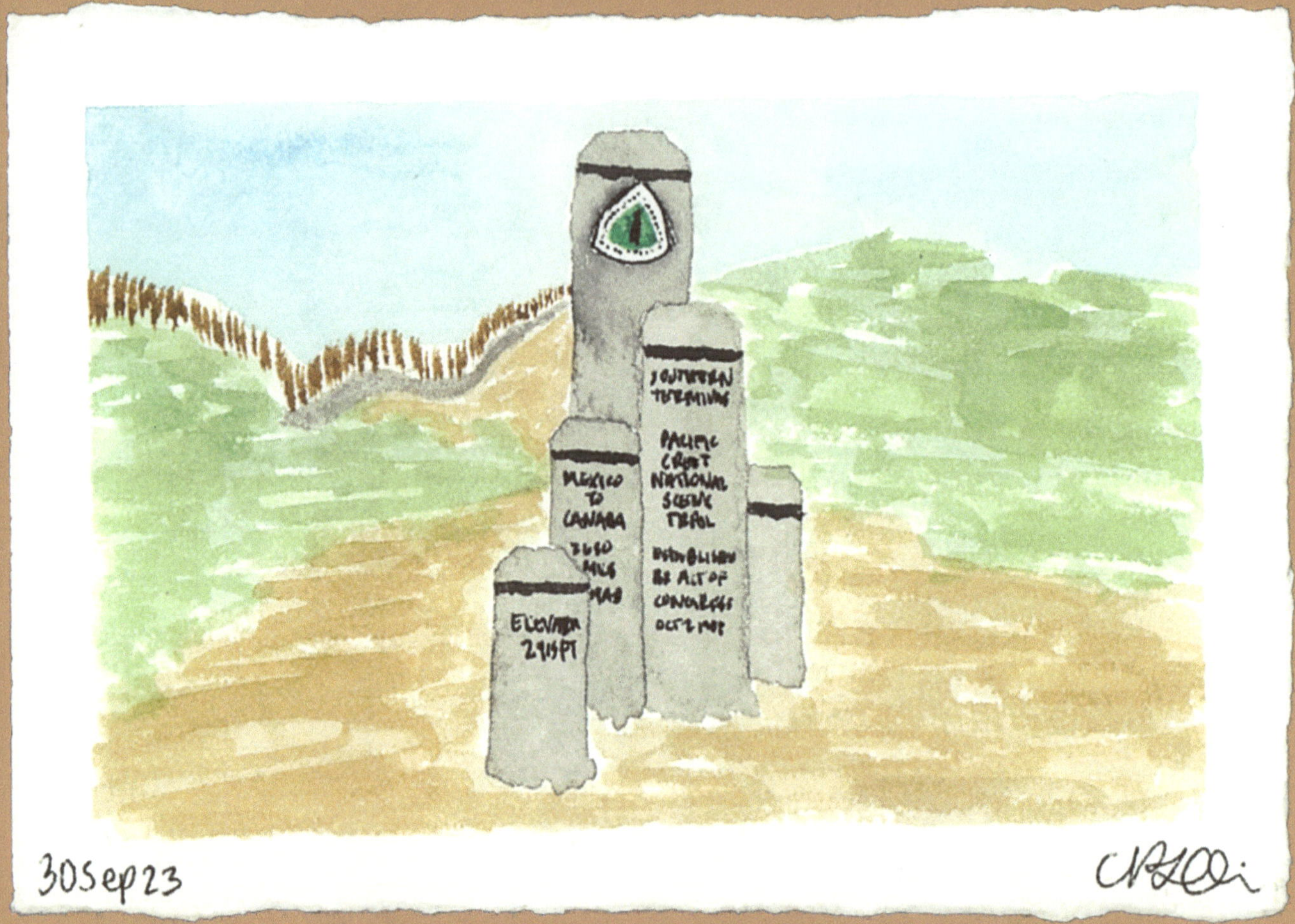

Total Trail Numbers
Southern Terminus at Campo, CA to
Northern Terminus, then Manning Park, BC

Trail days:	167	Average miles per hiking day:	18.66
Hiking days:	142	Fewest miles per hiking day:	3.07
Trail miles:	2655.1	Most miles per hiking day:	31.84’

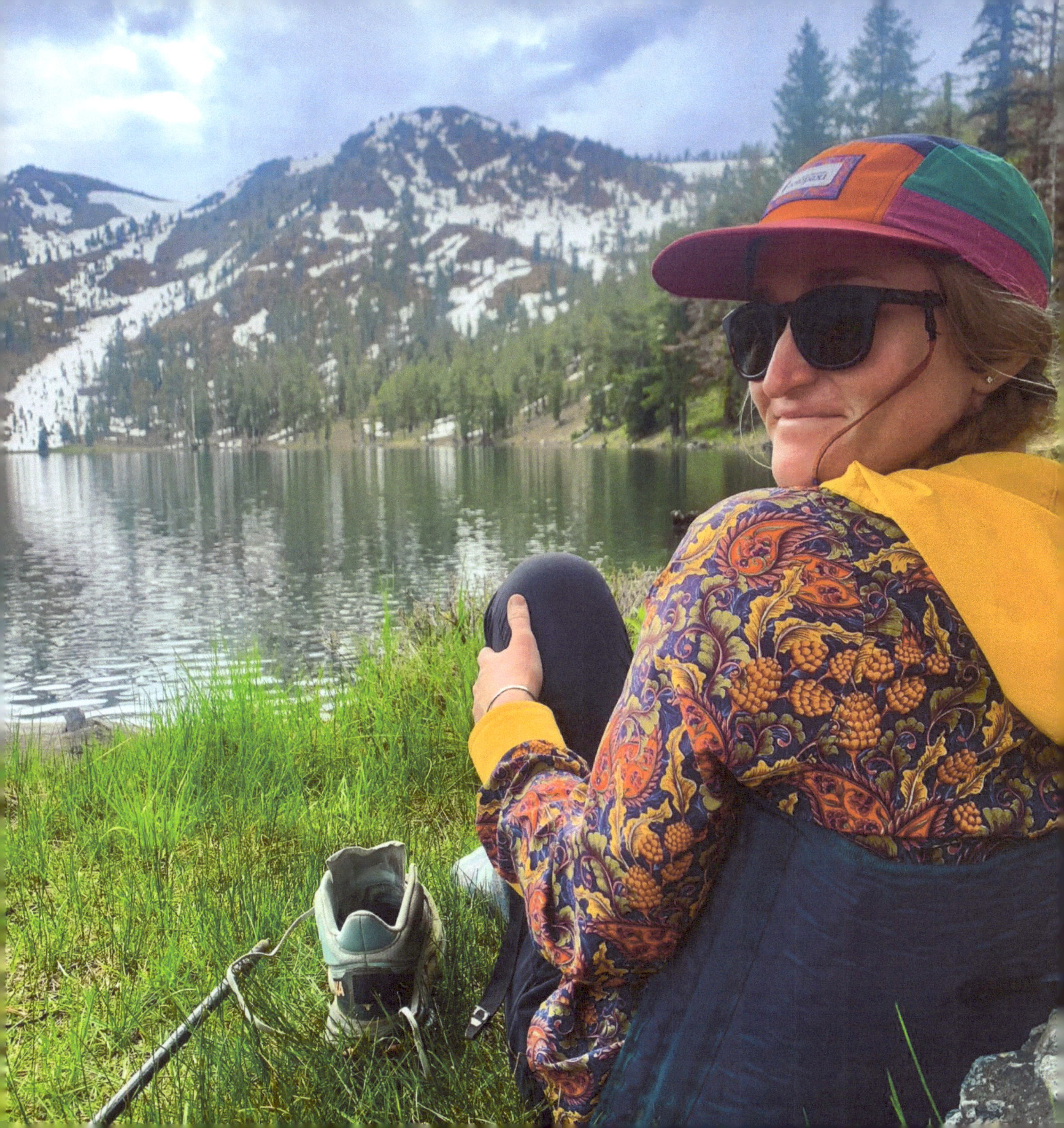

Hiker Box: Packing List

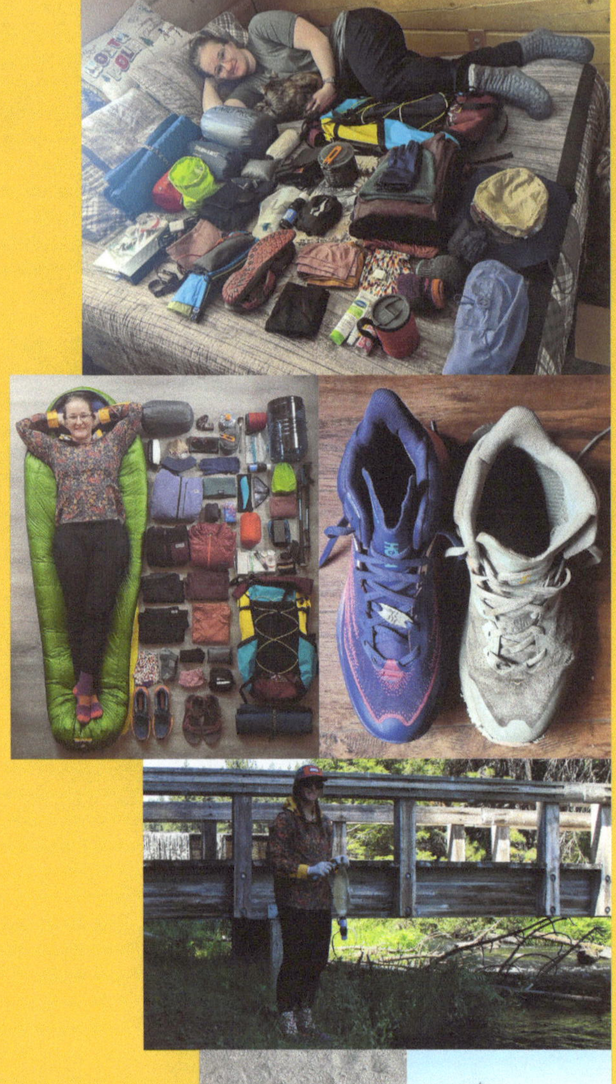

Worn bottom to top:

- 2023 Hoka Speedgoats Mids GTX Wide
- Darn Tough socks full cushion!
- Injinji liner toe socks essential for blister prevention
- UltraGam gaiters
- Mountain Hardware Dynama ankle pants
- Patagonia Barely Everyday underwear
- Patagonia Barely Everyday bra
- Jolly Gear Triple Crown button down long sleeve shirt
- Glacier Gloves prevents sunburned hands
- Garmin Fenix 7S watch
- Black Diamond Expedition WR 3 trek poles
- Dragon prescription polarized sunglasses
- Chums glasses strap
- Aftershockz OpenRun headphones
- Cotopaxi hat

On my back:

- ULA Circuit backpack
  - attached to shoulder strap:
    - ULA shoulder strap pocket
    - Garmin In-reach w/ hair rubber bands on carabiner
    - whistle
    - thermometer
    - Gerber knife
    - glasses cleaning cloth
    - Samsung Galaxy Ultra 22 phone
  - in pack's side pockets:
    - 2 1-liter Smart Water bottles switch to flip-caps so you can drink and walk
    - CNOC 2-liter water bag
    - Sawyer Squeeze w/coupler
    - pStyle I could pee.. standing up... w/my pack-on
  - in pack's outside pocket:
    - shit kit quart zip-lock w/trowel, wipes, hand sani, pack-out zip lock
    - ULA pack rain cover
    - Big Agnes Copper Spur 1P tent poles & MSR 6" tent stakes
    - Big Agnes Copper Spur 1P bikepacking footprint
    - Kahtoola micro spikes depending on section
    - Black Diamond Expedition WR 3 whippet attachment depending on section
  - strapped to outside of pack:
    - Crazy Creek Hex 2.0 essential for back support while painting. everyone was envious. I could sit on ANYTHING! slope, flat ground, stump, rock, in my tent!
    - REI camp towel
    - Teva sandals
  - in pack's hip pockets:
    - Cerave sunscreen
    - Purell hand sani #2

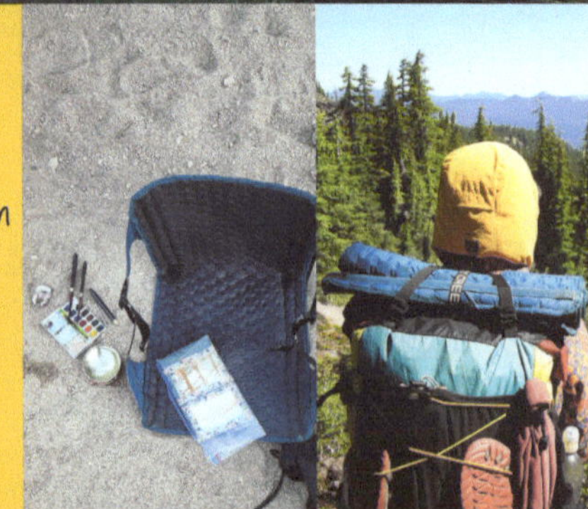

- Burt's Bees chapstick
- Picaradin bug spray *depending on section*
- head net *depending on section*
- lots of snacks

- <u>inside pack bottom to top</u>:
  - <u>bottom of pack inside a trash compactor bag liner</u>:
    - Big Agnes Rapide SL insulated sleeping pad
    - Cocoon silk sleeping bag liner *depending on section*
    - Western Mountaineering Versalite sleeping bag
    - Goose Feet down socks
    - REI sock liners
  - <u>quart zip-lock for electronics</u>:
    - wall plug
    - 2 USB-C charging wires with adapters
    - Nitecore 20000 mAh battery
    - Black Diamond Spot 400 rechargeable headlamp
  - <u>quart zip-lock for toiletries</u>:
    - toothbrush
    - toothpaste
    - assortment of meds
    - Cerave face lotion
    - tweezers
    - nail clippers
  - <u>gallon ziplock for painting supplies</u>:
    - Moleskin journal
    - Arches watercolor paper
    - 4 brushes
    - Windsor & Newton paint set
    - washi tape
    - Pilot G-2 0.5 mm pen
  - <u>Big Agnes sleeping pad air bag</u>: *dual-use as clothes sack*
    - midweight top & bottom thermals
    - beanie
    - Gortex gloves
    - Patagonia Nano Puff jacket
    - Outdoor Research Trail Mix fleece *depending on section*
    - 1 extra pair of Darn Tough socks
    - 1 extra pair of Injinji toe socks
    - 1 extra underwear
  - Big Agnes Copper Spur 1P tent body
  - North Face Summit Series Rain Jacket
  - REI full zip rain pants
  - bear can or Ursack *depending on section*
  - Jetboil Stash
  - lighter
  - small fuel can
  - Flip Fuel device *never have to buy fuel! Just transfer from hiker boxes*
  - spoon

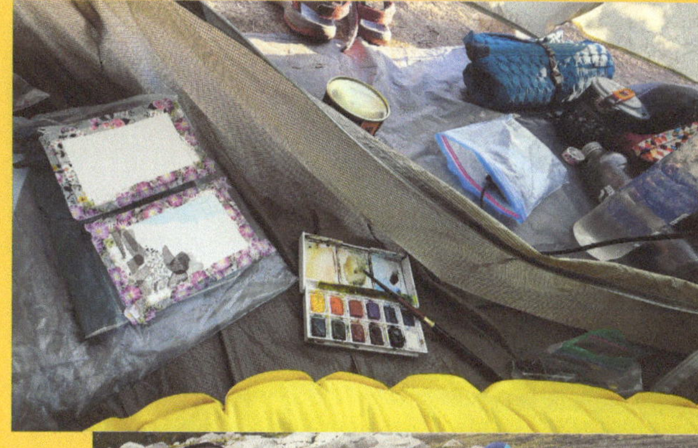

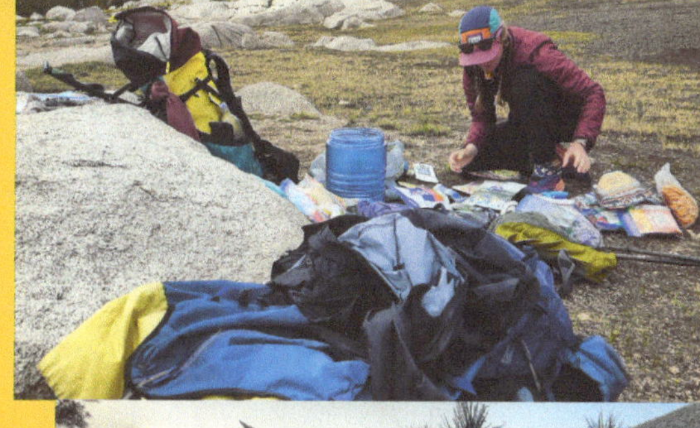

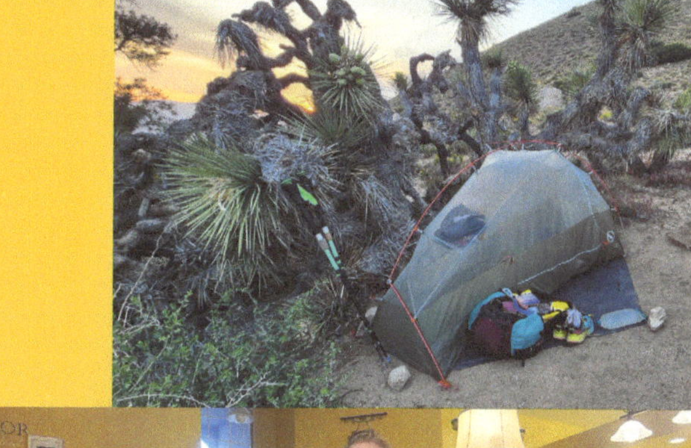

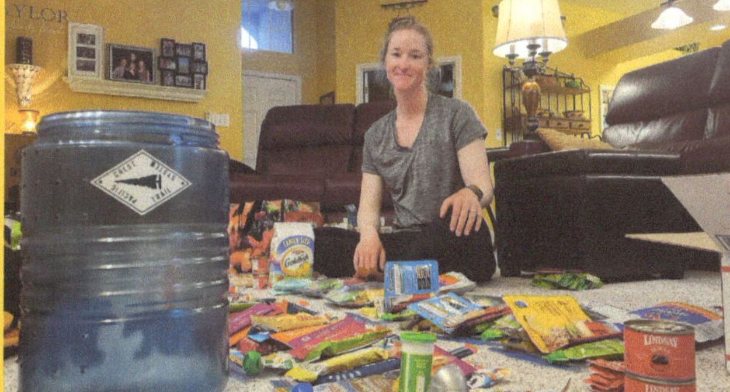

Hiker Box: Entertainment

Audiobooks:

- The Expanse Series and Novellas by James Corey
  - *Leviathan Wakes*
  - *The Butcher of Anderson Station*
  - *Caliban's War*
  - *Gods of Risk*
  - *Drive*
  - *Abaddon's Gate*
  - *The Churn*
  - *Cibola Burn*
  - *Nemesis Games*
  - *The Vital Abyss*
  - *Babylon's Ashes*
  - *Strange Dogs*
  - *Persepolis Rising*
  - *Tiamat's Wrath*
  - *Auberon*
  - *Leviathan Falls*
  - *The Sins of Our Fathers*
- *Remains of the Day* by Kazuo Ishiguro
- *Solito* by Javier Zamora
- *Angela's Ashes* by Frank McCourt
- *Born to Run* by Christopher McDougall
- *Braiding Sweetgrass* by Robin Wall Kimmerer
- *Killers of the Flower Moon: The Osage Murders and the Birth of the FBI* by David Grann
- *Crying in H Mart* by Michelle Zauner
- *The Overstory* by Richard Powers
- Red Rising Trilogy by Pierce Brown
  - *Red Rising*
  - *Golden Son*
  - *Morning Star*

Podcasts:

- *Dirtbag Diaries* by Duct Tape Then Beer
- *Wild Ideas Worth Living* by Shelby Stanger and REI Co-op
- *Rough Translations* by NPR
- *Out Alive* by Backpacker Magazine
- *The Daily Rally* by Outside
- *Outside Podcast* by Outside

Music:

- 99,892 minutes (65 days)
- Top Band: Ray Bull
- Top Album: *Strange Trails* by Lord Huron
- Top 3 Songs:
  - "Name Something Better" by Ray Bull
  - "Meet Me in the Woods" by Lord Huron
  - "I Don't Think We Should Wait" by sir Was

Hiker Box: Wildlife of the Trail

- Birds
- Snakes*
- Cows*
- Tiger
- Horses
- Ducks
- Deer
- Grouse
- Pikas
- Marmots
- Mountain lion*
- Bears*
- Dogs*
- Mountain goats
- French trail goat
- Llamas
- Porcupines
- Coyote
- Elk
- Owl
- Fox
- Cats
- Squirrels
- Chipmunk*

*close encounters

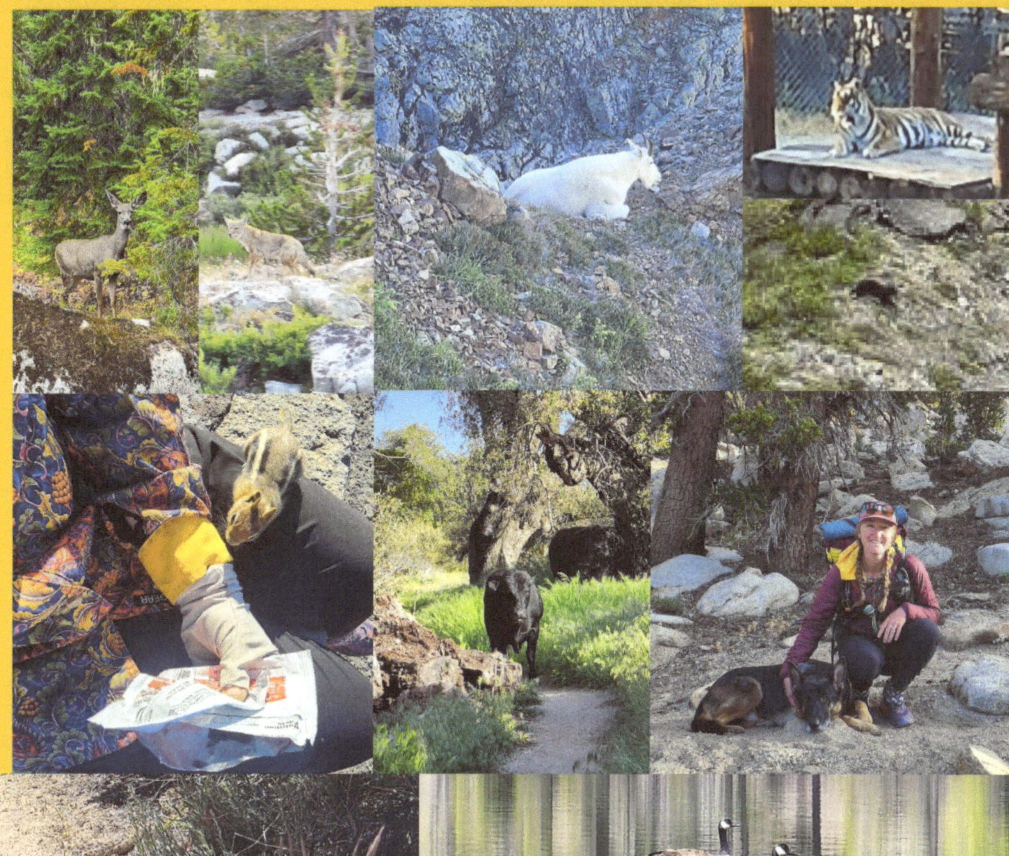

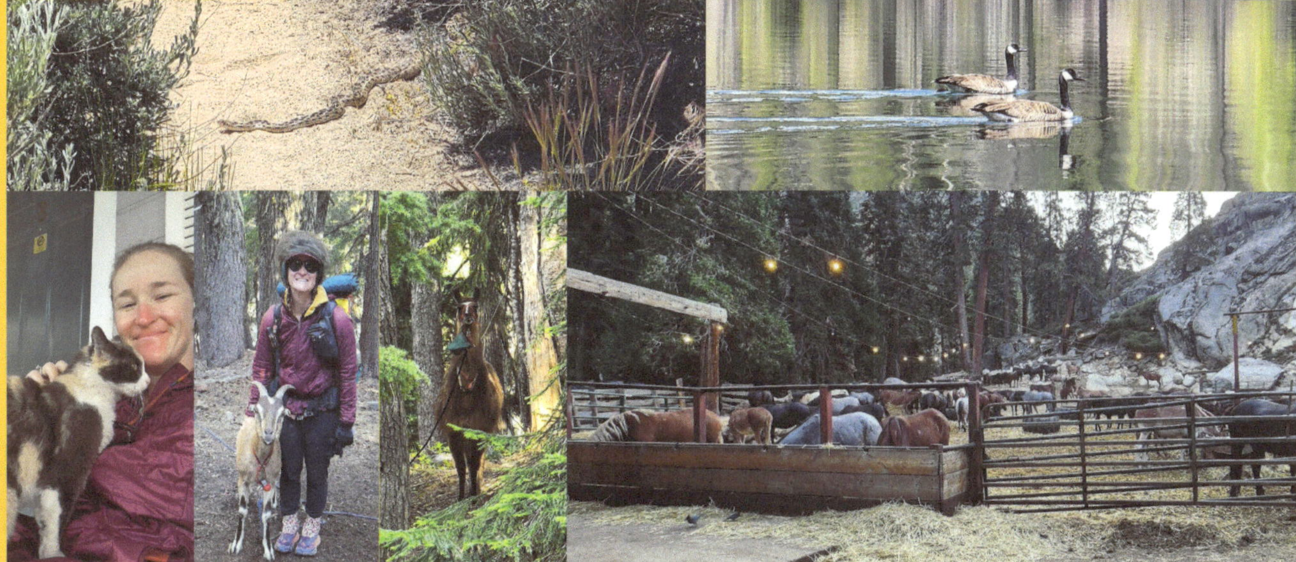

Thank You Notes

I was fortunate to have a strong support system every step of the way. This book is a testament to that journey, fueled by a lifelong dream and the amazing people who helped make it a reality. Thank you to those who were in my life before, during, and after the trail.

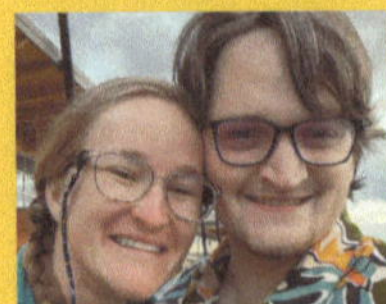

Thank you to my husband Bogdan who offered unwavering encouragement and understanding. My Bogdan who flew from Alaska and met me on trail just to hang out on zero days, who got severely altitude sick while hiking with me in the Sierra, who helped me video chat with our kitties, who surprised me at the Northern Terminus, and whom I missed the most.

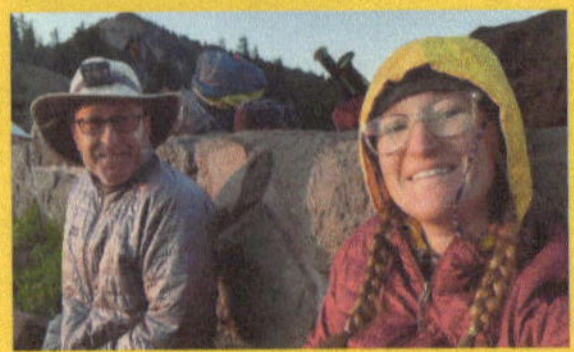

Thank you to my parents. Thank you to my dad Mark Taylor who I called on trail when I needed someone to understand and empathize with my aching feet and tired body. I called on him as a trusted and seasoned hiker to validate my flip-flop decisions. By this time in my dad's life, he was 61 years old and content with having completed every section of the PCT in California. However, his original goal was rekindled by my calls, and he decided to join me to hike all 455 miles of Oregon. Additionally, when I was hiking through the Sierra Nevada, my dad day-hiked 14.7 miles round-trip, from Onion Valley, up and over 11,709-foot Kearsarge Pass, to Charlotte Lake Junction to meet me with a fresh sandwich for lunch and a 7-day resupply. Thank you to my mom Kathy Jo Taylor for her boundless love and willingness to ensure I had everything I needed to succeed. A flip-flop thru-hike required more logistics than my original plan, and I was fortunate to have my mom located in Central California to be my personal trail angel. She helped me resupply and relocate and hiked with me for a few miles as she picked me up or saw me off at trailheads. She also shared her support with my fellow thru-hikers by providing trail magic of fresh fruit, yummy snacks, and cold drinks. Returning to the trail as an adult to hike with my dad and receive my mom's support just as it was in my youth was a sincerely meaningful experience.

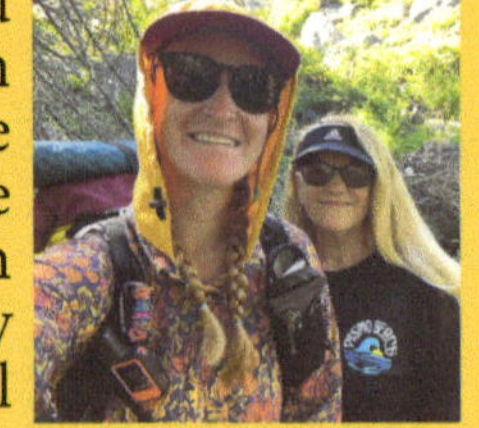

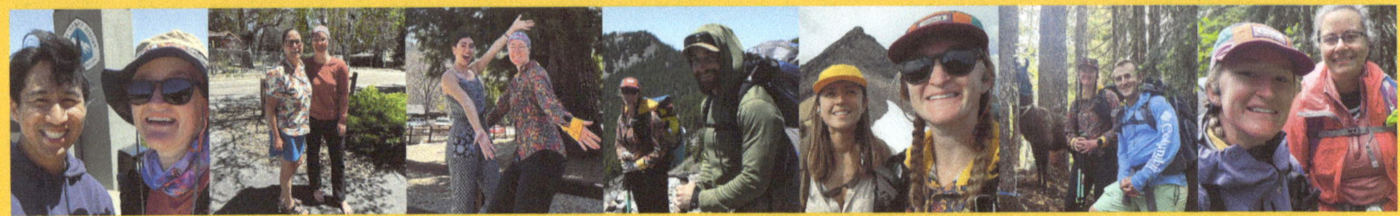

Thank you to my friends. Trevor for picking up where we left off a decade ago to enable my first steps at the Southern Terminus. Donna for hosting me in Idyllwild and being a comforting presence from my life in Alaska. Bill for hiking with me through the fear-mongered snowy section near San Jacinto. Jazmin and Vince for drinking wine and eating ice cream with me in the desert. Thank you to Alex for the constant reminder that I am her coolest friend, and T for telling me that I can and I will. Zac for becoming my brother on trail and conforming to my early morning hiking schedule. My best friend Nikole for letting me drag you into the worst day of your life and sticking with me for a week of high mileage days through

Southern Washington. Keane for hiking and meeting llamas with me, and Sam for making those logistics happen. Amber for the scavenger hunt near Mt Hood and for being my trail angel in Northern Washington. Thank you to the G8 Summit: Sara and Evie for being my pack color advisors, Gage for being my biggest cheerleader during my prep phase, Rich for hanging out with Bogdan while I was gone, Clare for answering my sonic boom questions, and Micky for the shoe lace charms that made me smile every time I put my shoes on sore feet.

Tim Royce is not only my editor but also my good friend. We met while both on active duty at Eielson Air Force Base and formed a remarkable friend group, bonding through camping, fishing, playing board games, and art. Tim closely followed my PCT journey and was a champion for my trail project. Upon returning home from trail and attempting to create this book, I quickly realized formatting an entire book was beyond my skillset and the project halted for months. Tim noticed that I had stalled and emphatically reached out to offer his expertise. He is the reason this book materialized after two years. Thank you, Tim.

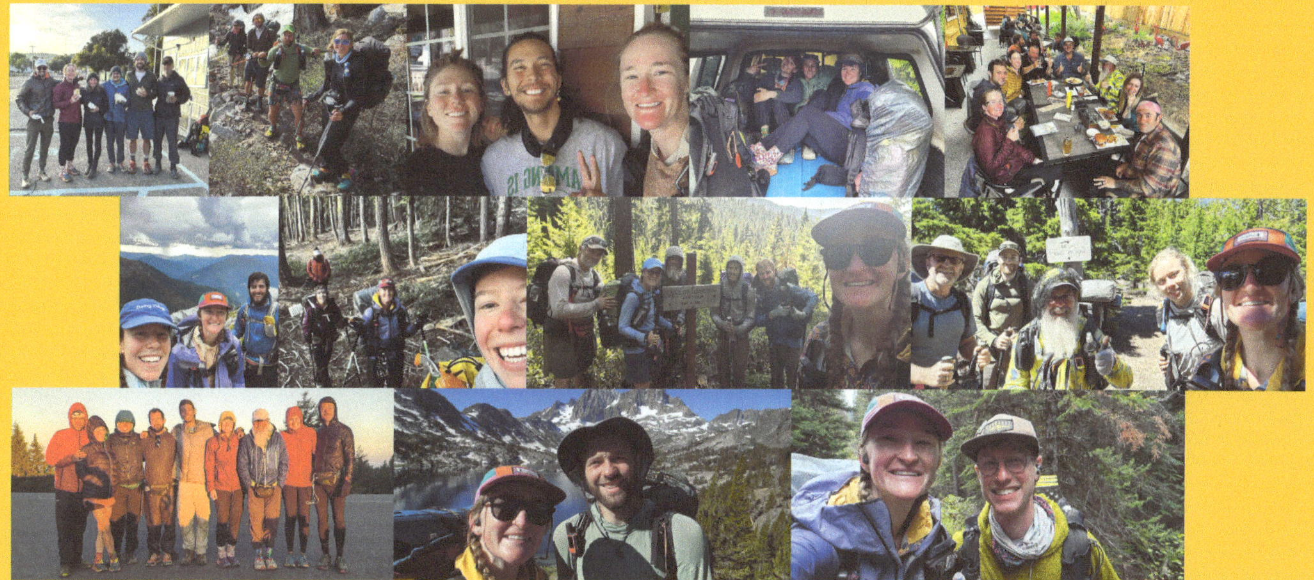

How do I even begin to express how much I appreciate the other hikers I shared the trail with? The PCT is a place where strangers become friends and friends become tramily. Thank you to the hundreds of hikers who made an impact on my hike or changed my perspective on life. If you are reading this and you remember me from the trail, whether we filtered water together once, hop-scotched on trail for days, camped together one or many nights, shared a shady lunch spot, or met in a laundromat, please know that I remember you and appreciate our moments together. Thank you to the Royals, Bless and Prince, for being the first ones to speak the idea of this book into existence. Thank you to Potatoes for sharing Rachel as a trail angel, feeling like a lifelong friend from the start, and waiting for hours for me to catch up to you at Palisades Lakes because I didn't want to be alone anymore after the lightning storm. Thank you to Toasty for giving me your oatmeal bowl to use as a water cup for painting (I still use it). Thank you to Party Trick and Checklist for having deep conversations, to Trip and Navigator for being there when I was hyperventilating after a bear incident, and to Otter for being a gentle soul who is empathetic to everyone around. Thank you to Maestro for my first commissioned watercolor project.

It would be nearly impossible and way less fun if the trail existed without trail angels and trail magic, both to be coveted and never taken for granted. I surely cannot remember every instance, but I would be remiss to not give thanks for some specific examples.

Thank you to trail angels throughout Southern California. Thank you to the trail angels in Julian who gave hikers long rides into town so we could get free pie at Mom's; the family at the campsite near Julian who gave me a pork chop and pesto pasta for dinner; and whoever left fresh fruit and cold drinks in coolers in Warner Springs. Thanks for the water tank at Mike's place; to Nitsy who picked us up and sheltered hikers during a storm; to whoever stocks beer and fresh water at the I-10 underpass; and to the wind farm near White Water Preserve that has a hiker hangout area with coolers of cold drinks. Thank you to trail angel Tiana in Big Bear who forwarded my late shoe delivery and returned my wallet when I left it in her van; to Misty for the hitch into Wrightwood; and to the lady day hiker near Mill Creek Fire Station who gave me her leftover homemade vegetarian Korean sushi for dinner. Thank you to the lineman worker who gave us a hitch to get burgers at the 49er Saloon and then offered us his cash and weed because he thought we were unhoused; to the guy who gave us a hitch back to trail in Acton in an old cop car and showed us the tigers; and to the gay couple at Vasquez Rocks who gave me warm pastries for breakfast. Thank you to everyone who tends to water caches in particularly scarce sections throughout the desert like Kelso Road.

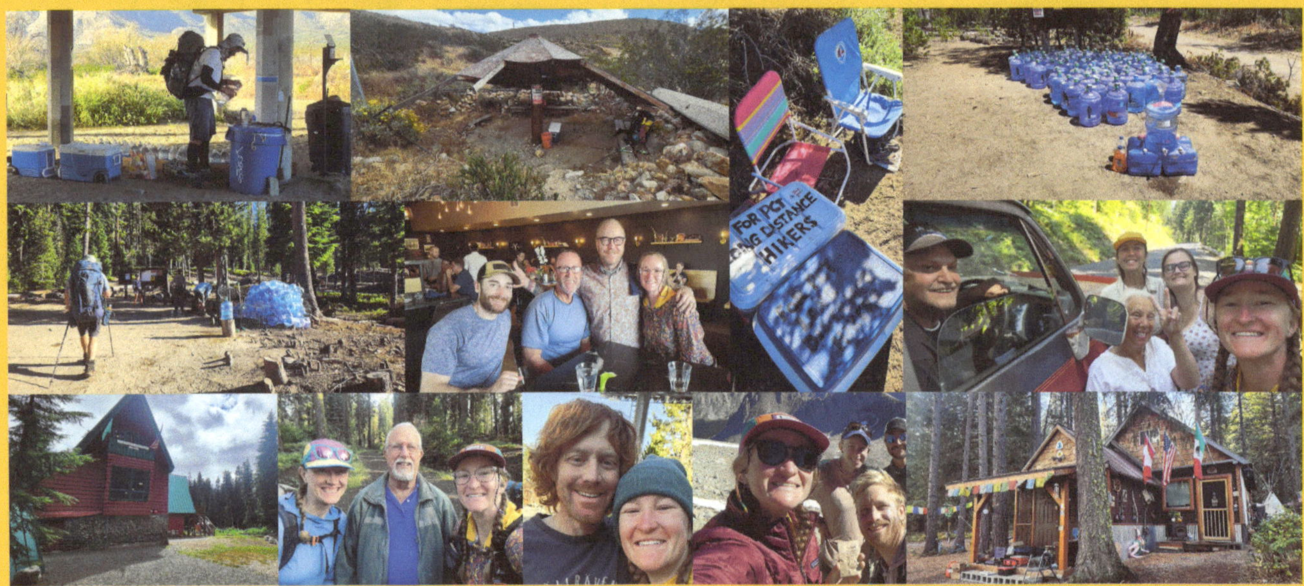

Thank you to trail angels in Northern California. Thank you to Titanic and her parents for the puppy chow, brownies, peanut butter rice crispies, and fudge bar. Thanks to Chief Bug for sharing your homemade dehydrated burrito dinner leftovers; to the young teen in the black truck for the hitch into Burney; to the vets at the Burney VFW for the beers; and to Jim for the ride back to trail. Thank you to the trout fishermen at Britton Dam for the beer and apple; and to the ladies hiking in the Trinity Alps who gave us a whole loaf of bacon bread and a handful of strawberries. Thank you to John and Goose for the rides to and from Etna and to Derrick at Etna Motel for doing our laundry for us. Thank you to the community of Siead Valley; to Cherry for taking care of hikers at Wildwood RV; to Bill for providing delicious family dinners for hikers;

and to Heather at the cafe for feeding us and continuing her mom's legacy. Thank you to the gals with the dog named Otis who gave me half a breakfast burrito and a can of kombucha.

Thank you to the trail angels and trail magic in Oregon. Thank you to the people who set up a whole trail magic camp for hikers and took fireball shots with us after crossing the California-Oregon border and for the trail magic coolers at the beginning of Oregon. Thank you to Teal who provided great company and a lift to where I needed to go and to the trail angel in Ashland who stored some gear for me. Thank you to the guy at Crater Lake who gave us a ride to get the rim camping permit; to the mushroom pickers who shared their morels; and to the boy scout near South Sister who shared pudding, pineapples, and cookies with us. Thank you to the local hiker, Brad, who gave us oreos and shared his favorite view in all of Oregon with us; to Big Lake Youth Camp for breakfast and a great hiker hangout; to the person who resupplies the trail magic cooler near Santiam Pass; and to the day hikers in the white BMW for the hitch to Sisters. Thank you to Garret Peck for the hitch from Sisters to Bend, the bottle of wine, and treating us like movie stars at your restaurant Rancher, Butcher, Chef. Thanks to trail angel Tom for the ride back to trail and to the day hikers for the snacks near Lolo Pass.

Thank you to the trail angels in Southern Washington. Thank you to Chris and Lori for picking us up in your old red Scottsdale pick-up and showing us the hospitality of Carson and to Pam Seaman for getting us back to trail. Thank you to the guy with fresh donuts for hikers; to the community of Trout Lake for catering to hikers' needs with rides and a stocked store; and to Dave and Maggie for the treats. Thank you to Susan for the professional physical therapy recovery tips and to the Washington Alpine Club for hosting hikers and making hot meals.

Thank you to the trail angels and trail magic in the final chapters of my journey through Central California and Northern Washington. Thank you to Pounder in Quincy for sheltering hikers from Hurricane Hilary; to John for the ride back to trail; and to the bow hunter south of Donner Pass who shared his water. Thank you to the lady in Granite Chief Wilderness who gave me her spoon after I lost mine; to the local campers who gave me rides to and from Kennedy Meadows North; and to Prez for hosting me in Mammoth. Thank you to the trail runners who shared their snacks and sang happy birthday to me on the top of Forester Pass and to the couple in Stehekin who bought me dinner.

Thank you to my uncle, Eric Taylor. In 1985, when my Uncle Eric was a Federal Forest Ranger, he was part of a crew that worked on the last 5 miles that would complete the Pacific Crest Trail near Acton, California. As the trail was nearing completion, the crew replaced old damaged signs with shiny new ones. My uncle kept one of the old damaged signs in his personal collection for almost 40 years. He had dreams of completing the trail, but life happened, and he never had the chance. Upon my return from trail in the fall of 2023, I arrived at home to a large box waiting for me. In that box was a letter from my Uncle Eric explaining the story behind the authentic PCT sign that now proudly hangs in my home. Thank you Uncle Eric for giving me a gift that only you could give and that every thru-hiker dreams of.

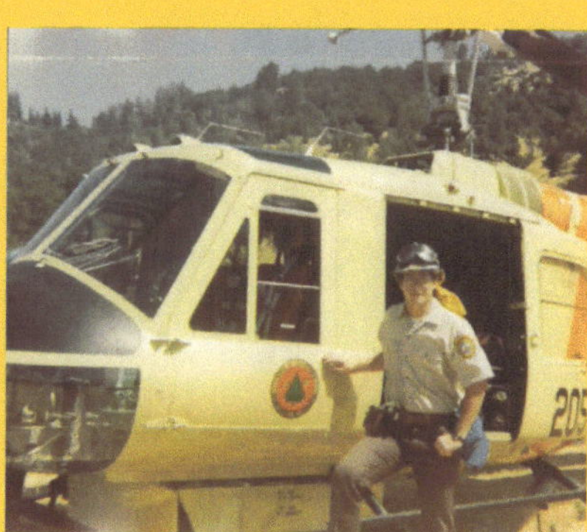

Finally, thank you to every single one of you holding this book, whether you know me personally or have stumbled upon these pages. Your willingness to delve into my story and explore the Pacific Crest Trail through my paintings means more to me than words can express. It's a truly incredible thought, knowing that something I created is in the hands of so many people I know and love and potentially in the hands of people I've never even met. If you've read this far, I invite you to reach out and share your own story with me.

For this, I thank you all.

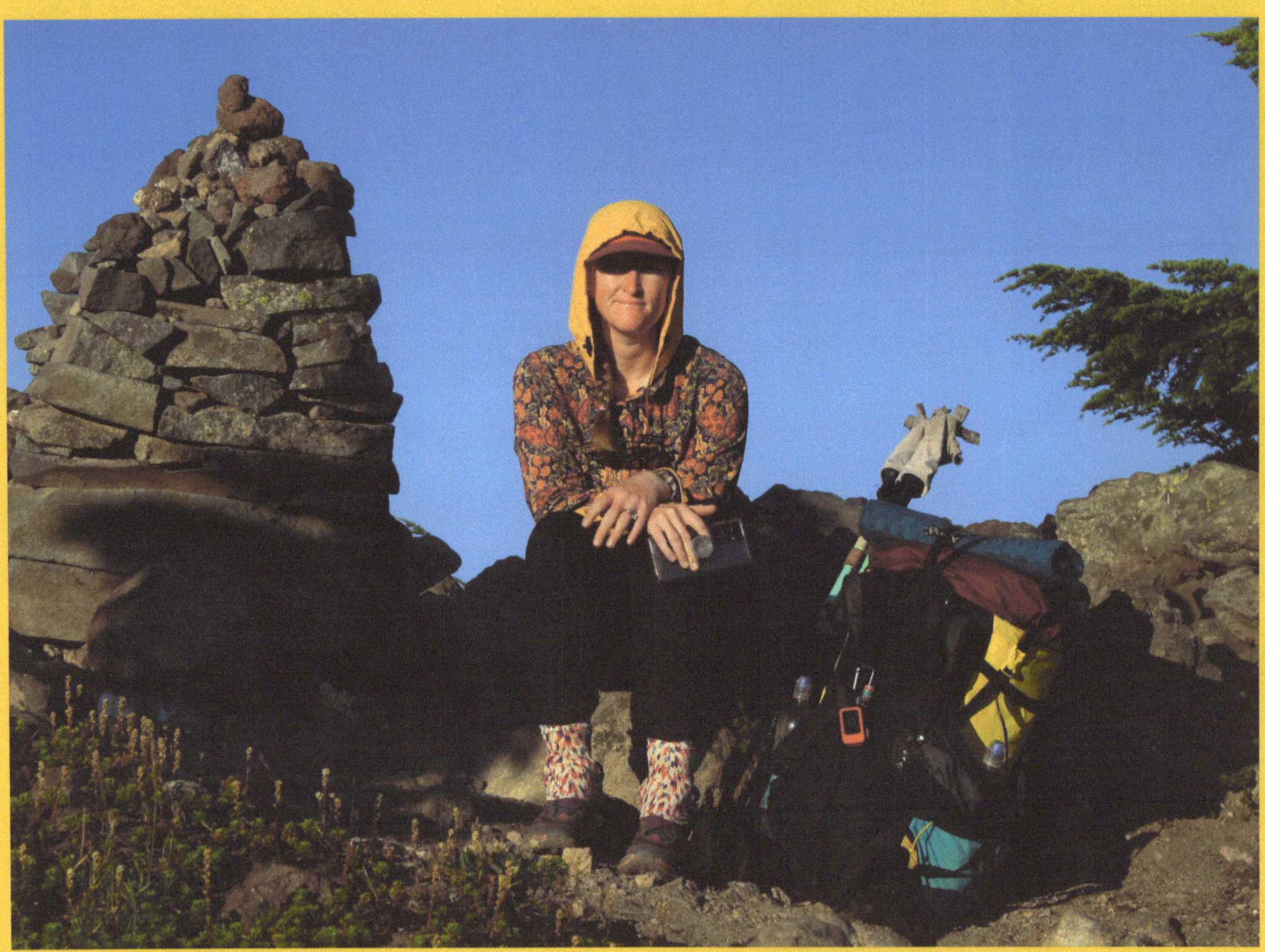

Contact Info

Email: nikkioniu@gmail.com
Instagram: nikki.draws.lines

About the Artist

I currently live in North Pole, Alaska with my husband Bogdan and our kitties. I spend my time skiing, snowboarding, hiking, biking, running, and eating Bogdan's tasty cooking. I enjoy traveling to see family, playing board games, and adventuring with friends. I also continue my practice of daily watercolor paintings in Alaska and while traveling. I am a seasonal worker. In the summer, I am a Forester for the State of Alaska, flying around the Interior in a helicopter and hiking to remote sites for Forest Inventory and Analysis. In the winter, I am a Pro Ski Patroller for the Fairbanks Ski Coalition at Ski Land. I also serve part time in the Alaska Air National Guard.

About the Editor

Tim Royce is an artist and editor based in Aurora, Colorado who specializes in portrait drawing and landscape painting in both oils and acrylics. He lives with his partner Beau and is also roommates with his dog Buck (pictured below), who once ate an entire shareable bag of Brownie M&Ms. Tim enjoys hunting and fishing and still likes to come back to Alaska for fishing trips with Bogdan and me. Tim has impeccable music taste (we share a love of sad, hokey cowboy music), and he guided my music discovery while I was hiking the PCT.

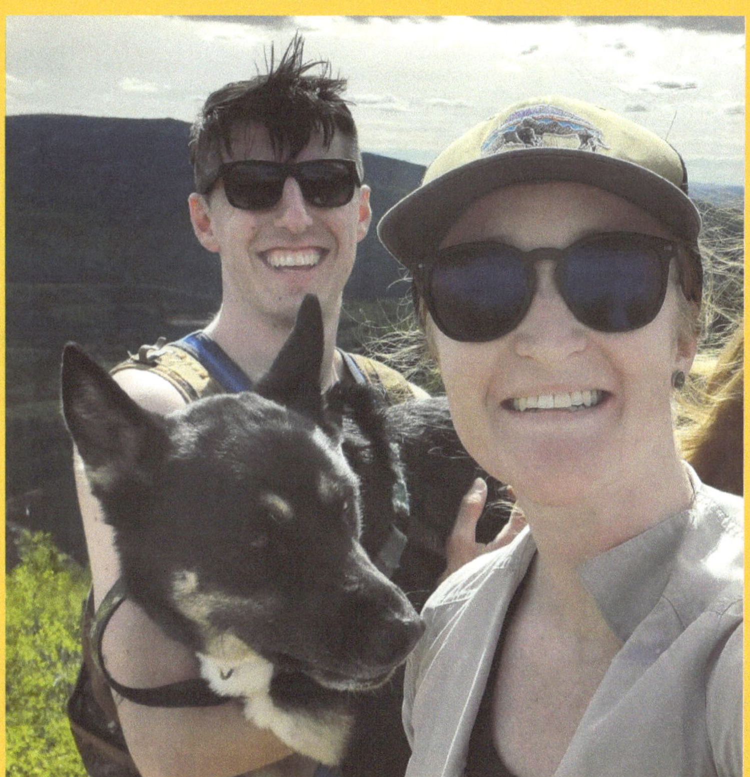

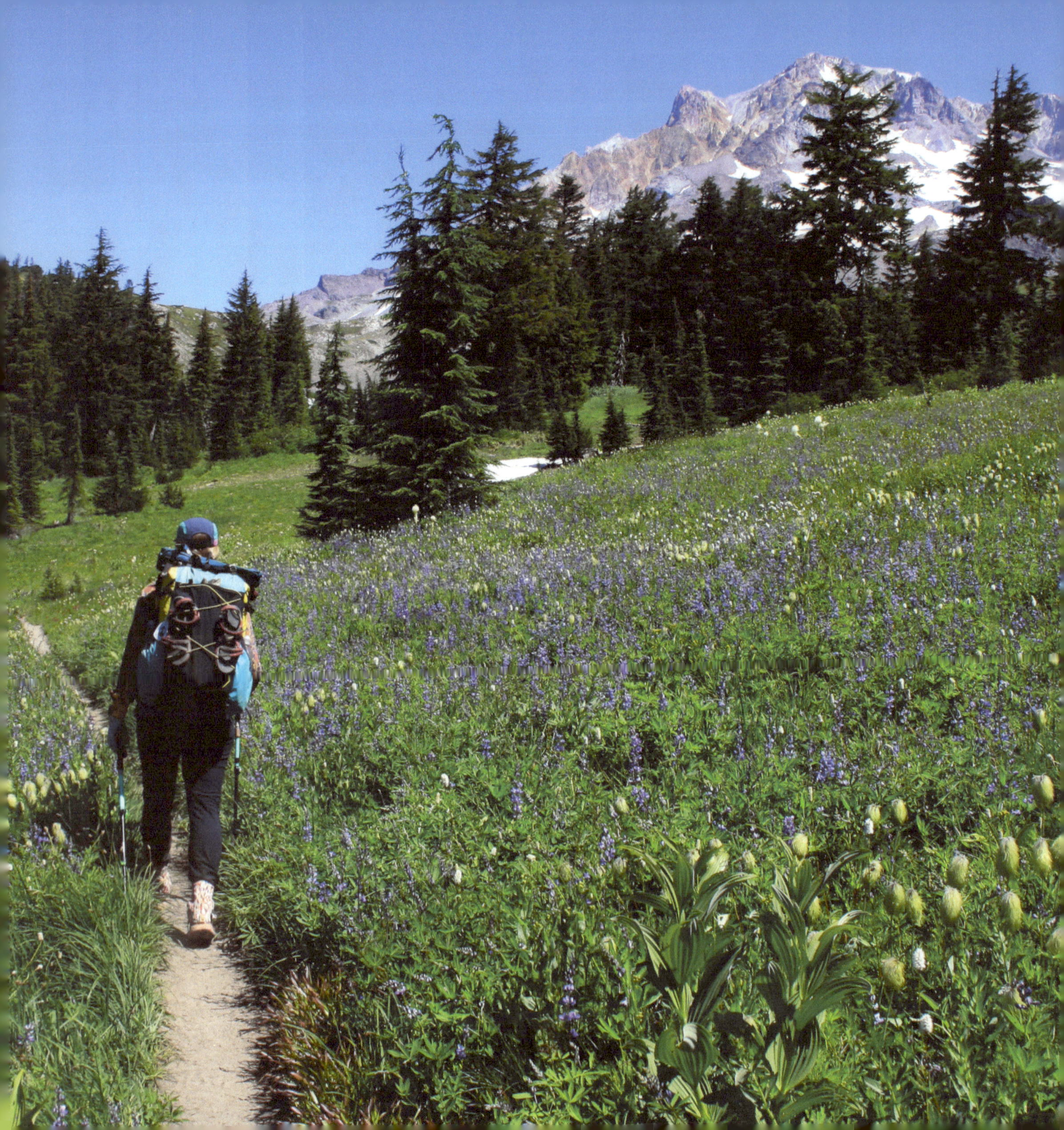

www.ingramcontent.com/pod-product-compliance
Lightning Source LLC
LaVergne TN
LVHW070213110826
845147LV00003B/568
* 9 7 9 8 2 1 8 7 8 6 7 0 0 *